THE LAND ON WHICH WE LIVE

Caitlin Press Inc.
8100 Alderwood Road, Halfmoon Bay, BC V0N 1Y1
www.caitlin-press.com

Text and cover design by Vici Johnstone
Image on title page: Fred Reed and Walter Horn driving a team of horses. Courtesy Audrey Woodman, Merritt, BC.
Cover images: Image A33886, Major Mathews Collection. City of Vancouver Archives. Background image of the Granberg Farm by Barbara MacPherson.

Printed in Canada

Caitlin Press Inc. acknowledges financial support from the Government of Canada and the Canada Council for the Arts, and the Province of British Columbia through the British Columbia Arts Council and the Book Publisher's Tax Credit.

Library and Archives Canada Cataloguing in Publication

MacPherson, Barbara, 1942-, author
    The land on which we live : life on the Cariboo Plateau : 70 Mile House to Bridge Lake / Barbara MacPherson.

ISBN 978-1-987915-36-5 (softcover)

    1. Pioneers—British Columbia—Cariboo Plateau—Biography.
2. Frontier and pioneer life—British Columbia—Cariboo Plateau.
3. Cariboo Plateau (B.C.)—Biography. 4. Cariboo Plateau (B.C.)—History.
I. Title.

FC3845.C29Z48 2017   971.1'75   C2016-907718-7

THE LAND ON
WHICH WE LIVE

Life on the Cariboo Plateau:
70 Mile House to Bridge Lake

BARBARA MacPHERSON

CAITLINPRESS

The rolling Cariboo landscape at Eagan Lake.

For my parents, George and Agnes Spanks, whose strength of character and adventurous spirit has always been my inspiration.

CONTENTS

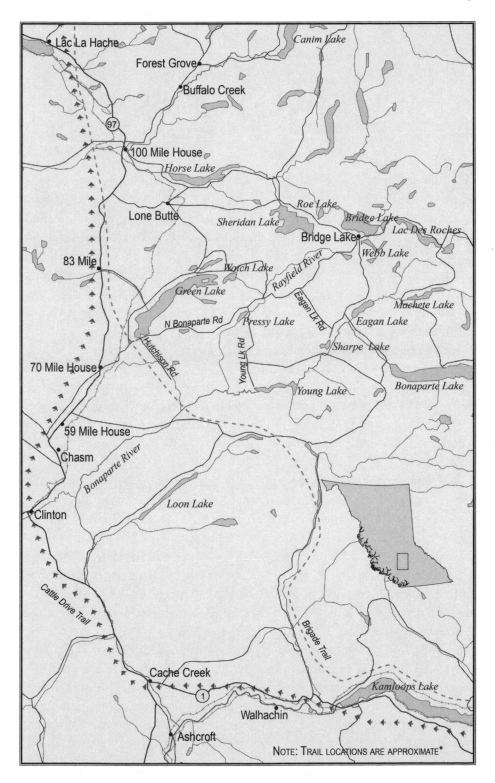

NOTE: TRAIL LOCATIONS ARE APPROXIMATE*

ACKNOWLEDGEMENTS

I would like to especially thank Jean Nelson for her encouragement and support for the initial idea for this book and also during the four years it took me to complete it. She has been a great influence on my life since I was a child and continues to be today. I would also like to express great appreciation to Sharon Hansen for all her help during the process. As the child of original settlers who knew everyone from Lone Butte to 70 Mile House, she helped to find, identify, and fill in the stories on many of the lesser-known individuals. I'd also like to particularly thank Audrey Woodman, Dave Law, Russell Ross, Deann and Glen Cleveland, Connie Greenall, Helen Horn, Diane Cleveland, Rose Scheepbouwer, David Park, Jack Black, and Lynn Watrich for their help on families other than their own. Thanks to Harold Mobbs for the copy of Reverend Stanley Higgs' memoir. Two of the people who went above and beyond to help me with information are no longer with us: Mae McConnell of 70 Mile House and Howard Malm of Roe Lake. They were two of the most informative and supportive people and their loss is immeasurable to their communities.

I owe a great debt to local memoirs that speak of early pioneers and the culture of their time: *The Rainbow Chasers,* by Ervin MacDonald; *The Homesteader's Daughter* by Marianne Van Osch; *Bridge Lake Pioneer* by Charlie Faessler; Eva Wrigley's *To Follow a Cowboy*; and Floyd Tompkins' *Honest Memories of One Man's Life*. Leonard Larson's unpublished memoir was also a great source. As well, newspaper interviews with old-timers in which they related their memories were full of wonderful information. Of special note are the writings of Roy Eden, who painted indelible pictures of early life in the North Bonaparte.

I am very grateful to everyone who contributed information. Virtually everyone I contacted for facts on their families—over 120 different people— were friendly, helpful, and incredibly supportive of the whole project: Faye Ryder, who shared the intimate letters and poignant stories of her family, the Ryders and the Andruses; the family of pioneer surveyor Geoffrey Downton, who so trustingly sent me their grandfather's original diary from London,

England, without even knowing who I was; people who lent me their treasured scrapbook collections without a second thought; people who let me borrow original photos, some right off their walls; people who trusted me with the intimate stories of their lives. I am awed by their faith in humanity and generosity. Thank you to each and every one!

I would also like to thank John Belshaw of Thompson Rivers University for his suggestions in analyzing my statistical data, Kathy Paulos of the Ashcroft Museum for going above and beyond in searching for information, Dr. Diana Kelland of Nakusp for her advice on puzzling medical data, and Art Lance of the Friends of Bridge Lake for geological information. I would also like to thank Elizabeth Pete, B.Ed, Treaty Coordinator for Canim Lake, for her invaluable input into "The First People" chapter. I'm very grateful to the Columbia Kootenay Cultural Alliance for financial support in the first year of my project. I'm also grateful to the BC Archives: without its free online access to birth, death, and marriage certificates, information would have been much more difficult and expensive to obtain. Thanks to the members of my long-time writer's group in Nakusp, who have been unfailingly encouraging. And a most especial thanks to my husband, Gary, for his patience, support, and encouragement during the process and to my children for their unfailing support as well.

INTRODUCTION

As a child living in Bridge Lake, I often wondered about the abandoned homesteads my brother and I would find in our exploratory tramps through the bush. A cabin sat across the lake from where we lived, mysteriously abandoned with plates still on the table. On the property next to us were the foundations of a half-built cabin. Who had owned these places? Where did they come from and where did they go? We wondered too about the people who lived in the wilderness south of us. Standing at the Bridge Lake Store, signposts on the road south pointed to Green Lake, Watch Lake, and North Bonaparte. We'd never gone there and speculated about who lived there and what that shadowy country was like.

Many years later, embarking on the journey of writing this book, my curiosity was finally satisfied. What gratification there was in finding the stories of all the people who had lived in the countryside around us, some so long forgotten no one now remembers that they ever lived there. My questions were finally answered.

The Land on Which We Live: Life on the Cariboo Plateau from 70 Mile House to Bridge Lake covers a specific area and time period—from 1871, when the first family arrived at 70 Mile House, until 1959, nearly ninety years later. Although there were technological advances during those years, the culture of the area did not change dramatically. By the beginning of the 1960s, however, the countryside had become transformed by better transportation, roads, and communication. The old ways of life began to disappear and with it, attitudes and aspirations changed. I wanted to capture life as it was before that transformation began and look at the population who settled there in a way that evokes the kind of people they were. I have tried to identify virtually everyone who ever lived there, but of course, there were undoubtedly many settlers who mutely came and went and left no paper trail.

Some of the families who settled in the district had a huge impact, and in a few cases, recent generations of the families still live there. Some people were in the area for only a few years before they had to admit defeat and move on. Many of those names are completely unknown to present residents. It was exciting to uncover those lives and discover Mormons, English ladies,

French-Canadian trappers, Dutch linguists, Russian spies, and Texas cowboys among the varied settlers who came to this part of the Cariboo. Their stories one and all are fascinating and inspiring. So many suffered tragedies and blows, and yet, heroes in their own lives, they just kept on living and fighting, putting one foot ahead of the other. I have nothing but admiration for them. I could be accused of seeing them through rose-coloured glasses, but that is the only colour that discerns both the truth and the mythology at the core of every family's story.

At 4 years old, I was introduced to life in the Cariboo when my father, a dreamer and adventurer, took our family from the city to Bridge Lake in 1946. The war barely over, he wanted us to experience a "natural" life in the wilderness. Eventually that dream was crushed by lack of experience, lack of money, my mother's ill health, and the lack of higher education in the area. We were one of the families who didn't quite make it, but what we took away in 1958 was the experience of a remarkable, vivid life in the middle of the bush, one that strongly influenced our present values and beliefs.

As far as possible, I tried to find and identify everyone who had settled in the area up to 1959, conducting genealogical research on over 250 families or individuals. My sources were: interviews with residents and their descendants; Crown grant land records; pre-emption land maps; town directories; voters' lists; censuses; vital statistics records, including birth, death, and marriage records and other genealogical documents; cemetery records; published and unpublished memoirs; and books, articles, and newspaper clippings. To identify the year in which many settlers arrived, I have used the pre-emption date for their property, unless I knew otherwise—but this may not always be accurate. Virtually all the settlers would have scouted out their land before they actually filed; the lapse between their investigations and formal filing for the pre-emption could vary from a few weeks to perhaps as long as a year.

As far as is humanly possible, I have tried to verify facts and keep the book as accurate as possible. However, official sources such as censuses, town directories, vital statistics documents, and even cemetery records can contain many inaccuracies. This is to say nothing of human memory recorded in interviews and memoirs. There is probably not a single published history or genealogy without a mistake, and I'm sure mine is no exception. I apologize in advance for any errors that might be present.

"TELL ME THE LAND ON WHICH YOU LIVE..."

Spanish philosopher Jose Ortega y Gassett once famously said, "Tell me the land on which you live, and I will tell you who you are."

This would perhaps be an accurate statement for those who lived on the Cariboo Plateau. With an elevation of 1,067 metres (3,500 feet) to 1,219 metres (4,000 feet), severe winters, a short growing season, and a lack of good agricultural land, the landscape was a challenge. The people who managed to stay and thrive in such an environment were a special breed. Tough and resourceful, they were individualists who wanted to live life in their own particular way.

The Cariboo Plateau is volcanic, part of the Fraser Plateau. Most soils are glacially derived, with a high proportion of clay. The flat to undulating terrain of the main plateau gives way to rolling hills bordering the North Thompson valley to the east. The eastern region in the sub-area around Bridge Lake, Lac des Roches down to Eagan Lake and Sharpe Lake, can be described as "aspen parkland." The area is characterized by grassy meadows and tall aspen trees, along with evergreen trees. Farther south, the land is more poorly drained, resulting in marshes, alkaline lakes, and smaller aspen trees. The differences are a result of variations in topography, rainfall, fire history, and human impact history. Natural meadows with swamp grass (sedges) and some open grasslands encouraged settlers who were looking for grazing land for cattle. Bridge Lake and Lac des Roches at the northeast (and highest) corner of the area drain eastward into the North Thompson River, whereas the rest of the area drains directly into the Thompson.

The area covered in this book is a specific area in the South Cariboo, a rough rectangle of about 216,000 hectares (540,000 acres), with 70 Mile House at the southwest end, bordered by Young Lake, Eagan Lake, and Lac des Roches on the east side; Bridge Lake and Roe Lake on the north; and 83 Mile-Taylor Lake to the west. Within this loose area, there is also a circle of larger lakes, beginning with Green Lake, Watch Lake, Sheridan Lake, Bridge Lake, Lac des Roches, Machete Lake, Eagan Lake and ending with

Young Lake at the south end of the circle. Surrounding and within this circle are at least forty smaller lakes. The Bonaparte River rises within this area. The branch that was once the North Bonaparte and is now called the Rayfield River, rises south of Bridge Lake. The Rayfield River meets the part of the Bonaparte River that first flows from Machete Lake to Eagan Lake to Sharpe Lake. (Oddly enough, this was called the South Bonaparte in early maps and the 1911 census, even though it was actually north.) From there, the Bonaparte drains into Young Lake and then runs south of Chasm, finally joining the Thompson River at Ashcroft.

Before any white settlers arrived, the Cariboo Plateau area of Bridge Lake to 70 Mile House was occupied by the Tsq'escenemc ("broken rock") band, later called the Canim Lake Band. The Tsq'escenemc are part of the lakes people of the Northern Secwepemc and archaeologists have defined them as inhabiting the plateau between the Fraser and Thompson rivers, with their headquarters at Canim Lake. It wasn't until 9,500 to 10,000 years ago that the area was ice-free and suitable for habitation. About 4,500 to 5,000 years ago, the cool, moist climate saw a dramatic rise in the fish population, although the number of larger mammals and plant diversity was lower. This encouraged people to settle in the area. Archaeological studies have dated various sites, such as pictographs at Mahood Lake, to some 5,000 years ago. The Tsq'escenemc began to inhabit the land at that time and their traditional hunting and fishing territories spread out to include the many lakes in the region. Because of their proximity in the south, east, and west to other bands, they ranged closely within their own territory but went north to hunt as far as Horsefly, Quesnel Lakes, the Clearwater Lakes, and up into the Caribou Mountains opposite the Yellowhead Pass.

It wasn't until the Cariboo gold rush in 1862 that any appreciable European impact was felt in the area. Ex-miners, speculators, and land-seekers began to settle in the Cariboo and word started to spread. Gradually, most of the choicest country in the Cariboo-Chilcotin suitable for large cattle ranches was taken up. By the early twentieth century, not much prime land was still available. But for the wave of settlers arriving in the South Cariboo in the early decades of the century, there were still opportunities in the 70 Mile to Bridge Lake area for those who wanted to have a modest-sized ranch. Crown land was available for pre-emption until 1970, although by the late 1940s, most suitable land had already been pre-empted. However, there were plenty of opportunities to purchase relatively undeveloped properties for a reasonable price and a homestead style of life was still possible for many years.

Most, if not all, of the homesteaders who came to the district in the settlement years from 1871 to 1959 originated in warmer areas and were probably shocked by the severity of the winter. Few came from the Canadian prairie provinces, where they might have been better prepared for bitter cold. The Americans who came were experienced farmers and travellers, but they would likely have found the winters hard to take. Later settlers from England would have been even more dismayed.

Eventually, of course, the settlers either adapted to the harsh conditions or left. In fact, a huge percentage did leave: of the over 250 families and single men who settled between 1871 and 1959 from the North Bonaparte to Bridge Lake and Roe Lake, a quarter lasted only one to five years. A little over half managed to hang on for fifteen years. Less than a quarter of the total stayed for the rest of their lives.

The fact is that most of the settlers were dreamers and romantics looking for an ideal life. Many had moved from place to place in search of this dream. From the Americans in the earliest decades who'd moved from state to state before they came, to the veterans of World War II who had their heads filled with ideas of independence and a free, unregulated life, the new occupants were willing to take a chance, although few actually knew what they were getting into. They were adventurers and risk-takers, whether they were old hands like Andy Whitley of the North Bonaparte, who'd tried all kinds of farming and ranching before he came in 1909, or like Arnold Cornish in Bridge Lake in the 1940s, who'd lived in the city all his life and dreamed of riding a horse over his own meadows and fields.

The area from 70 Mile to Bridge Lake was attractive to many who had these dreams but not much money to back them up. Because the area was not top-quality farm or ranch land, there was little competition for parcels of land. Later, when homestead land had all been taken up and property had to be purchased, prices were more affordable than in areas such as the Okanagan. Many of these properties also bordered a lake. If they could make a success of it, titleholders were monarchs of their own personal domains. For some, this would be the only time in their lives that they owned a large chunk of land.

Some managed the feat of pre-empting enough land to make a viable ranch by pooling their resources with brothers in their family. There were at least thirty groups of brothers who purchased or pre-empted land together. There were also a few partnerships. It seemed to be a good solution, but didn't always work well, especially if the brothers or partners had differences of opinion.

No matter how you managed to obtain the land of your dreams, it still cost money to live. No one made much money but most had more than one source of revenue to put food on the table and hopefully pay the bills. When the Great Depression hit, residents were able to weather the lean years better than their urban counterparts because of their diverse skills. They were also able to garden, hunt, and raise animals to provide food for the table.

Family unity was a valuable commodity, not to be taken lightly. If anything went wrong, this could have a devastating impact. The death of one of the adult members of a family, the disruption of divorce, family disagreements—any of these events could have a harmful effect on the ability of the family and the ranch to function and survive.

Almost as essential as family unity was the support of friends and neighbours. Without social services, medical facilities, ministerial counsel, or any other form of societal assistance, life would have been much more difficult without the aid of other community members. Neighbours were not just friends you socialized with, but people who also pitched in to help with building, haying, and other ranch work during busy seasons. Just as importantly, they became stand-in midwives, doctors, counsellors, and undertakers.

From the first people, the Tsq'escenemc, to the hopeful settlers who arrived from 1871 to 1959, the Cariboo Plateau was a place that shaped and formed those who lived there. Ortega y Gasset's observation that the land on which you live speaks of who you are was never more true than it was in the Cariboo. Tough and unrelenting with its flinty soil and harsh weather, the landscape was tempered by beauty: grassy meadows and rolling hills, picturesque lakes, white-trunked poplar trees, silence and seclusion. Those people who made it their home were stamped by both the toughness of the land and the rewards of its beauty.

THE FIRST PEOPLE

The Tsq'escenemc—part of the Lakes division of the Northern Secwep-mec, along with the Hat'inten and the Green Timber—were known as Styetemc. They lived during the winter in underground homes known as *s7istktn* (also known as *kekulis*). Extended families of about fifteen to thirty persons wintered together, relying on dried fish, meat, and berries, and roots and medicines, usually stored in cache pits nearby. Seasonal activities included making clothes, repairing woven baskets and fish nets, and making tools and implements.

In the springtime, the group would split up into smaller divisions and begin the springtime gathering of fresh roots and medicines. They watched for many indicators that let them know which plants were ready for harvesting, or when it was time to fish the streams and lakes. When the leaves started growing on the birch trees, for example, the sap was running, and the bark could be removed for basket making. Summer camps had circular or lean-to dwellings made of lodgepole pine, reeds, bark (cedar, if available), and skin mats. People looked forward to fresh fish, migratory birds, and roots.

Many gathering activities continued on into the summertime. Harvesting "chiefs" would go out to check resources and relay this information back to the people. There were fish camps along the many streams and lakes. At each camp, drying structures were built and the fish dried. Along the river, salmon were air-dried. In the Bridge Lake to 70 Mile area, the main fish was trout; those desiring salmon could go east to the Clearwater River or west to the Fraser. Sometimes, relationships helped determine in which direction a small group would travel.

Fall was dedicated mainly to hunting caribou. This meant travelling to the mountains in late summer and camping for at least two to three weeks. This gave the people enough time to harvest the caribou and dry the meat for transporting back to the winter camps. During this time, mountain whistler (marmots) would be harvested for food and for making winter gloves. The fat of the animal would be rendered for "butter." Dried caribou hides would be sewn into large bags for storing dried meat. When horses became available, these large bags would be strapped onto the sides of pack horses when it was time to travel back. Food harvesting of roots, nuts, and berries continued into the fall. Fall fishing for char took place in certain lakes (for example, Horse Lake). The vast knowledge about harvesting resources was passed down to the younger generations, who also travelled out to the land with their families.

Sometime before white settlement began, perhaps about two hundred years ago, a great fire swept through the South Cariboo, driving out all the large animals such as moose, elk, and caribou. Fish in the creeks were killed and it was years before the stocks recovered completely. It was a time of great deprivation for the inhabitants of the country. Not until the second decade of the twentieth century did moose finally return to the area.

The Canim Lake people had a huge network of trails criss-crossing the entire countryside. These trails connected trade routes, villages, camps, and choice hunting and fishing locations. They often linked to other band territories. The Clearwater Trail was one of the most important routes and led from the south side of Canim Lake all the way over to the Clearwater River and on to the North Thompson. The present Interlakes Highway from Bridge Lake to Little Fort generally follows this Indigenous people's trail from Bridge Lake to Chu Chua, where the Tsq'escenemc and Simpcw (Chu Chua) people travelled back and forth. Other trails went from Green Lake to Bridge Lake and Horse Lake to Sheridan Lake. These trails would still have been well used when the first white settlers arrived in the early part of the twentieth century and may have been the basis for some of the roads that they established.

It's not known what the population of the Canim Lake people was before the Cariboo Gold Rush. The entire Secwepemc (Shuswap) nation was estimated to be between 7,000 and 9,000 people in 1862, but that was soon to change. This was the year construction began on the Cariboo Road and with it came smallpox. The disease created devastation among the Secwepemc and the death toll was high. Many small communities were completely decimated and never recovered. The few that did survive were greatly decreased in size.

Disease continued to be a threat, as was the arrival of white settlers. The few white people who settled in the North Bonaparte before 1907 would have had little impact, but after that, lands that the Tsq'escenemc ranged over began to be taken up by an influx of homesteaders. This put pressure on the group, and as time went on, the places they had traditionally summered were no longer available. Another factor in the discontinuance of some summer fishing camps was that residents of the reserves had their movements restricted by a pass system: anyone wishing to leave their reserve would need to have a pass or they would be fined. In 1937, for example, a Canim Lake Reserve resident was fined $10.00 for visiting his relatives at the Canoe Creek Reserve.

Ed Higgins, who arrived at Roe Lake from Oregon in 1913, was very interested in his Indigenous neighbours and spent a great deal of time with them. According to Ed, the last years that members of the Canim Lake Band spent any amount of time summering in the Bridge Lake area were 1916 and 1917. Whether this was true for the Green Lake and North Bonaparte area isn't known, although the Mobbs children, whose family settled by the Bonaparte River in 1920, were said to have played with Indigenous children who lived at Turkey Gulch.

By the 1920s, homesteaders were living in every corner of the country from 70 Mile House up to Horse Lake. The white population was not overly numerous, but it was large enough to change the whole dynamic of traditional life. Virtually all the newcomers had cattle, ranging from thirty to well over a hundred head, and the livestock grazed on land that had formerly been used for foraging for traditional foods. There was also competition for the fish and wildlife that the band had depended on for their sustenance.

Despite this, the many encounters between the Indigenous people and the new settlers seemed sociable and cordial. Most of the memoirs written by residents mention friendly encounters with individuals who lived there at the time, such as Billy "English" Decker (or Deka), Cashmere, and others. Despite the fact that the new settlers were causing dramatic changes in their lives, most of the Canim Lake people were welcoming and often helpful to the newcomers.

In the lower part of the countryside, around 70 Mile House and Green Lake, members of the Stswecem'c Tgat'tem (Canoe Creek) Band also mingled with the newcomers. Roy Eden, an early settler around Green Lake, wrote about the summer of 1907 when he worked for the Boyds at Green Lake, as did several members of the band:

> That first summer—for me—went all too soon. Jim Boyd took me with him to the hay camp at the big "Green Lake" meadow which was close to the [later] Flying U Dude Ranch... The haying crew at that time was made up of him and myself along with about 15 Indians. Most of them came from the Canoe Creek Indian Reservation. Most of them used to trade at the 70 Mile Store when Jim's father was alive, and Jim had known them since he was a small boy. The old Chief of the Canoe Creek Reserve, Louis Tin Musket, was one of the crew and for years to follow he was a good friend of mine. In the evenings they used to play the Indian game called "La Hell" [lahal] and they let me sit at the end of one row and showed me how to keep the proper time beating with two drumsticks. The

Billy "English" Decker of the Canim Lake Band and his family. Sociable and fond of travelling, English is mentioned in nearly every pioneer memoir of the area. A visit from English Decker was always memorable. Courtesy Robert White, Forest Grove, BC.

following is a rough description of how it is played. There is a row of 5 or 6 Indians on each side of a small campfire. Each side has a certain amount of pointed sticks stuck in the ground, and each side has a "loader" who sits in the centre of the row and is the only one who makes the signs, the rest just chat... The "loaders" or medicine men give all the signs and they have the big cowboy handkerchief tied to the back of his neck and hanging down as a sack in front of him so he can hide his hands. They use two bones taken from a deer's foot, one of the bones has a black thread tied around the centre of the bone, the other is plain. In the opposition, the leader has to guess (by signs only) which of the opposition leader's hands the bone with the black thread is in when he holds out his closed hands—if he guesses the correct hand, the opposite side has to pay with one of the pointed sticks. Apparently, before the game even starts, the different sides have made their bets among themselves of all personal effects: including horses, blankets, saddles and most anything!

Louie Tinmusket (or more properly, Louis Mtinmeshen), actually settled in the area for a while. In the 1930s, he ran a small ranch somewhere in the 70 Mile area, probably along with his daughter and son-in-law, Elizabeth and Joe Alexander.

The Canim Lake Reserve, established in the 1860s, is located east of 100 Mile House at the southwestern end of Canim Lake. "Canim" was the word for a large canoe in Chinook jargon and was often pronounced "cinim." Courtesy Robert White, Forest Grove, BC.

Today, the Canim Lake Band has 608 registered members; of these, 420 still live on the reserve at Canim Lake. Their website outlines how they have dealt with the dramatic cultural change:

> The Canim Lake Band are a progressive people, striving for self-sufficiency through education, economic development, social development, and overall management of its lands and resources. We have a strong leadership in council as well as within the community, nation and province overall. We are a proud nation, with a rich heritage and culture. We have a unique position within the surrounding community and its economy. We are integrating our historic past and technological present to meet our present needs.

LAND SETTLEMENT
1871–1959

Patterns of Settlement

The Cariboo-Chilcotin region opened up for settlement beginning in the gold rush years. Aspiring ranchers realized the possibilities of the open grazing land in the Chilcotin and Cariboo countryside from Lac La Hache up to Prince George. Until those choice ranching territories were gone, few looked at possibilities east of the 70 Mile House. From notations written on early pre-emption records, it seems that the whole area northeast of 70 Mile House as far as Horse Lake was called "North Bonaparte" in the earliest years. This area was among the last in the Cariboo to be settled.

Members of the Park family heading north on their epic road trip in 1922 from Missouri to the Cariboo. In 1920, the entire family had come by train to Ashcroft, expecting to find a developed ranch on their land in the North Bonaparte. Shocked to find this was untrue, they soon returned to Missouri. But their son Jack wouldn't give up. Along with his two children, Buster and Virginia, and his sister, Roxie, and her husband, Paul Hanke, he returned in 1922, driving two thousand miles in a Model T Ford and pickup truck. Courtesy Gene Park, Langley, BC.

The region was known to some, however, since the second fur brigade trail ran through its heart. In the 1820s, the Hudson's Bay Company established trade routes into the Interior. The first brigade trail came up from the south and passed to the north of Bridge Lake, Sheridan Lake, and Horse Lake. The second trail passed through the Bonaparte Plateau, heading north from Loon Lake to the west end of Green Lake. From there it proceeded west of Horse Lake, where it connected with the original fur brigade trail and on to other existing trade routes. These trails were traversed twice a year by pack trains of two or three hundred loaded horses.

Cattle drive routes paralleled the second trail, one of those coming from south of Clinton east to the Bonaparte River, crossing the Bonaparte, then heading past the west end of Green Lake and then north.

After the gold rush hit the Cariboo, construction began on the Cariboo Wagon Road in 1862. Those who travelled these roads and trails would have had a good chance to observe the countryside. But perhaps anyone who entertained thoughts of taking up land around 70 Mile House would have had second thoughts as the country began to rise dramatically from Clinton to the Cariboo Plateau.

It was another forty-five years before any serious attempt was made to settle on land east of 70 Mile House. Excluding the population of the roadhouses on the Cariboo Road at 59 Mile, 70 Mile, 74 Mile, and 83 Mile, only four households, two composed of bachelors, settled in the district between 1871 and 1904.

In 1907, settlement began in earnest, mostly by land seekers from south of the border. Everyone had to go through a certain process to acquire land. In the earliest days, most of the land had not been surveyed and would only be officially mapped after a pre-emption had been filed, sometimes years later. Undoubtedly, most, if not all, potential settlers scouted out the area first, searching for a suitable piece of land. They were allowed to apply for a quarter section (160 acres) at a time and would be looking specifically for open meadows and potential grazing land for cattle. The applicants then visited the Clinton government office in person and applied for a pre-emption on their selected piece of land, which would usually (but not always) be given a lot number at that time. In order to obtain a Crown grant and the title to their property, the applicant was obliged to make improvements on their land to earn a Certificate of Improvement. If necessary, they had to become a naturalized Canadian citizen. The fee was often paid in installments, especially in the early years. Up to 1913, settlers had to pay $1.00 per acre for their Crown land, a considerable sum for those days, since most parcels were 160 acres. When the fee was paid in full, the settlers would then get their official title.

After 1913, the price dropped to $1.00 for the entire parcel; no doubt the earlier settlers were disgruntled about having paid much more. After World War I, if the applicant was a returning soldier, documents had to be provided to verify that fact. They would then be granted their pre-emption, rather than paying the $1.00 that it cost at that time. Prices varied during the years after that, but they remained very low and affordable for the aspiring settler. Once applicants had received title to their first parcel of land, they could then apply for another, a strategy most settlers followed. It was valuable to have adult members of the family who could apply for land at the same time, as this sped up the process of establishing a viable ranch.

By the end of 1909, twenty-two individuals and families had settled between Pressy Lake and Bridge Lake. Hardly a land rush, but this was to be the pattern. By the time the 1911 census was taken, there were thirty-two households, twenty of them families. The population from 57 Mile House up to Bridge Lake was only 115 people. It was not an easy life for those early pioneers, and it wouldn't be for many years to come. This was a remote, isolated region, one that would never support any sort of town, although a few scattered stores, schools, and community halls eventually served as centres.

As was the case throughout most of the rural areas of British Columbia, men dominated the landscape. Well over half of them were single, and they had few chances for marriage: only 8 per cent of the women were also single. Over half of the households that arrived had children, although there were no facilities for education until 1914.

The 1911 census revealed that 70 per cent of the population had originated in the United States, primarily Washington State. The rest were Canadian. Most of the American household heads were middle-aged, implying that they had tried living several other places before arriving in the Cariboo. Typically immigrating to the Cariboo from Washington, Oregon, or Idaho, their actual origins were usually much farther east. They were descendants of restless parents and grandparents who had migrated throughout their lives from eastern states such as New York and Pennsylvania to the midwestern states of Missouri, Iowa, and Kansas. From there, they moved in an upward arc to Wyoming, Idaho, and Montana, finally reaching the promised lands of Oregon and Washington. This was usually a serial migration, in which they spent a year to three years in each state until they reached the West. It was quite common for every child in the family to have been born in a different state. One wonders how the wives and children withstood the constant uprooting. But there was a positive side: because of continual migrations to new territory, most of the Americans were experienced farmers and had a good idea of what was needed to set up a homestead.

A rare photo of an original group of settlers who travelled by wagon train from Rathdrum, Idaho, to the Cariboo. It's possible they were in eastern Washington in this photo. From left to right: Hazel Nichols; Inez Rodman (in shadow); Eva Andrus and her baby, Janie Andrus; Vivian Rodman in front; Cora Nichols; Sarah Nichols; Lawrence Thomas; Mrs. Chisholm and Everett; Jack Chisholm; Willis Nichols; Jim Nichols; Mr. Sparks kneeling with son Clifford; Hiram Andrus; Mr. Thomas and Art Foster by horses. Mrs. Sparks, photographer. Courtesy Yvonne Fraser, Port Alberni, BC.

The year 1914—the year the greatest number of settlers arrived—saw a different mixture of incoming people. Over half the households were from British Columbia, although many of these were recent immigrants to Canada. Only four households were from the US, in contrast to previous years. The majority chose to pre-empt land in the North Bonaparte, with only four or five settling at Bridge Lake, Roe Lake, or Horse Lake.

The years from 1907 to 1920 saw the arrival of the greatest number of settlers, with a total of over one hundred families or single men. However, for the next quarter-century, the number of newcomers was only about half what it had been in "the boom years." Fewer people were from the US. Several were recent English immigrants but the largest percentage of newcomers were either from BC or other Canadian provinces. Over half the newcomers moved to Bridge Lake, Roe Lake, and Sheridan Lake, while the remainder chose Eagan Lake and the North Bonaparte.

Although the incoming number was smaller, the immigrants from this time period tended to stay longer. Over a third remained for between twenty and ninety years; over 60 per cent of those lived in the Bridge Lake and Roe Lake area. The population in that district seemed to be the most stable, perhaps because of the fact that there were advantageous developments during

In 1903, Elizur and Amelia Chapman moved their family of four children, from Utah to Alberta. They moved to North Bridge Lake in the twenties but left in 1926.

the years: jobs opened up with the Department of Highways, and supplies were available, first at the Bridge Lake Trading Post, then at the Bridge Lake Store. Neighbours were closer; schools remained open continuously.

Things changed considerably in the ten years that elapsed between the 1911 census and the 1921 census. Although many of the original settlers from 1911 had departed, the population had more than tripled. Where there had only been settlers up to Roe Lake, now settlement had spread to Horse Lake and Lone Butte. There were only thirty-two households in 1911; in 1921, there were one hundred. However, the composition of the population hadn't changed that much. There were still over 40 per cent more men than women and the number of children per capita had actually declined. The biggest change was in the nationalities of the newcomers. Fewer people had come from the US and for the first time, immigrants from England, Scandinavia, and Europe were arriving, most settling at Horse Lake or in Lone Butte.

In the years from 1921 to 1959, well over 120 new families arrived, but of those, at least 75 per cent had moved on by 1960. Of all the people who originally settled in the district up to 1959, only a small percentage still have descendants in the area. Many of these are descendants of pioneers that arrived in 1912 and 1913: the Cleveland, Larson, Horn, Nath, Malm, Higgins, and Granberg families. At Watch Lake, descendants of the Eden family, who originally settled in 1911, still live in the area. The Park family still owns land on the Young Lake Road, although no one lives there on a permanent basis. Some families have summer homes, reluctant to let go of the last vestiges of their pioneer ancestors.

THE ROADHOUSES

70 Mile House (1871–1954)

Built in 1862, 70 Mile Roadhouse was on the border of the North Bonaparte country, and therefore, their owners could be considered the first settlers. The roadhouse changed hands several times in its first ten years: Charles Adrian, G. W. Wright, J. M. Rodgers, and Edward Fisher were all entrepreneurs leasing, renting, or selling the enterprise to various people. Rodgers and Fisher were said to have purchased the 70 Mile House in 1869. Sometime after that, John and William Saul took over the roadhouse.

Although the Saul brothers are famous in the history of the south Cariboo, facts about them are scanty and conflicting. Perhaps because there were four brothers who arrived in the country at varying times, accounts are contradictory and confusing about which brother did what and when. Genealogical records helped to sort things out.

There were actually four Saul brothers: John, Thomas, William, and Isaac, all of whom left their family farm in London, Ontario, and followed each other to the Cariboo. Although they appeared not to have any great wealth or status in Ontario, each of the Saul sons turned out to be adventurous, enterprising, and entrepreneurial. Together, they played an important part in the development of the South Cariboo as landowners, businessmen, and politicians. The brothers partnered together in different pairs and also partnered with other people, such as Edward Dougherty, William Innis, J. Rogers, Robert Beard, Richard Walters, and possibly James Robertson. Since they didn't have a great amount of money of their own, perhaps these associates lent financial support to the various ambitious Saul ventures.

Although John and William Saul may have come to British Columbia to work on the G. B. Wright road-building crew on the Cariboo Road, it wasn't long before they saw other opportunities. By late 1862, John had formed an informal partnership called Saul and Company with William Innis (or Innes), who was also working for the Wright road-building crew. Some accounts state that it was Isaac Saul and William Innis, but it was without a doubt John Saul. At that time, Isaac still lived in Ontario.

Mail day at 70 Mile House, pre-1900. 70 Mile House was the doorway to the North Bonaparte-Bridge Lake area and an essential part of the area's development. For many years, the only way into the region was the road from 70 Mile House; settlers depended on the mail and freight that arrived there. Courtesy Earl Cahill, Clinton, BC.

The pair established the 59 Mile House and were also said to have built the 61 Mile House. A traveller named Harry Jones recorded in the summer of 1863 that he stayed at the 59 Mile House, which was up and running as an inn at that time. "The proprietor [John Saul] was very kind," he noted, and went on to write that he and his companions were treated to a good meal and sent off to bed. The roadhouse was built on Lot 384, which the two leased from the BC government. It's not known how long John Saul and William Innis ran the 59 Mile House but it was still known as Saul's House in 1866.

A year earlier, in 1865, John went into ranching and he and William Innis purchased Lot 159 at Round Mound, near Clinton, from James Robertson. A few years later, John bought Innis out; the official document states that Saul and Company was an informal partnership and not incorporated. At that time, they may have sold the 59 Mile House, although no documents have been found recording that transaction. The *British Columbia Directory, 1882–1883* states, "Along the wagon road after leaving Clinton, the first place of public accommodation is the 70 mile house, 23 miles from Clinton." There was no mention of any stopping place in between.

By 1871 or 1872, Saul and Company (which now comprised John and William Saul) took over the 70 Mile House from Rogers and Fisher. It is possible that Rogers stayed on as a partner for a year or two. In the *First Victoria Directory, Fifth Issue, and British Columbia Guide* of 1874, Saul and Rogers were listed as living at "70 M. Post," although this was the last time Rogers was referred to. About this time, John sent for his youngest brother, Isaac, to come from Ontario with his family and run the hotel.

After the purchase, the Sauls added a second storey to the house, as well as building a two-storey addition. With these improvements, the roadhouse now had a dozen bedrooms that could be used for guests. The Sauls also acquired a dairy herd that they pastured at Green Lake Meadows. This was to provide dairy products for the roadhouse. John and William established

William Saul, one of the four Saul brothers who played a role in the development in the South Cariboo. William was a Member of Parliament for a few years. Image H-00841 courtesy of the Royal BC Museum and Archives.

their own brand, registered to J. and W. Saul. The herd, the brand registration states, ranged in the Upper Bonaparte and Green Lake. A wagon road was built to the area, as evidenced by the *British Columbia Directory, 1882–1883*, which states: "From this point [70 Mile House], a trail on which a wagon easily travels leads to Green Lake… Along the northern side of which the old trail of the Hudson's Bay Company formerly passed, and where mouldering huts of more recent date still remain as mementos of the passage of early gold seekers."

While Isaac and his wife, Sarah, ran the 70 Mile House roadhouse, John concentrated on ranching at the Mound Ranch. William had pre-empted the adjoining lot and the two combined their efforts at stock raising. In 1884, John was listed as a justice of the peace in *Henderson's British Columbia Gazetteer and Directory*, as well as being the first commissioner for liquor licences. By this time, he was in his sixties and had made out his will. His brother William was his sole beneficiary.

John moved to Ashcroft for a few years, where he was said in an 1886 newspaper article to be working at Harper's Mill "growing wonderful melons." By the time the 1891 census was taken, he was back in Clinton and a year later, was once again a justice of the peace. In 1894, John, who never married, died at the age of 73 after a ten-day bout with pneumonia. He is buried in the Clinton Pioneer Cemetery.

William Saul, who also never married, was born in 1836, the third-oldest Saul brother. He and John probably came to the Cariboo together. According to his obituary, he was in partnership with Edward Dougherty of Maiden Creek in a ranch on Chimney Creek before he pre-empted land at the Mound about six kilometres (four miles) out of Clinton.

In 1872, William entered the world of politics. Thomas Basil Humphreys, a well-known figure in early British Columbia politics, was serving as a representative for Lillooet in the BC legislature. His running mate died in office in 1872 and William Saul was elected to take his place as the junior representative for the district. However, William Saul and Humphreys had diametrically opposing viewpoints and Humphreys felt that he needed to oust Saul. He challenged Saul to resign and run the election over again. William accepted the challenge, confident in his backing. All was well in the Saul camp until polling day. Saul was ahead in the race, but Humphreys had an ace up his sleeve. Formerly, Chinese labourers had not been allowed to vote because they were not British citizens. Since Humphreys, a former miner, knew them all well, he found a scheme to use their allegiance. He had his Chinese friends declare that since they were all natives of Hong Kong, a British possession, their votes were valid. Humphries won over Saul by a margin of four votes. Saul ran again in 1878 and served as a member of the opposition.

Sometime after his brother John's death in 1894, William sold their property at the Mound and moved into Clinton, where he had a small residence. In 1898, he served as a justice of the peace and was listed in this capacity until 1916. During that time period, he was also appointed as a stipendiary magistrate for Clinton (one source says 1905; another says 1908). In 1913, he was transferred to Lillooet, then returned to Clinton in 1916. Suffering from chronic heart disease, he resigned from his post and died two weeks later in Clinton in April 1916. At that time, he was the last Saul brother left in the Cariboo. He is also buried in the Clinton Pioneer Cemetery.

Thomas Saul, the second-oldest of the Saul family, was not mentioned in any record in the district until 1877, when he pre-empted Lot 14 at Dog Creek. He may have stayed in Ontario until that time, taking care of their mother's farm. Thomas was listed in directories and in the 1881 census as a mail carrier in the Dog Creek area, but he also raised horses on his land. A family memoir states that Thomas and his brother William built up a herd of horses, but it may have been Isaac who did so. Since Isaac filed for a pre-emption on a parcel of land next to Thomas at Dog Creek in 1879, this suggests that the brothers may have gone in together on this venture. In July 1884, Thomas and an unnamed assistant drove a herd of horses from the Cariboo to, presumably, Fort Macleod in Alberta. Since Fort Macleod was a fairly new headquarters for the Northwest Mounted Police, it can be conjectured that Thomas had a contract with the NWMP to provide horses for their members. While fording a river near Fort Macleod, Thomas was swept away in the current and drowned. Thomas is buried at Fort Macleod, his grave marked by an impressive monument. According to a descendant, this monument was erected later by the remaining Saul brothers. Whether or not the horses were ever delivered or the Sauls received their money for them isn't known. Thomas was 52 at the time of his death.

Isaac Saul, the youngest brother in the family, married Sarah Quinn in 1865 in London, Ontario. In 1871 or 1872, Isaac and his family moved to the Cariboo to join his brothers, John and William. Perhaps not quite certain of how things would work out at 70 Mile House, Isaac retained his farm in Middlesex and rented it out. Whether Isaac contributed financially towards the venture isn't known, but he was listed as a hotel keeper and dairyman at 70 Mile until at least 1884.

Isaac and Sarah remained at the 70 Mile House for fifteen or sixteen years, running the hotel, feeding the guests, and later running the dairy at

Green Lake as well. One of their guests, Sarah Crease, mentioned them in her diary entry for September 11, 1880: "Reached 'Saul's' 70 Mile House at 5:00 pm, sun warm and bright… Had excellent supper, delicious bread, butter, and cream. Mrs. Saul quiet and thoughtful woman with small children. Room clean, beds wide, but blankets smelled of cats!"

The Sauls' life during this time was fraught with problems and tragedies. Two of their seven children died of diarrheal disease. Isaac may have lost money on the horse-raising venture with Thomas and, adding to this, was the fact that their farm back in Ontario was in trouble. A family member who was purportedly taking care of collecting rent from the farm had pocketed all the money. Sarah returned to take care of the matter and it went to court, but amazingly, they lost their case. This no doubt forced Isaac and his family to move back to Ontario in order to save their farm. Family letters confirm that they left British Columbia in 1886, and the roadhouse was sold at that time to Bill Boyd. However, records show that Isaac returned to the Cariboo more than once to take care of affairs.

The four Saul brothers were indelible characters in the history of the Cariboo. The scanty mentions of them in diaries of the time refer to at least two of them as kindly—John Saul at 59 Mile House and Sarah Saul at 70 Mile House. William was well liked enough to be elected as an MLA for the Lillooet district, although one account stated that he had a narrow mental horizon. Narrow it might have been, but he and his brothers were no slouches. Enterprising and opportunistic, they built and ran roadhouses, ranched, operated a dairy, raised horses, became justices of the peace, liquor commissioners, magistrates, and members of the provincial legislative assembly.

The next owners of the 70 Mile Roadhouse, the Boyd family, became even more legendary in Cariboo history. Running the 70 Mile Roadhouse from 1886 to 1918, a period of thirty-two years, Bill and Mary Boyd and their children pulled together through thick and thin. Many stories have been written about the affable Bill Boyd, about the courage and strength of his wife, Mary, after his early death, and about their flamboyant younger son, Jack Boyd of the Flying U. The five surviving Boyd children all distinguished themselves in various ways, and as a tightly knit family, they were a formidable unit.

Bill and Mary Boyd didn't marry until comparatively late in life. Bill, who was of Irish descent, was born in Perth County, Ontario. The farming life was not for him, and early in the 1870s, he arrived in British Columbia with a Canadian Pacific Railway work train. After living in Victoria for a short time, he made his way to the Cariboo. *Henderson's Directory* for 1882 lists him as

A rare photograph of the entire Boyd family about 1902 at 70 Mile House. From left to right: John (Jack); William Jr.; Mary with Herbert; Catherine; Sarah (Tottie); James; William Sr. with Ira. The next year, the Boyds lost two of their children, Catherine and Herbert. Two years later, Bill himself also died. Courtesy Bonnie (Boyd) Pyper, Kamloops, BC.

the road superintendent in Clinton. By 1886, he was living at 70 Mile House and working as a stockman.

Meanwhile, Mary Nicholson, his wife-to-be, was making her way west. Born in Flat River, Prince Edward Island, Mary had an intrepid spirit. She left PEI for Boston, where she worked for a few years as a governess. When she learned that her uncle Ewan Bell was going west to Clinton in the Cariboo district of British Columbia, she took a chance and went with him. There she met Bill Boyd, and they married in November 1886. She was 29 and Bill was 37, so they wasted no time in making a new life for themselves and took on the 70 Mile Roadhouse almost immediately.

Under their ownership, the roadhouse continued to thrive. In 1887, their first child, James, was born. By 1902, they had their family of five boys and two girls: James (Jim), Catherine, William (Bill), Sarah (Tottie), John (Jack), Ira, and Herbert. Their life was a busy one. While the children were young, Bill farmed and managed the cattle and dairy stock by himself. Mary cooked and ran the roadhouse. Censuses show they had at least four and possibly five employees. Mark Wade, an engineer on the Cariboo Road, visited the family and wrote colourfully about it in his memoir, *The Cariboo Road:*

Jack Boyd and his wife, the former teacher May Hunter. The couple ran the Flying U Ranch together for many years. Eventually, Jack's good times faded away: his marriage fell apart and he sold the Flying U. Courtesy Bonnie (Boyd) Pyper, Kamloops, BC.

[The 70 Mile House] was occupied in my term of residence in Clinton by William Boyd and his family. Boyd was one of the characters of the district, always to the fore at dances as a "caller-off," a good-hearted, unpolished soul, with strong prejudices, honest as the day, an Orangeman. He it was who drove me at the tail-end of one winter, my introduction to that part of the country, from Clinton over Pavilion Mountain to visit the wife of a farmer, Irish as was Boyd, but Roman Catholic. At the patient's house was a priest. Oil and water do not mix very well, but quite as well as the Orangeman and the curé.

An often-repeated story about Bill Boyd has been somewhat exaggerated. Various accounts state that he died of a gunshot wound from a hunting accident, some saying it was shortly after the event, some that it was years later from the lingering effects. But the "Kootenay Mail" column in a Revelstoke newspaper dated April 14, 1894, tells the real story:

Shot, Not Quite by a Stranger

William Boyd, who keeps the 70-Mile House, Cariboo road was accidentally shot on the 20th inst. While returning home from Clinton he passed a stranger and offered to take his overcoat on with him so as to ease the stranger's load. When Boyd got home and took the things out of the rig, he threw the overcoat and other articles on the floor, when a pistol went off. The bullet entered Boyd's side above the hip, circled around the body and now lies buried in his shoulder. The doctor says that no vital part has been touched and unless blood poisoning sets in, there will not be much danger. Mr. Boyd is well known amongst old timers here and is a very popular host. He is rapidly recovering.

A strange enough story on its own, and one which Boyd descendants verify is the true version.

During the years that the Boyd family owned the roadhouse, they enlarged the accommodations to twenty-eight rooms and built a freight shed. A post office was situated there, and as time progressed, a telephone and a telegraph office were added. There was also a general store that stocked basic supplies. To warm the hearts of weary travellers, they also sold liquor by the bottle or glass, something not all roadhouses offered.

Many well-known people stayed at the 70 Mile Roadhouse, including Judge Matthew Baillie Begbie and the poet Pauline Johnson. The famous packer Jean Caux, nicknamed Cataline, stopped often. Roy Eden, who homesteaded around Watch Lake, tells of meeting Cataline in 1907 when he first went up to the Cariboo as a boy of 16 and worked at the 70 Mile:

It seemed to me that every day that summer there was always something happening of great interest. The road houses in those years were doing a good business, and most every night the place was crowded. It was that summer when I saw my first real pack train, when the famous packer "Catalina" or Catalan made an overnight camp close to the 70 Mile House. I had quite an interesting talk with Jean Caux, one of the first and the last of the old Cariboo Packers—a most interesting old fellow. I cannot remember just how many mules were in his train, it must have been around 75 with what the packers rode themselves.

Life was going well. Business was brisk and the Boyd family was active and happy. But in 1903, that all changed. The oldest daughter, Catherine, had suffered from a severe bout of strep throat the year before and wasn't recovering.

She developed pyaemia, a strep infection that was invariably fatal before the advent of antibiotics. Her parents sent her to Clinton to be cared for by a doctor, but she died in March 1903. The *Ashcroft Journal* published its condolences:

> There is sorrow at the 70-mile House because of the death of Mr. W. Boyd's eldest daughter, Katie. The deceased was 13 years of age, and succumbed last Monday morning, after a lingering illness of about a year. The funeral took place at Clinton on Wednesday. Many friends from all parts of Cariboo and Lillooet districts extend their sincere sympathy to Mr. and Mrs. Boyd.

There was more to come for the grieving family. Three months later, their 11-month-old son Herbert died of meningitis in Clinton after a two-week illness. The family was still reeling from shock when another black cloud appeared on the horizon. Bill, always strapping and energetic, wasn't feeling well and gradually went downhill. Early in 1905, he visited Vancouver, hoping to find out what was wrong with him and regain his health. But the news wasn't good. Bill was diagnosed with kidney cancer, and although he had some treatment, he didn't rally. Finally, in August, he went down to Vancouver and was operated on at St. Paul's Hospital. He never recovered from the operation and died on August 16. His friend, Jack Cunningham of 74 Mile, signed for the body when it arrived in Clinton. Bill was only 56 years old.

Mary was now left without a husband and had barely recovered from the loss of two of her children two years earlier. The family ranged from the eldest, Jim, who was 18, to Ira, who was 6. Her surviving daughter, Tottie, was 12. They did the only thing they could do—rally together and carry on. Money was found to send Jim to the Vancouver Business Institute (now Sprott Shaw College) in Vancouver, which had just opened in 1903. This training gave Jim the skills to become a forester in later years. While he was there, he met Roy Eden, who later pre-empted land at Watch Lake, and also Henry Koster, who later owned the huge Empire Valley Ranch.

Tottie was her mother's right hand. As well as cooking, cleaning, and attending to matters that concerned the running of the roadhouse, she was just as proficient at the outside ranch chores. According to an article by Molly Forbes in the *Clinton Pioneer* in 1966, she could "hitch and saddle, drive and ride any kind of horse, or pick a hawk out [of] a tree at 200 yards." Later, she learned how to drive a car too, and confidently drove the Ford back and forth to Clinton. In 1909, the 70 Mile House became part of the telegraph line. Tottie had taken a course in Vancouver and she, along with Jim, took over the operation of the telegraph.

By 1911, when the census was taken, Mary was still running the hotel and was also listed as a freighter. Her son Bill was working on their farm and doing odd jobs on a government survey; Tottie was living at home; Jack was working as a cowboy on their farm at Green Lake; and Ira was still only 11. Jim was living separately, closer to the 74 Mile House and had a Chinese cook and a domestic worker. In 1913, Jack pre-empted Lot 3782 at Green Lake, which eventually became the Flying U Ranch and was a separate unit from the Green Lake Ranch that the Boyd family owned.

The news of World War I filtered into the Cariboo and the Boyd boys, always up for a challenge, enlisted as soon as they could. Losing the help of her older sons during the war period made Mary rethink her life and once the boys were back and beginning to set up their own individual lives, she saw the writing on the wall. Sometime around late 1918, the Boyd family sold the roadhouse to Fred and Agnes Cummings and bought the Bell ranch near Clinton on the Kelly Lake Road.

Several sources have named "R. D. Cummings" as the new owner, but in fact, it was *F.* D. Cummings. According to *Wrigley's British Columbia Directory*, there was an R. D. Cummings living in Ashcroft selling insurance at the same time that F. D. Cummings was running the 70 Mile, so they were two different people.

Fred Cummings and his wife, Agnes Smith, came from Nova Scotia with their children and in 1914 moved to the Cariboo, living in Springhouse, Clinton, and Ashcroft. By 1918, they had taken over the 70 Mile Roadhouse. Agnes became the cook, cleaner, and postmistress at the roadhouse, and Fred also did teamster work while running the establishment. Geoffrey Downton, who was surveying the North Bonaparte and Bridge Lake area, used Fred's services several times in 1920. The surveying camp had to be moved from place to place, and Cummings had a wagon and team of horses they used for transport. He also had a car. Fred was a bit of a daredevil and Downton had an interesting ride one day: "Tuesday, Aug 10th, drove to 70 Mile House with Cummings. Experienced a rough and hair raising ride over rough roads at top speed."

By 1921, Agnes and Fred had eight children ranging from a few months old to 14 years of age. Two of the children had been born while they owned the roadhouse. Since Agnes had the job of operating both the post office and the inn, as well as raising her young brood, she must have been a very busy woman. Her predecessors, Sarah Saul and Mary Boyd, had been in exactly the same position: many children and a stunning load of work.

In 1922, Fred and Agnes sold the roadhouse to Matt Porter and turned to farming in the North Bonaparte. A newspaper article in the *Ashcroft Journal* stated that in May 1922, F. D. Cummings was renting the former

Mawdsley farm, which was on the North Bonaparte road. There he raised sheep and ran a dairy. Sometime in 1923, Agnes and the children moved to Roe Lake, perhaps so the children could go to school. The next year, the family moved to California, where they spent the rest of their lives.

The new owner of the 70 Mile Roadhouse, Matt Porter, was destined to become one of the most beloved characters in the South Cariboo. Charles Marshall Porter, as he was always known on official documents, went by his nickname "Matt." Born in 1882 in Bruce County, Ontario, Matt became a tinsmith apprentice. In the summer of 1914, he arrived in the North Bonaparte with his older brother William. William filed for a pre-emption on Lot 4469, three kilometres (two miles) east of Little Green Lake. A month later, Matt filed on the adjoining Lot 4470. With 320 acres between them, they worked together to establish a cattle ranch. In 1919, *Wrigley's British Columbia Directory* listed them as "Porter Bros., cattle & horse ranching." That same year Matt Porter became the postmaster at the North Bonaparte post office and the brothers had a mail stage for pickup and delivery at 70 Mile House. By 1920, Matt had moved out to the 70 Mile House. Surveyor Geoffrey Downton stated in his daily diary on July 30, 1920: "Mr. Porter at 70 Mile House badly hurt in auto accident at 69 Mile—Doctor arrived 7 PM." A week later, he noted that "Mr. Porter who was seriously injured in auto

Matt Porter at 70 Mile House, driving a stagecoach with a handsome team of horses, probably during the 1920s. The sign on the building tells about the services the roadhouse offered. Matt used many modes of transportation for mail and freight: horse and buggy, sleigh, a Pierce-Arrow sedan, and a delivery truck. Courtesy Mona (McConnell) Sturges, San Diego, California.

Posing out in the snow, Matt Porter (far left) and "Ma" Porter (seated, centre) have a good laugh at 70 Mile House with staff, guests, four dogs, and two bagged deer in the background. Courtesy Mona (McConnell) Sturges, San Diego, California.

smash is progressing favourably." No other source mentions this accident, so it appears that Matt didn't suffer any long-term effects.

Matt's goings and comings were a bit confusing during this time period. When the June 1921 census was taken, both Matt and William were listed as living at the North Bonaparte ranch. They were both recorded as ranchers, with no mention of a postmaster's job. Living with them were three employees who did general work: Thomas English and William Rushworth, both listed as ranchers, and Ed Rioux, a trapper. As well, Isabelle McConnell, later known as "Ma," made her first appearance in the Porter household. She was working there as a housekeeper, along with her son, Ashley, who was 11. It was noted that she also worked at a "cookhouse" and according to family lore, this was at a local tie mill. Isabelle was a busy woman, but she had to be in order to make a living. Her husband, David, no longer lived with the family and was in Manitoba.

In 1922, Matt purchased the 70 Mile Roadhouse business from Fred Cummings. When the Cummings owned it, Agnes had done all the cooking, cleaning, and various other jobs around the roadhouse. Now that she was gone,

Matt needed someone to fill her place. Isabelle was the natural choice. As well as being a conscientious worker, she was a renowned cook.

According to *Trails to Gold*, Vol. 2, she was working as a cook at 59 Mile House when Matt recruited her, offering her twice the going rate to come and cook for him at the 70 Mile House. But it is also possible that Isabelle was still cooking at the tie mill, as she had been a year earlier.

Isabelle worked for Matt for several years as an employee, but things changed after her husband David's death. The story goes that she gave Matt an ultimatum: since she was uncomfortable living under the same roof with a bachelor now that she was a single woman, it was either marriage or she moved on. On April 10, 1931, she and Matt went to Ashcroft and made it official. Matt was listed as a 48-year-old bachelor and Isabelle as a 46-year-old widow on the marriage certificate. On the bottom, the certificate shows Matt's somewhat flowery signature and Isabelle's more practical one. From then on (and perhaps before), Isabelle was known affectionately as "Ma Porter."

Matt took care of the weekly mail route, a ninety-five-kilometre (sixty-mile) round trip that could take up to three days to complete. Together, the two ran the 70 Mile House for over thirty years, often housing road crews, survey crews, and other workers. They both had big hearts and often helped

70 Mile House was always a popular place to stop, no matter what the year. In the 1940s, an unidentified man poses by two automobiles from the period. Courtesy Harold Mobbs, Lone Butte, BC.

Water Witching
Mae (Bryant) McConnell, 70 Mile House

"Get a nice green, limber red willow branch with a fork in it. Hold it in both your hands until you feel it pull. When you can't hold it up any more and the stick pulls down, you know there's water there. Then cut a straight stick 4' long. Hold it by the end and the number of bounces means the number of feet you have to go down to reach the water. Then when the end of the stick goes around and around, that means how many gallons per minute you'll get when you pump it."

Mae successfully witched thirty or forty wells in her time. Her husband, David, believed in the method, but it wouldn't work for him. For her, it worked so well and the pull was so strong, the bark would peel off in her hands.

others. Floyd Tompkins, in his memoir, *Honest Memories of One Man's Life,* recounted how he was taken under their wing for a while:

> I rode the little mare that [my brother] Earl had given me, bareback, for 23 miles out to 70 Mile House to the Porters' where they were meeting lots of people every year, as they ran a roadhouse and the post office. It didn't matter how green you were, as long as you were willing to work. They always had fun with you, and I liked to help so this made it a very pleasant place to work. I was still only 14 years old and was working for my board. [My friend Howard Reaugh] Kinik and I always had good clothes to wear and a couple of dollars in our pockets. Mrs. Porter was good to us, and she loved kids. She was a wonderful cook and loved people. We all worked at putting up the hay at the Thompson Meadow, which was about 13 miles north on the Cariboo Road. It was a big meadow that put up about 100 tons of swamp hay. After haying was done, there was bird hunters coming up. They wanted someone to show them some geese and the lakes of where they were at. Mrs. Porter said that she was sure I could do this, as I knew quite a bit of country around the area, and she told me how to hunt the geese and how much I should get for being their guide...

Matt was a man with many interests. He was a talented tinsmith and blacksmith, teaching his grandchildren, particularly Stallard McConnell, the tricks of the trade. As a charter member of the South Cariboo Historical Society, he had his own collection of historical artifacts, including many collected from Indigenous people. According to his obituary, he had certificates for service with the Rocky Mountain Rangers and a Royal Canadian Air Force certificate for aircraft detection during World War II. There have been stories written about Matt's fondness for alcohol and his irresponsibility, but surviving family members dispute this. While he was an interesting, colourful person, the truth is that he was more dependable than some writers portrayed him. This is not to say he didn't enjoy a wee nip now and then.

Through good times and bad, the 70 Mile Roadhouse continued to thrive. Prices were always reasonable, Ma's cooking was legendary, and the Porters were willing to house and feed any kind of crew that came along. But both Matt and Ma were getting older. On September 16, 1954, five days after his last postal run, 72-year-old Matt died of pneumonia at home. Isabelle, by then 69, retired and rented out the 70 Mile House, first to William Goodrich and then to Jack Parrot. When the roadhouse burned down two years later, she had a small house built on the location and lived there until her death in 1968. Matt and Ma are both buried in Clinton, pioneers of the South Cariboo who will always be remembered.

74 Mile House (1896–2017)

The 74 Mile House was first developed by Sergeant-Major John McMurphy in 1862 and was run by him and his family until 1865. After that year, it was leased out to others but eventually business dwindled to non-existent. Jack Cunningham changed all that.

John (Jack) Cunningham was born in 1869 in Scotland and immigrated to Canada in 1887. By 1891, he was living in Clinton, BC, working as a farm labourer. A few years later, he started thinking about owning land. He filed two different pre-emptions in 1894, but changed his mind and cancelled them. In January 1896, he filed for a pre-emption on Lot 570, 160 acres at "74 Mile Post."

Not too long after he arrived in the Cariboo, Jack arranged for his 19-year-old sister, Margaret, to join him. In a land of bachelors, she was highly eligible, and by November 1892, she'd married Thomas Barton of Clinton, a road inspector. The Bartons were big-hearted people, known for their kindness to others. In 1896, Jack again sent back home, this time for his fiancée, Margaret Clark, 21. When Margaret arrived, she was accompanied by John's sister Isabelle, who was also 21. In 1899, Isabelle married William Kelly, who had a saddle shop in Clinton.

Jack built a log cabin on his property, and in December 1896, he and Margaret were married. While they spent their first winter in the cabin, Alexander (Sandy) Innis, an expert axeman, constructed the 74 Mile Roadhouse. In 1898, their first child, John Kenneth (called Kenneth), was born. Ethel Henrietta (Rieta) followed in 1901, Thomas Norman (Norman) in

1902, and Margaret in 1905. All the children were born at the 74 Mile House. Jack became district road superintendent and relied on Margaret to run things when he was away. Their inn was doing well and the cattle herd was growing. Life was good.

Then, in 1910, like the Boyd family at the 70 Mile House only five years before, their world came tumbling down. Kenneth got the measles, a common enough childhood disease. But he rapidly developed acute peritonitis and died at home on November 10. The day of his death, Jack came down with influenza, which grew increasingly worse and developed into pneumonia. On November 24, exactly two weeks after Kenneth's death, Jack died too.

It's hard to imagine carrying on with normal life after two such tragedies. The grief that Margaret felt must have been intense, but she couldn't afford to let it take control. Her three other children had to be taken care of, the roadhouse had to be run, the cattle and livestock had to be attended to. Unlike the Boyds, though, Margaret's children were all young: in 1910, Margaret was only 5, Rieta was 9, and Norman was 8. But, like all country children, they helped out and did chores. Eventually Margaret hired Frank Mills to work as the ranch foreman while she took care of the roadhouse. Jack's sister Margaret and her husband, Thomas Barton, had come back from up north and were no doubt a help to the struggling family.

The roadhouse continued to thrive through the years. As well as appreciating its good reputation for meals and comfort, many of the travellers knew of Margaret's circumstances and made sure they patronized her business. The children, as they grew older, took on more and more responsibility. By the time they were in their early teens, they were able to handle chores such as dehorning and branding, hauling hay from the meadows with a four-horse team, rounding up the cattle herd, and all the myriad other jobs that had to be done. Eventually, Norman ran the ranch with the help of a hired man, Rieta worked with the horses, and Margaret, the youngest, helped with running the roadhouse. But fate was about to deal them another blow, described in a news story in the *Ashcroft Journal*:

Ashcroft Journal, December 8, 1923: 74 Mile House Burned Down

Another old land mark in the shape of the 74-Mile House, on the Cariboo Road, was totally destroyed by fire on Monday night last, being a total loss to the owner, Mrs. J. Cunningham, who has resided there for a number of years. The fire started during the night from some unknown origin and the occupants were forced to flee in their night attire. They had time, however, to save the piano before the fire reached that part of the house. Part of the building destroyed was built during the early days of freighting on the Cariboo Road, while other parts were added later. The property was partially covered by insurance. Mrs. Cunningham and family are taking up temporary quarters at Pollards' ranch, Clinton.

A new roadhouse, this time a large frame building, was soon rebuilt on the same spot with the help of family and friends. Life carried on once more. During the 1930s and 1940s, the family capitalized on the new trend of dude ranches. Discovering a niche that fit well with their own beliefs and lifestyle, they advertised an opportunity for young boys in urban areas to experience country life. They soon became so popular that they were unable to accommodate all the applicants. Teenaged boys from Vancouver and Victoria, sometimes twenty at a time, spent summers and holidays at the 74 Mile. Living in small cabins and eating meals at the roadhouse, they helped out with ranch chores and learned essential country skills. Margaret had a big heart and during World War II took in two children from London who had been sent to Canada to escape the bombing. Their parents had been killed in an air raid and Margaret raised them until they were old enough to go out on their own.

Margaret's own children developed into resourceful people in their own right. Rieta, the oldest daughter, was well known for her horsemanship. No one could handle a horse like she could. She developed a taste for racing at a young age, and when she was only 14, rode against professional jockeys at the Clinton track. Mr. R. F. Leighton of the BC Riding Association wrote: "Miss Cunningham's riding record is, as far as I am aware, unbeaten, and her average for the last two years (1924–1926) is right at the top." In an unnamed newspaper of 1926, an article appeared entitled "Cariboo's Favourite Jockey Started Racing Career as Girl of Fourteen." Journalist Louis Lebourdais concluded the article by stating:

> She sits her horse like a centaur, and it is a pleasure to watch her ride, but this is not her only accomplishment. She is equally at home at the wheel of a high-powered automobile, or perched on the precarious seat of a "bucking" mower as it bumps over the uneven surface of some wild hay meadow. And in the ballroom, her well-fitting riding togs exchanged for the conventional evening gown, her favor is much sought, for she dances with as much charm and gracefulness as she rides.

Apparently, helping to run a roadhouse developed many skills: Tottie Boyd of the 70 Mile House had also been praised for almost exactly the same characteristics.

The second 74 Mile Roadhouse. The Cunninghams built the first 74 Mile Roadhouse in 1897 and this building burned down in 1923. They rebuilt soon after but the second roadhouse suffered the same fate, burning down in 2010 after standing for 86 years. Courtesy Earl Cahill, Clinton, BC.

Rieta was as tough to catch as some of the livestock she had to round up. She was independent and also had a great sense of responsibility towards her family and the ranch. Not about to give that up easily, her answer to her many suitors was always "maybe"—never "yes" or "no." But finally she met a young man named James Dougherty who was able to persuade her to give up the single state. Part of a telephone crew stationed at 74 Mile House, James was from Montreal and had been in the air force. About 1942, they married and sometime later purchased a ranch at Graham Station in the Green Lake area from Fran Walsh. James, brought up in the city, found it hard to adjust to the remoteness and isolation of the Cariboo. He eventually had a breakdown, and he and Rieta divorced. After the sale of their ranch, Rieta settled for a few hectares on the highway with a saddlehorse and a few head of her original herd of cattle. Finally, her health forced her to move to Kamloops, where she died in January 1980 at the age of 79.

Norman, although ranch-born and -bred, had many other interests besides being a cowboy. He was fascinated by engines and machines, and despite his difficulties getting an education, was a voracious reader. He also enjoyed music and was interested in the world at large. In 1919, he travelled to California with his friends Carr, Minnie, and Deloy Cleveland from Eagan Lake. The brothers were visiting their family in Mendocino County and the party also made a visit to San Francisco. For young Norman, who had never been away from the Cariboo, it must have been enthralling.

Despite his other interests, Norman settled down to ranch life and made a success of it. In 1930, he married Mary Dorothy (Molly) Wilkinson, a teacher from Jesmond, BC, and they ran the 74 Mile ranch together. Four boys were born to them over the years: Kenneth, William (Bill), Gordon, and Earl. Their family life was a happy one and the boys all grew up helping to run the ranch. They learned to break horses and regularly participated in rodeos.

When the Cariboo Road was rerouted in 1948 and no longer went past the 74 Mile Roadhouse, Margaret closed the roadhouse, retired, and handed over the reins to her son Norman and daughter Rieta. She continued to live at the ranch until her death at 91 in February 1966.

The third generation of Cunninghams were all becoming adults. As Bill, Norman and Molly's second son, got older, he worked for others as a ranch hand, sometimes at the Flying U Ranch. A few of the young women who worked there had their eye on him, but apparently, he wasn't up for grabs. Joan McPherson Dunbar, who wrote an article published in the *100 Mile Free Press* about her memories of working at the Flying U in 1948, tells the story: "A few permanent cowboys were on staff and the first night I looked over the corral fence and watched a quiet young man working with a young horse. He was so gentle and had the manners of what we now call a true 'Horse Whisperer.' His name was Billy Cunningham, however Olga (Rust) had already staked him out."

Bill and Olga married in 1954 and moved into a large log home at Bullock Lake, although there was no running water or power. Their family of five boys and a girl were raised there, and Bill ran a herd of a hundred head of cattle. In 1975, Norman passed away, and the 74 Mile ranch was handed over to Bill, although he and his family continued to live at their Bullock Lake home. Five years later, that house burned down. Bill and Olga and their family moved into the old roadhouse, virtually unchanged. Room numbers still hung on the bedroom doors; the original furnishings still graced the rooms.

In 2000, Olga passed away and Bill was left in the rambling old roadhouse alone. With the help of his sons and grandsons, he continued to run the ranch as it had been run since 1896. Another kind of death occurred when fire again struck in 2010. The 74 Mile ranch house, which had stood for eighty-six years, was burned to the ground; only the original barn remained standing. With the help of his sons, a new house was built for Bill. He passed away in 2016.

Margaret, the youngest daughter of the family, married Leonard Sadlier-Brown in 1929. Leonard, a recent widower, was a police constable stationed at 100 Mile House. He became the first motorcycle policeman on the road and patrolled from Ashcroft to Williams Lake. The couple moved to McClure.

In 2011, there was a huge reward for all those years of working the ranch and remaining on the land. At the Kamloops Cowboy Festival, the Cunningham family—all five generations—were inducted into the BC Cowboy Hall of Fame. The vice-president of the BC Cowboy Heritage Society, Mark McMillan, remarked that "[t]here are hundreds who have been nominated and are on a waiting list and at the moment, do not qualify as above average to make the BC Hall of Fame. This is not the hall of average; the Cunninghams are special. Every generation has been involved with both rodeo and working ranch."

83 Mile House (1933–1950)

The 83 Mile House changed hands many times through the years. It was originally developed by Thomas, John, and Richard Walters in 1862. In 1866, it was purchased by Albert Crysler, who ran it for two years and then sold it to Murdoch Ross. Steve Tingley was the next owner, acquiring it in 1897. At the peak of its operation over the years, Tingley renovated and enlarged the operation and ran it until 1905. David Stoddard of Clinton purchased it at that time and sold out in 1915. The new owner was the government-backed Soldier Settlement Board, who put two inexperienced veterans, Tony Orford and Jack Templeton, in charge. The roadhouse burnt to the ground in 1922.

The 83 Mile Roadhouse in a photo said to be taken in the 1860s. During the gold rush, all the roadhouses were bustling with activity. Image A33886, Major Mathews Collection. City of Vancouver Archives.

Records are murky after that date. However, in 1933, the 83 Mile was revitalized with the arrival of the Walsh family from Nelson. Francis (Frank) Walsh and his family owned and ran the 83 Mile Roadhouse for many years and members of the family still live in the district.

Frank Walsh was born in Ontario and was perhaps destined to be in the roadhouse business: his father James was listed as a saloon keeper in the 1881 census and as a hotel keeper in the 1891 census. Sometime around the turn of the century, Frank moved to British Columbia. In 1907, he married Anne Cruikshank in Nelson, BC, and the couple had three children over the years: Doreen, Francis Jr. (Fran), and Monica.

The 1921 census listed Frank as a waiter in a restaurant in Vancouver, but he had other plans for the future. Searching for a different life for their family, he and Annie saw that there were opportunities along the Cariboo Road. Roadhouses catering to travellers dotted the expanse of the road and most seemed to thrive. Although Frank was the one with experience in that direction, they decided that Annie would try it out first and see if this was a viable option. Annie, a strong, independent woman, took on running the 87 Mile House for a year or so. Their son, Fran, and youngest daughter, Monica, went with her. Frank remained in Vancouver, working and saving money, along with Doreen, who was training to be a teacher at the Normal School.

Annie came home with good reports on the possible success of running a roadhouse and in 1933, they purchased the 83 Mile Roadhouse. Ironically,

The 83 Mile Roadhouse. Frank and Annie Walsh purchased the roadhouse in 1933 and built a thriving business. While they didn't provide rooms, they had a store, restaurant, and gas pumps. After Frank's sudden death, they sold out in 1946. Courtesy Marilyn Walsh, 70 Mile House, BC.

two days after their arrival, history repeated itself and the building on the property burned down. The family was lucky—they hadn't even had time to unpack, so they lost very little. With the $200 of insurance money they were awarded, they lost no time building another house, which became part roadhouse, part living space.

The 83 Mile Roadhouse quickly became a going concern. Although they didn't offer accommodation, the Walshes had a restaurant, some convenience products, and gas pumps at the front. The piece of property they'd purchased included a large acreage and they were able to raise several milk cows. The milk provided butter, cream, and ice cream for the restaurant.

The family worked together, everyone handling his or her own job. Frank manned the gas pumps and ran the restaurant; Annie was the cook. Monica milked the cows and took care of the chickens and small livestock; Fran did the haying and looked after the cows and horses.

When World War II broke out, Fran enlisted and went back east for training. After his return from the war, his parents gave him a large portion of their property. He made it into his home, running it as a ranch, as well as working as a log builder. He married Marilyn Bunker in 1951. Part of their property remains in the family today.

The 83 Mile Roadhouse continued to run until Frank's sudden death in 1946. The family made the difficult decision to sell and it was purchased by Erwin A. Brandley, a druggist from Williams Lake. As is usual when a business changes hands, Brandley set about making changes. He hired Frank Granberg to build a new, larger log roadhouse. After a few years, he sold out and returned to Williams Lake. The new owners, a German family, soon had an unpleasant surprise: they learned that the government had plans to reroute the Cariboo Road, bypassing the 83 Mile House. Not to be outwitted, they had Frank Granberg and Fran Walsh take the building apart, log by log, and move it to a new location by the rerouted highway.

After her husband's death, Annie purchased property at Green Lake. Always an intrepid person, she built her own house and lived there until her death in 1956.

GREEN LAKE, WATCH LAKE, AND THE NORTH BONAPARTE

During the tenure of the Boyds at 70 Mile House, the North Bonaparte country to the east finally saw its first settlers, a few intrepid souls. The first, as far as is known, were partners Alexander (Sandy) Innis and Robert Jamieson. They'd been living in the vicinity of Clinton and they'd ridden around the territory and were familiar with it. In 1891, Alexander applied for a pre-emption of Lot 786 on the Bonaparte River. Lot 786 straddled both sides of the Bonaparte along the cattle drive trail.

Although Innis was the owner of the property, gaining title in 1905, it's likely that his partner Robert Jamieson was the one who lived there full-time. In fact, that area was referred to as the Jameson Place (although the correct name was Jamieson). Surveyor Geoffrey Downton specifically referred to this place in 1920, which was apparently unoccupied at that time: "… went down Fly Creek with party and commenced survey of [Lot 4906] (Edward Mobbs, returned soldier). Moved this P. R. a quarter mile south of place described to take in the flat below the 'Jameson Place,' Lot 786, on the Bonaparte River." The 1901 census shows Alexander Innis lodging at 83 Mile House, working as a carpenter (he built their large horse barn), and Robert Jamieson farming on the Bonaparte. *Henderson's Directory* for 1901 and 1902 for 70 Mile House listed Jamieson as a "farmer and stock-raiser on [the] Bonaparte."

Sometime between 1891 and 1894, Robert, who was not a young man, married an unnamed Secwepemc woman. He fathered three daughters with her, and in 1900, it seems that she died in childbirth (Robert, listed as a widower in the 1901 census, had a baby daughter, Rose, who had been born in 1900). As far as is known, Louisa Jamieson, the eldest daughter of Robert and his wife, born July 9, 1894, was the first baby born to a white settler in the North Bonaparte country.

Five years after Innis and Jamieson settled Lot 786, a young man named John Currie pre-empted Lot 656, somewhat north of the partners and along the Brigade Trail. Currie was from New Westminster and married Florence Hacker a few weeks after his land application in October 1896. By that time, it was the beginning of winter, so perhaps they spent the winter at the coast and moved up in the spring. Arriving in the Cariboo at the beginning of November without a house built would have been foolhardy.

John Currie and Robert Jamieson, as neighbours, were many kilometres apart on a rough trail, but that would have made little difference. No one was daunted by distance or weather conditions in those days. Robert, along with a John Ferry, vouched for John on his Certificate of Improvement in 1901. Florence probably became friends with Mrs. Jamieson and when Florence's second child, John Jr., was born in August 1899 at home (his birth certificate says his birthplace was "Brigade Trail"), it could very well have been that Robert's wife helped to deliver him.

Two years after his wife's death, Robert died in Ashcroft in 1902 at the age of 64. Sandy Innis completed the improvements on the pre-emption and applied for the Certificate of Improvement in March 1905. Since most records show he continued to work as a labourer and itinerant carpenter, he may never have lived on the property again and may have let it revert to the Crown for unpaid taxes. As far as is known, no one else ever lived on the place.

The Curries, meanwhile, continued to work diligently on their homestead. By 1901, John had built a dairy, two stables, barns, and corrals. As well, he had been working on a wagon road from his place to Green Lake. Geoffrey Downton, in his 1920 diary, frequently mentioned the "Curry Trail" or the "Curry Road." Since Downton was referring to travelling north from the Currie place to Tin Cup Mountain and Mount Begbie, it seems certain that Hutchison Road was once the Currie Road. If historical maps of trails in the area are correct, this would originally have been the Brigade Trail.

After Jamieson's death in July 1902, the Currie family were the only settlers in the wilderness that stretched northeast from 70 Mile House. But not for long. Later in the year, two Scottish ranching brothers, Samuel and Robert Graham, moved east from their ranch at Kelly Lake in the Chilcotin. They pre-empted land around Green Lake and drove their large herd of cattle from Kelly Lake to their new homestead.

The Graham brothers had first emigrated from Scotland to Manitoba, where their older brother James lived. According to an entertaining article written by P. W. Luce in the *Vancouver Sun* in 1951, they arrived in Canada with a belt of gold strapped around their waists. However, they never spent a penny they didn't need to. All that booty never tempted their Scottish souls. Although they both applied for homesteads in Manitoba, they gave that up and turned to working in railroad construction. "Sam was a teamster, and a good one," the article stated, and "Bob did anything around the camps and did it well, unless it was cooking. He was terrible at that. So was Sam." The Grahams ended up owning a good string of horses, wagons, and quite a bit of equipment.

British Columbia and the Cariboo appealed to the brothers and they decided to go into the cattle business, establishing a ranch at Kelly Lake. Bob took care of their 150-odd head of cattle and Sam hauled freight on the Cariboo Road. His earnings went into obtaining more stock and improving their ranch.

The brothers needed some good natural meadows and found what they were looking for in the North Bonaparte. In July 1901, Sam applied for a pre-emption on 320 acres on the Upper Bonaparte River. A year later, his brother Bob filed for a pre-emption of 160 acres in the 83 Mile Creek and Green Lake area. The Grahams must have sold their Kelly Lake place, perhaps to one of the larger ranches in that area. By 1904, they had built a house and stable at Green Lake, had twelve acres under cultivation, and had completed some fencing. But in August 1907, a house fire consumed their dwelling and they lost everything they had, including all the paperwork on their pre-emptions. Fortunately, the land office had made provisions for such occurrences. The brothers made a legal declaration that they'd lost their paperwork in a fire, the land office accepted their word for it, and they both gained title in 1911 to their respective pieces of land. Three years after the conflagration, they had regained all their losses. As well as rebuilding their house, they erected a stable, hay sheds, cattle sheds, and corrals. The Certificate of Improvement stated that they'd also constructed a dam and had done further clearing.

The Grahams were progressive farmers. The brothers created a series of flumes and ditches on their places to carry water several kilometres to irrigate their hay fields. According to the *Vancouver Sun* article, they were the first in the Lillooet land district to raise two crops of rye in a year. Some of these flumes survived for many years after their deaths. The sturdy house they built in 1908 is still standing today, a testament to their fine workmanship.

The brothers were both quite well educated, and Bob served as the justice of the peace in the earliest years in the North Bonaparte. "He resigned when he discovered that he had been tricked into certifying that the necessary improvement had been done on a homestead for which patent was sought," the *Vancouver Sun* article stated. "He could not reconcile his Scottish conscience to official misconduct." Bob also had a political bent and ran for the Liberals against Archie MacDonald of Clinton. The *Vancouver Sun* tells the humorous story:

> It was Bob who served as standard-bearer early in the century
> in a forlorn-hope campaign for the Liberals in the East Lillooet

district. He had no chance whatever against Archie MacDonald, owner of the general store in Clinton. Bob Graham didn't open his purse strings for the campaign. He rode his pet mare around the grub line to canvas the voters, talked crops and cattle, berated the government, slept in the hired man's bed, and went his way after breakfast. There was a tradition that a candidate should bring a bottle with him when making the circuit. Bob conformed to this, but there were critics who said the whiskey was a little weak.

After the election the Grahams continued to get their supplies from Archie MacDonald's store in Clinton. Sometimes they were not satisfied and then Sam would write a sarcastic letter fairly dripping with insults and slander. Bob Fraser, the manager, would pin up the letter for all the customers to see "that Sam Graham had gone on a rattlesnake diet again."

On one occasion Sam ordered twenty-five cents' worth of Epsom salts and demanded good value. Bob Fraser sent him a 100-pound sackful, which he scooped up from a lake near Clinton that had a natural deposit of the stuff. "It will probably take all this to get the bile out of your system," he scribbled in an enclosed note.

Bob secured the job of census enumerator for the 1911 census and travelled from 70 Mile House up to Bridge Lake. No doubt he had good visits every place he stopped, as he and Sam were popular, congenial people, despite Bob Fraser's comments. They were friends with Judge Matthew Begbie and on his horseback trips to Barkerville to conduct court sessions, Begbie would often stay overnight at their place.

Although neither Bob nor Sam ever married, they were far from reclusive bachelors. They liked to have a female face around and employed several different housekeepers over the years. The housekeeper usually also did ranching chores. In the 1920s, a niece from Manitoba, Jean (daughter of their brother James), moved to the area to live with them and help out.

Jean's life came to a tragic end a few years later. Her obituary in the *Ashcroft Journal* of November 28, 1925, tells the sad story:

Jean Mills Graham, niece of Sam and Robert Graham of Green Lake, committed suicide on Friday of last week by discharging a .22 rifle shot into her temple. Miss Graham arrived from Scotland [error: should be Manitoba] a few years ago and lived with her uncles ever since. No motive has been given for the deed, but the unfortunate lady is reported to have been subject to fits of melancholy. She was alone in the house at the time, Sam having gone to Clinton and Bob being out in the field. She was about 38 years of age. The funeral took place at Clinton cemetery, and the sympathy of the community is extended [to] the unfortunate woman and the Graham Brothers in whose home she resided...

Bob and Sam Graham were a well-loved pair of Scottish brothers who lived at Green Lake. Arriving in 1902, they ran a thriving ranch until their deaths in the 1930s. Courtesy Robert and Gayle Fremlin, 70 Mile House, BC.

It was said that she was refused burial in the Clinton graveyard because of the nature of her death, but the authorities must have relented. A large white headstone marks her grave today, undoubtedly erected by her uncles.

In 1931, *Wrigley's British Columbia Directory* noted that the Graham brothers had a housekeeper named Nellie Gray living with them, but the next year Dora Graham, Jean's younger sister, arrived and lived with her uncles. In 1935, she married local rancher John McGillivray.

Life with Sam and Bob was never dull. Stories about the pair and their hijinks still circulate around the country. Both of them were fond of a wee nip now and then, and Bob especially relished meeting up with Matt Porter when he did the mail rounds. They'd share a bottle together.

One day, it was discovered that the liquor cupboard was empty. One of the brothers went to the store and got a bottle of rum, emphasizing that this one was to be saved for medicinal purposes. One afternoon, one of them said, "You know, I'm feeling a mite under the weather. I think I'll have some of that rum to help me out."

"Ach, too bad," the other brother replied. "I was a wee bit under the weather myself the other day and I'm afraid I drank it all up."

Perhaps after this, Sam played a joke on his brother and hid Bob's bottle in their grandfather clock. Eventually, Bob found it. The next time, Sam hid it in an old shed with a scythe propped against the door inside. Bob hunted for it one evening and when he poked around in the dark shed, ran into the scythe and bruised himself. "Who put that there?" he roared.

Sam replied in his rolling Scottish brogue, "Robbie, I did it."

"Weel, that was a damned churlish thing to do," Bob muttered.

The joke was on Sam in another story. It may have been Nellie Gray who was working for them at that time. Whoever the girl was, she was washing some of the brother's good clothes and used white gas to clean the stains. When she was finished, the gas was quite dirty and she pondered about what to do with it. The Grahams had a two-seater outhouse, so she decided to pour the leftover gas down one of the holes. Not long after that, Sam strolled into the outhouse with his pipe. When he was finished, he emptied the ashes from the pipe into the other hole. There was a tremendous *kaboom!* and Sam came running out of the outhouse with his pants around his ankles. Bob looked at him in astonishment and said, "What's the matter with you, Sam?"

"I nae know, Robbie, it must have been something I ate!" Sam replied.

Robert and Sam continued to ranch until their deaths in the mid-1930s, and by that time, the countryside was full of other settlers, although the Curries had moved to Prince Rupert. Their first new neighbour appeared two years after their arrival, driving a herd of livestock from Washington. Pre-empting land along the North Bonaparte River southeast of Green Lake in November 1904, Henry Atwood was the first (but not the last) American to come to the North Bonaparte. Once he reached Green Lake, there was no road, so he had to blaze his way east, following a route that would approximate where the road is now, past Pressy Lake and up as far as what is termed "the Forks," where his land lay. Within the next five years, Henry built a house and stables and did some fencing.

Apparently, Henry was a very short, powerful man. Hardly more than five feet tall, he was built like a granite block and was just as tough. Henry had a big saddle horse of his own that he babied. He'd brought it from Washington and called the horse "Fox." When he wanted to mount Fox, he'd kick his left leg up to catch the stirrup, then haul himself up with his quirt and lines around the horn of the saddle. Once safely in the saddle, he could ride for days without fatigue on cattle drives, sometimes to Ashcroft. Most of the time, he was in the lead and took care of hard-headed steers who tried to make a break for it. One of his favourite expressions was "By gad!" but he used much more colourful language when he needed to. Though he was a very sociable person, he let others do the drinking when the crew ended up in a bar after their arrival with the cattle herd. He was content just to swap stories with his many friends. Henry turned out to be one of the few Americans who actually stayed and made the North Bonaparte their permanent home. When he died in 1933, his obituary in the *Ashcroft Journal* revealed the kind of person he was:

> Too much cannot be said as to the splendid humane character of the late Mr. Atwood. He was every man's friend and his home was always open to all neighbors and strangers alike, and they were welcome to food and shelter. The number that paid their last respects at the funeral in a district where settlers are so few and so far scattered, testifies to the esteem in which he was held by the whole community.

Three more years went by before anyone else made an attempt to settle in the area. In 1907, John Franklin (Frank) and Harriet Pressey, along with their family of six children ranging in age from 4 to 20, emigrated from Yakima, Washington, and pre-empted a quarter section beside what is now Pressy Lake. The Presseys, an enterprising family, soon had a homestead built and instituted the first mail service for the North Bonaparte, although there was only a tiny number of customers at first. They left after only four years and moved to Saskatchewan.

Migration to the North Bonaparte began in earnest in 1908. It wasn't exactly that the trickle became a rushing stream, but the thirteen families and single men who arrived in 1908 boosted the population by a huge percentage. In the early summer, three families arrived from Washington: the large Lyman Price family from Addy, Stevens County; the Wilson family, also from Addy; and the Simmons family from Idaho, possibly tag-alongs. The adult sons of all these families were planning to establish themselves with their own ranches and each family worked together as a team to achieve their goals. Family members spread out to Eagan Lake, Sharpe Lake, Bridge Lake, and the Little Fort-Blackpool region.

The Prices chose to settle in the North Bonaparte and a son, Port, pre-empted land closer to Bridge Lake. They carved out a wagon road from Atwood's as far as they could, and later, the MacDonalds worked from the Bridge Lake end, so that a wagon road was finally in place from 70 Mile House to Bridge Lake. Lyman Sr. and Linda Price had a tightly knit family of six grown sons and one daughter: Curtis, Port, Dell, Levi, Eugene, Lyman (who had the somewhat strange nickname of "Rats"), and Lindaett. Lyman Sr., Curtis, Dell, and Eugene lived out their lives in British Columbia; their mother, Linda, her daughter, Lindaett, and sons Levi and Lyman Jr. returned to Washington. One son, Port, ended his days in California. The original pre-emption of Lot 1494 was purchased by Johnny Hansen from Lyman Jr. ("Rats") and it became the Horsehead Ranch.

Maurice and Margaret Mawdsley with their first child, Stanley, in 1905, three years before they arrived in the North Bonaparte in 1908, having come from the West Kootenays. Within two years, Maurice had built a house, stable, chicken house, blacksmith shop, and cattle corrals, dug a well, and made a start on fencing—more or less single-handedly. Courtesy Jack Mawdsley, London, Ontario.

The only settlers from British Columbia to arrive in 1908 were Maurice Mawdsley and his family. He and his wife, Margaret, and two small children pre-empted a quarter section not far from the Presseys and set to work building up a homestead. Unlike the other new settlers, Maurice had no grown sons or brothers to help, making it a much more challenging venture. Nevertheless, over the years he managed to establish a homestead, blacksmith shop, and acquired a total of 640 acres. Margaret did a stint as postmistress. The family left in 1920.

Autumn 1908 came and with it, another group of three families who filed for pre-emptions: the Andruses, Nichols, and Chisholms. Travelling by covered wagon from Idaho, these three families were very different from the strong group consisting of the Wilsons, Simmons, and Prices with all their grown sons. Hiram Andrus's family was quite young and he had no adult sons to help him out. James Nichols had only a few children, none of them of an age to do heavy manual labour. John Chisholm was with his wife and young stepson. Nevertheless, they all made the challenging decision to pre-empt land east of Pressy Lake. James Nichols was close to the North Bonaparte wagon road (if one could call it that), but the Andrus and Chisholm families moved a few kilometres east. The Andruses and Chisholms would have had to forge a wagon road to their properties, although it is possible there might have been a traditional trail, since Indigenous people were known to have lived at Young Lake. This was the beginning of the Young Lake-Boule Road. These families had chosen their land fairly late in the season, giving them little time to build shelters before the snow and cold of winter arrived. Hiram Andrus, who lived the farthest from anyone else, had a daughter barely a year old as well as three young stepdaughters. Their beginning did not bode well for the family.

The year 1908 ended with the countryside in the grip of the usual severe Cariboo winter. One wonders how the settlers fared during this time, since most had come from Washington, with its milder weather. Scattered the nearly eighty kilometres (fifty miles) between 70 Mile House and Bridge Lake, few people were close to each other. Spring finally arrived and in the late summer of 1909, Andrew and Emma Whitley, along with their children, Bill and Pearl, arrived from Asotin County, Washington, pre-empting land a mile or two north of the Presseys.

The Whitleys were notable, because they were the first family in that part of the country who remained for the rest of their lives. The distinctive house they built is still standing (as of 2017). Constructed of logs, the outside was finished with fir shakes. The home, which also served as a post office for a time, became a stopping-place for many of the new settlers of the area. The road was hardly more than a wagon trail and people

Bill Whitley, the son of Andrew and Emma Whitley, who settled in the North Bonaparte in 1909. The Whitleys were among the most well-known and well-respected families in the entire area. Bill married Della Sneve and also lived on the Montana Lake Road and in Roe Lake. Courtesy Yvonne Fraser, Maple Ridge, BC.

were exhausted by the time they'd reached the Whitleys'. There could be ten to fifteen people staying there overnight, resting and regrouping around the big barrel heater. If someone was short on cash, you could go to Andrew and he'd see what he could do. If any of the women needed advice or reassurance, Emma was there with sensible guidance.

In 1910 and 1911, the Watch Lake area began to open up. Brothers Roy and Stan Eden from Vancouver had been in the Cariboo before, but officially filed their pre-emptions in November 1910 and May 1911. The Edens were an adventurous family and were joined for a while by their sister Muriel and their father, Benjamin. In 1916, their brother Frank also pre-empted land at Watch Lake. Stan, however, ended up being the only one who stayed for a lifetime. He and his wife, Sadie McMillan, had four children who were a vital part of

The McGillivray Family. Left to right: Shirley (daughter of John McGillivray and his second wife, Dora Graham), John Sr., his grandson John, and his son John. Originally from Scotland, John Sr. and his two sons, William and John, arrived in the Cariboo in 1915. Courtesy Keith McGillivray, Kelowna, BC.

the ranching community and many of whose descendants still remain in the area.

The area around Bonaparte Forks saw its first settler around this time: Daniel Morrison, who arrived in 1910, stayed about six or seven years and then moved on. Daniel Puckett was the first to settle near Young Lake, in 1911, and stayed about the same length of time. They were both bachelors.

In 1913, John McGillivray and his two sons, John and William, who were all originally from Scotland, settled in the North Bonaparte. Between the three men, they accumulated several parcels of land and established a thriving cattle ranch. The sons eventually moved away and their father married Dora Graham, Robert and Sam Graham's niece. After running the ranch for over thirty years, in 1946 John moved to Armstrong with his family.

The beginning of World War I in 1914 signalled a whole new influx of settlers, the greatest number that arrived in any one year. Bill Anderson took over the Andrus place on Young Lake Road and Fred Campeau pre-empted land farther east. At Green Lake, Ed Rioux, who later became the foremost trapper in the area, pre-empted land, as did the Prydatok brothers, Bill, Harry, and Steve, who had originally come from Galacia in Poland. Harry went on to establish the Graham Dundun Ranch and Steve the VT Ranch.

The Prydatok brothers were well liked in the community, a fact Leonard Larson of Bridge Lake talked about in his memoir:

> Steve [Prydatok] was a good neighbour and was liked for all of his funny sayings. I remember him telling me of a time that he was at the Flying U, at this one Saturday night dance. Whenever you saw a bunch of people gathered around you could bet that old Steve would be in the middle of it all, telling some of his funny stories. This time Steve was telling me, "You know, I get too many drinks in me and these girls, they start looking pretty nice. Maybe I would like to kiss them. Then I stop and I think, Steve, you are a married man with a wife and child. So I take mine hand and lead mine self home."

Steve Prydatok of Green Lake with a moose he'd bagged for the family larder. Moose were plentiful at that time and part of every family's diet. Courtesy Olga Burr, Kamloops, BC.

John (Jack) Maindley, William and Clara Kearton, and James and Bessie Firrell took up land at Watch Lake. The Keartons and Firrells remained in the area for many years. Stewart Haywood-Farmer and his family settled at Pressy Lake for a few years, then moved to land near Taylor Lake. In the Little Green Lake area, the Porter brothers, Bill and Matt (Matt later bought the 70 Mile Roadhouse), arrived from Ontario and set up a cattle operation.

David Hutchison, originally American, arrived in the North Bonaparte that year and established the XH Ranch, destined to become one of the largest in the area. Situated on what was once called the Curry Road (now Hutchison Road), Dave and his family lived in the area for forty-six years.

A group of settlers from the Lower Mainland comprised of the Andrews, Millard, and Marsden families took up land near Bonaparte Forks, a relatively remote destination. An early homestead map shows only a wagon trail from their place to the end of Hutchison Road. Establishing mixed farms and dairying operations, they lasted until 1925 or 1926 and then returned to the coast.

Settlers who arrived in the next few years tended to go to Bridge Lake and Roe Lake, but one notable family arrived in 1917, the DuBoises. Pre-empting land near Bullock Lake, the DuBois family had come from Alberta, where John was as unwelcome as a snake at a garden party. He'd been charged with rustling but no one could make a conviction stick.

Mildred and Stewart Haywood-Farmer out riding on their property at Taylor Lake. Arriving in 1915, they first lived at Pressy Lake, then Taylor Lake. Later, they moved to Kamloops because of the difficulty of educating their children in the Cariboo. Courtesy Frank Haywood-Farmer, Kamloops, BC.

In 1919, two Dutch families arrived and settled on the Young Lake Road area. Pleun Herwynen and his wife, Betsy Okon, set up a dairy operation on an isolated parcel of land and lived there for almost ten years, while the Scheepbouwer family chose land close to the road. Jacob and Catharina Scheepbouwer, originally from Holland, immigrated to the US in 1906 and after living in Alberta for some years, came to the North Bonaparte in 1919. With their six children, Frances (Fanny), Nellie, Jake, John, Bill, and Annie (four other children had died young), they settled on Lot 1387 near Pressy Lake. Jacob and Catharina died in the mid-1950s and two of the sons, Jake and Bill, ran the ranch along with their wives until they sold it in 1964. John married Minnie Eden and lived on Grant's Mountain; Bill married Rose Park and they bought a ranch between Lillooet and Lytton. Jake married Ann Sworyk and they purchased a place north of 70 Mile House. Fanny moved to Oregon, Nellie ended up at 100 Mile House, and Annie moved to Vancouver Island. The Scheepbouwer Ranch is now owned by the Blue Goose and is run as an organic cattle operation.

The next year, 1920, saw the arrival of the Mobbs family. Edward Mobbs, born in England, immigrated to Canada in 1907. After a stint serving in World War I, he married Marion Jackson in England in 1920. The couple moved to Edward's previously pre-empted land, Lot 4906 near the Bonaparte River. Four children were born there: Frances, Walter, Fred, and Ben. They made a decision to leave their remote, isolated homestead and purchased property from the Edens at Watch Lake in 1928. At that time, Marion became the teacher at Watch Lake School. They developed their property into a tourist lodge called the Lake View Ranch, which was sold to the Horns and Edens in 1950. Edward and Marion moved to Kamloops and eventually their children also left and established themselves elsewhere.

About the time the Mobbs arrived, the first wave of the Park family left Missouri, bound for the North Bonaparte. Their story perhaps exemplifies the experience of many new settlers, who knew little about the land they were heading for. The Park family was made up of Overton and Mattie Park and their sons Jack and Arlie, as well as other children.

It all started with their colourful son Jack. While living with his first wife and family in Kemmerer, Wyoming, he made friends with a rancher who told him about land he had purchased, sight unseen, from a former homesteader in the Cariboo. The rancher was rhapsodic about the property in the Cariboo. "It's a fabulous place," he told Jack, with "acres of fields where you can grow anything."

Jack must have talked about the opportunity to his parents and family. Eventually, the family bought the ranch, sight unseen. In 1920, Overton, Mattie, and most of their children moved to this wonderful, fertile place, despite the misgivings of their family in Missouri. Overton had his farm machinery shipped to Ashcroft and the family travelled there by train. They arrived in Ashcroft, hungry and tired, and went to eat breakfast at a local café. As they sat around the table, they heard a commotion and looked up to see the Chinese cook bursting out of the kitchen, chasing one of the customers around the café with a big knife. Mattie was horrified. "What a country!" she exclaimed. "They kill men before breakfast!"

Theresa and Arlie (Pete) Park and their family settled at Canyon Ranch in the North Bonaparte. Courtesy Rose (Park) Scheepbouwer, Vernon, BC.

Looking like characters out of the Wild West, James Ryder, Arthur Rodman, and Hiram (Hite) Andrus pose at 59 Mile House in 1911 after the wedding of their children, John Ryder and Ethel Rodman. Hite Andrus was Ethel's stepfather. The Ryders owned the 59 Mile Roadhouse at that time. Courtesy Yvonne Fraser, Port Alberni, BC.

Overton managed to obtain a car and they made their way along the rough highway to 70 Mile House. There, they had to turn right and drive several miles along the even rougher North Bonaparte Road. When they reached Young Lake Road, they turned right again. A few more bumpy miles and they had reached their highly anticipated destination, the ranch of their dreams.

They couldn't quite believe their eyes. Where was the cleared land, the waving fields of hay, the lush vegetation? In front of them was nothing but acres of jackpine and rocks. Stunned, they did the best they could with what they had. Overton traded the car to Matt Porter for a far more practical team of horses.

The Gammie family. Left to right: Jessie (Bert's mother), Bert, and Ruth, along with their children, George, Lynn, and Donna. The Gammies purchased the Flying U Ranch from Charlie Wilkinson and ran it for many years. Courtesy Lynn (Gammie) Watrich, Kamloops, BC.

Matt threw in a cow for good measure. There was no use for the farm machinery, so Overton just left it in Ashcroft. It was already October and getting cold, so they needed shelter as soon as possible. Everyone pitched in to build a small log cabin, even though none of them had ever built one before. They threw a tarp over the top so they could stay in it until the roof was done.

No one is now sure how long the family stayed at their new property or how long they managed to survive the winter. Perhaps they realized the impossibility of it and moved to Clinton after the bitter Cariboo cold set in. By the time the 1921 census was taken, they were living next to the Pollards in Clinton. The Park family, along with Lyman Price, who had fallen in love with their daughter Verda, returned in disgust to Missouri. They had the farm machinery shipped back to Missouri and sold it by auction.

But Jack, who had stayed home during this sojourn, was not dissuaded. He and his children and a few other members of the family came up shortly afterwards to see what they could do with the property and stayed for a while, making improvements. Ten years later, in 1932, Jack returned with his new wife, Hazel, and settled down for good on what he called the Lost Valley Ranch. In 1940, his brother Arlie, Arlie's wife, Theresa, and their family emigrated from Missouri as well, purchasing a ranch of their own that they named the Canyon Ranch. Arlie and Theresa's journey was as arduous in its way as the Park clan's had been in 1920, but they were satisfied with their land and stayed for many years.

The Reinertson brothers—Reinert (Ray), Chester, Jake, and Clarence—as youngsters in the Peace River country. The four of them came to the Cariboo in 1935 and 1936, first living at Chester's place at Davis Lake. Since there was only the two-room homestead cabin, Chester and his wife, Laura, lived in the cabin and the other three Reinertson brothers slept in the barn and took turns cooking. Each of the Reinertsons made their own mark on the Cariboo. Courtesy Rodina Coldwell, Quesnel, BC.

The years from 1921 to 1929 saw many notable families settle in the area: William and Mary Jane Haines, who lived in three different places in the North Bonaparte; Havelock and Lydia Bryant, who settled around Taylor Lake; the Goetjen family; the Coulson family; Harvey and Orpha Boule; the Prest family; the Livingstons; Frank and Gladys Maddocks; Jack and Minnie Davies; and the Provo family. A few others also arrived in that time period and stayed only a few years.

From 1930 to the mid-1940s, several families moved in who became well known and important to the area's history. The Reinertson brothers—Jake, Chester, Clarence, and Ray—arrived from the Peace River and each followed their own path. Two newcomers ended up being successive owners of the Flying U: Charlie Wilkinson from Vancouver and Bert Gammie, who was originally from England. Other new residents were John Morris, Jack Dyer, Harry and Adriana Bowden, Floyd and Earl Tompkins, and Ted and Eva Wrigley. A short biography of each of these families can be found in an appendix at the back of the book.

EAGAN LAKE
AND SHARPE LAKE

Bill Hollanbeck from Michigan, the Wilson family, and the Simmons family arrived in the Eagan Lake area about the same time, in 1908. Both the Wilsons and the Simmonses were from Addy, Washington, and brought along their elderly mothers. With their arrival, the new settlers would have had to blaze a route from the North Bonaparte wagon road to their locations at Eagan Lake and Sharpe Lake. This would be the origin of the present-day Eagan Lake Road.

In May, Charles, one of the brothers in the Wilson family, pre-empted Lot 1439 at the east end of Eagan Lake. His pre-emption map names the river flowing through the property as the South Bonaparte River, although today it's known as Machete Creek. In 1911, most of the family was living with Charles on this property. The family stayed for only about ten years and many of their members ended up in the Little Fort-Blackpool area.

Established about 1930, the Eagan Lake School was built by locals on land donated by Carr Cleveland. The Cleveland, Park, Johnson, Francis, Larner, and Tuovil children attended the school, although there were never a great number of children at any time. It closed about 1949 when the number fell to below the minimum required.

From Isaac "Ike" Simmons at Eagan Lake to his sister, Maggie Case, in Idaho, 1919
70 Mile House, Aug 1919, Mrs. Maggie Case

Dear Sister,
I have just returned from a prospecting trip and expected to find a letter from both of you and Margie as I have visited with both of you since hearing from you. Mother is so very uneasy for fear that some of you are sick that I thought I would try again. Charley is busy with the hay. [The] hay crop is very short here this year. With the old hay that is left over he will perhaps have enough to see him through this winter. I think that my place is sold but do not know as yet. There has been a lot of places changed hands here this year and looks like a lot more will change hands this fall. Maggie, I am agoing to make this short so it will be easy to read and if you are very very busy, just stop long enough to say all is well here, Maggie Case. That will keep Mother from fretting. Tell Sherman if here now I could give him a big feed of redfish as the river is full of them now and they are fine…

Your loving brother, I. J. Simmons

Isaac Simmons, the eldest son in the large Simmons family who settled at Eagan and Sharpe Lakes in 1908. Isaac, an experienced woodsman and horseman, left about 1920 and moved back to Idaho. Courtesy Donna Woodruff, Newport Beach, California.

Bill Hollanbeck from Michigan had been working for the Boyds at Green Lake for at least a year, but in June 1908, he pre-empted land at Eagan Lake and established his own homestead. In 1914, he travelled to Ashcroft and married an English nurse named Nellie Cashmore, who was twenty years older than he was. The local story about lovelorn Bill was that he had written to a lady in Ontario, trying to persuade her to come out, but she kept the fare money and never arrived. Nellie, a widow, was indeed living in Ontario when the 1911 census was taken, and the facts show that she came to Ashcroft and married Bill. But there is no evidence of her ever accompanying him to the North Bonaparte. In 1921, she was living in Winnipeg, and Bill was nowhere to be found. Crown grant records show that he cancelled a

Matilda Simmons is pictured here in front of the Simmons home at Eagan Lake about 1910 with three of her children, twins John and William and baby, Charles. Charles was the first white child born in the Eagan Lake area. Courtesy Donna Woodruff, Newport Beach, California.

pre-emption on Lot 3875 in 1922. After that, Bill disappeared to parts unknown.

The Simmons family filed for their first pre-emption in June 1908. A large group of seven adults and two children, they accumulated at least four parcels of land through the years. One brother, William, along with his family, lived around Eagan Lake and the month they arrived, his wife, Matilda, gave birth to Charles, the first white child born in that particular area. The family's other properties were closer to Sharpe Lake. Considering there were four brothers who each wanted to establish a ranch of their own, this really was not enough property. One by one, the Simmons family moved away, the last two remaining brothers running a horse ranch until 1929.

In 1909, George Brown, who was originally from Oklahoma, pre-empted property first at Red Creek, then at Brown's Creek. George was a solitary, clever, industrious bachelor who prized his independence. When he found at the age of 76 that he wasn't able to take care of his place any longer, he moved to Kamloops. A few months later, in September 1945, he was found in a little cabin, dead of a self-inflicted gunshot wound. Carr Cleveland of Eagan Lake came down to collect his old friend's body and George now rests in the private Cleveland cemetery.

Carr Cleveland and Minnie Hansen's wedding in 1919. Carr came from California and settled on land around Eagan Lake in 1913. Minnie's family had come from Washington to Roe Lake nine years earlier. Together with their family, which grew to include five sons and a daughter, they ran one of the most successful ranches in the area. Courtesy Sharon Hansen, Vancouver, BC.

Carr Cleveland was a young man from California who left his comfortable family home in Mendocino County to homestead in the Cariboo. He first arrived in 1912 and rode through the country until the Eagan Lake area caught his eye. In 1913, he pre-empted his original quarter section of Lot 1430 and set to work establishing a ranch. After serving in World War I, he returned and married Minnie Belle Hansen, the daughter of another pioneering family. Together, they raised six children—Robert, Evelyn, Jamie, Weston, Eric, and Gary—and built the Cleveland ranch into a thriving venture. On what became one of the largest ranches in the district, the family raised cattle and sheep, had a tourist and hunting camp, and also brought in income from trapping. Each of the children ended up with their own chunk of land. After Carr's untimely death in 1953, Minnie and the children carried on with the home ranch, which is still in Cleveland hands at the west end of Eagan Lake.

Leon Borleske and his stepson Fred O'Toole from California filed for pre-emptions between Eagan Lake and Sharpe Lake in 1913 and lived there for only four or five years. Their property eventually became part of the Cleveland ranch.

Orren Johnson arrived at Sharpe Lake from Washington in 1921, pre-empting Lot 1405. That year, he married Elma Janes. With their family

Orren Johnson first settled in Sharpe Lake in 1921. Pictured here is the Johnson clan about 1934. On the left are Orren's siblings: Mark, Claude, Lester, and Audrey, with Orren on the far right. In the middle are Elbert, Elma, Wayne, and Zale, Orren's wife and children. In the rear is Elma's mother, Mrs. Janes. Courtesy Susan Profili, Castlegar, BC.

of six children, they later moved to property in the North Bonaparte and established another ranch. In 1935, Orren's younger brother Claude came from Alberta and pre-empted Lot 1421 at Sharpe Lake. After the breakdown of Orren and Elma's marriage, Claude took care of the family at his place at Sharpe Lake and Orren moved to property he had on the road to Little Green Lake, where he died in 1966.

The Tuovila and Francis families came to Sharpe Lake in the 1930s. They had been neighbours in Alberta. Tor and Svea Tuovila and their family of nine children settled at Sharpe Lake. Tor built log cabins and developed a tourist camp, but with the advent of World War II, demand dropped. In 1942, the family moved to Kelowna. Their oldest daughter, Stina, and her husband, Sherman Davis, joined them there.

A year after the Tuovilas arrived, they were joined by Ben Francis. Ben had no intention of ranching: he was coming to the Cariboo to save his family. He and his wife, Eva, had been living in Alberta and had six children: Edna, Louis, Roy, Ellen, Shirley, and Sheila. When Eva became ill and died at the age of 38, leaving Ben with six young children, Ben was warned by his wife's former nurse that authorities planned to take them away from him. So he followed his friends, the Tuovilas, to Sharpe Lake. Along with Ben's mother, the family moved in 1936 to Lot 1408 between Sharpe Lake and Eagan Lake. Ben ranched a little and also did mechanic's work. His daughter Edna married Alf Payne, who was living in the North Bonaparte. In 1941, the whole family moved to Kelowna.

The Richards family, consisting of Bernard and Margaret and their children, Stephen and Anne, came to Sharpe Lake in 1939 and resided on a 320-acre property. Bernard worked for Harrison's sawmill and had a few cattle. They left in 1966 and moved to Williams Lake.

BRIDGE LAKE AND ROE LAKE

Bridge Lake was first known as Great Fish Lake and early pre-emption re-cords used this name for some years. Jack Demming was the first settler in the area, as far as is known. He applied for an unnamed pre-emption in 1905 that was at Lac des Roches near Bridge Lake. He built a homestead there, along with a little trading post.

In the summer of 1907, Archie MacDonald and his four sons arrived at Demming's homestead. The MacDonalds, who were originally from Wash-ington, travelled by horseback from a homestead they'd had in Alberta, and, taking advice from people they'd met, travelled over the Mount Olie trail. They planned to explore the whole Cariboo from there, but when they ar-rived at the beautiful meadowlands around Lac des Roches, they knew this was where they wanted to settle. Although it was said they bought the land from Jack Demming, it doesn't appear that Demming ever actually owned it. Crown grant records show that Archie MacDonald was the one who applied for a pre-emption and gained title on that particular piece of land.

In August 1908, Theophile François (Frank) Rossi arrived from the US. Originally from a French-speaking region of Switzerland, he was the first to settle on the southeast side of Bridge Lake, on Lot 1446. Three months later, Charles Rouse from Wyoming pre-empted Lot 1443 at the southeastern end of Crooked (Webb) Lake.

Two people share the distinction of being the first settlers in North Bridge Lake. On June 13, 1908, Albert Wilson and Bill Bannon both applied for a pre-emption in the area, travelling to the Clinton land office together. Albert, a brother of the Wilson family who were living at Eagan Lake, settled on the northeast end of Bridge Lake and pre-empted Lot 1448 on the lake that today bears his name. Bill Bannon from Michigan pre-empted property farther west in North Bridge Lake. Eugene Brown, also a bachelor, arrived that month and filed on property by what is now Eugene Lake. Neither Wil-son, Bannon, nor Eugene Brown stayed long after they received title to their parcels.

The year 1909 saw a few new people in the Bridge Lake area. Ed Smith and his young wife, Martha, arrived from Montana. Their first child, Thelma, was born at Mount Olie during the journey. They pre-empted Lot 1485 and later Lot 1484 between Bridge Lake and Crooked (Webb) Lake. Three more children were born while they were in Bridge Lake: Clifton, Violet, and Goldie. Clifton was born in Ashcroft, but Violet was born in 1914 in Bridge Lake, the first white child to be born there. The family built up a dairy, then moved to Alberta in 1919. Their youngest child, Claudia, recalls her father reminiscing about Bridge Lake, wondering if the log house he'd built was still standing. He felt that if he went back to visit, he'd be able to find the cabin, because he had a unique method of log notching. But he never did return and died in 1980 in Cranbrook, 100 years old.

In September 1909, Arthur Rose arrived from Colville, Washington, and settled at the east end of Crooked (Webb) Lake. It's possible he was estranged from his family, since he left a wife and several small children in Washington. He left after four years; the border crossing record stated that he was going to Priest River, Idaho, accompanied by his friend Ole Ellingson, who went along for the ride. Ole returned but Rose never did.

The same month Rose arrived, Alexander and Agnes Burns, along with their three adult sons and a younger daughter made their entrance into the

The legendary Roe Lake bachelor Ole Ellingson (left) is pictured here with his friends Gordon King and Ed Higgins at a local picnic. The only time Ole was seen without his ample beard was when he was shipped home in a coffin. Wanting to ensure that it was really Ole, friends pried open the coffin lid and were shocked to see that he was clean-shaven and looked forty years younger. Courtesy Connie (Leavitt) Greenall, Kamloops, BC.

countryside. Originally from Montana, they settled at the lake that bears their name, Burns Lake. Alexander became the justice of the peace with a jurisdiction stretching from Bridge Lake down to the North Bonaparte. Together, the family pre-empted land around Burns Lake and amassed almost a thousand acres of land; one of the chunks was around Young Lake. In 1914, Henry and Samuel enlisted in World War I but only Henry returned; Samuel died in the 1918 flu epidemic in England. After his death, Alex, Agnes, and Grace moved to Savona and ranched there, leaving the Bridge Lake ranch for Henry and Peter. Peter died while working away from home in Spokane with a logging operation, and the remaining part of the family sold the Savona and Bridge Lake properties and moved to Clinton. After a few years, they moved on to California.

Another family arrived in Bridge Lake, settling near the Burns property. Harry Sargent, who was born in England, was a risk-taker who immigrated to Alberta and married Alma Brown there. They arrived in Bridge Lake in 1910 with five small children, and had two more after their arrival. On Vancouver Island, where they'd just come from, they'd spent the winter in a tent with children ranging in age from a few months to 7 years old. Harry applied for a pre-emption on Lot 1883 near Burns Lake and they lived there for a year or so. In 1912, he broke his leg and, unable to take care of his homestead, the family moved to the Port Price place in the North Bonaparte. The next year, Harry decided they would move to Australia. There, another seven children were born in the outback, and the numerous Sargent family, a tough and hardy bunch, became part of Australian folklore. None was tougher than their long-suffering mother, Alma.

A few single men swelled the numbers at about that time: Bruce Craddock, who settled near Montana Lake and remained until about 1932; Hugh (Paddy) Boyle at Twin Lakes; and Ole Ellingson at Roe Lake. Ole was said to have arrived from Washington a few years earlier, squatting on land in North Bridge Lake, but border-crossing documents show him coming to Canada no earlier than 1909. Ole became a legend around the countryside and is still fondly remembered. He built a unique cabin on his place where he raised horses, goats, and other livestock. His death certificate stated that he was married, although he was always known as a bachelor. One person who knew him well wrote: "Ole, being a quite secretive man, had told me stories that he had told no one else. He had been married three times in the States and all their names were Helens and he said, by God, they were full of it." This was no doubt highly exaggerated, and the truth will probably never be known about Ole Ellingson's marital status.

Hugh Boyle, known as Paddy, was born in Ireland and also had a somewhat mysterious marital status. Although Paddy arrived in Bridge Lake in 1909, he came and went with no one being quite certain where he was. He pre-empted the land at Twin Lakes in 1914, five years after he settled there, but in January 1916, he was living in Savona. That month he married a 32-year-old waitress named Mary Keefe or O'Keefe. The following October, Paddy enlisted in World War I and strangely enough, the address of his wife Mary was "c/o Chief of Police, Kamloops" on his attestation papers. Paddy returned to Bridge Lake sometime after the war ended. Perhaps Mary came with him and found that living in the bush was not for her. The 1921 census recorded Paddy as a farmer in Bridge Lake, married, but with no wife listed. His wife, Mary, was living in Kamloops, working as a maid in the hospital. Perhaps this was where the story came from that she was a nurse. Paddy left Bridge Lake sometime after 1935. Mary died in 1945 and Paddy in 1958. His death was a lonely one. Notes on his death certificate state: "This aged recluse was found dead on Sept. 2, 1958. Last seen alive on Aug. 10, 1958." At the time he was living at Bear Creek, eleven kilometres (seven miles) from Chase, BC, although no one knew how long he'd lived there. The fate of elderly bachelors or widowers could often be a sad, forlorn one.

The area now called Roe Lake saw its first settler in March 1910. Claude and Addie Roe from Washington arrived with their young son, but they lasted barely a year. Since the lake they settled by was named after them, the Roe family will never be forgotten. A few months later, another family came to Roe Lake, one that did stay. Frank and Dovie Hansen and their four children ranging in age from 2 to 14 were from Asotin County, Washington. They first settled at Roe Lake, then, eight years later, moved to property in Bridge Lake. They remained in Bridge Lake for the rest of their lives and their

Claude and Addie Roe, along with their young son, Ray, were the first settlers at the lake that now bears their name, although they actually homesteaded on Bridge Creek. After only a year or so, the family moved to Big Bar. Courtesy Lisa Hegle Sinks, Keizer, Oregon.

children and grandchildren lived most of their lives there as well. One of their descendants, Sharon Hansen, wrote about the family's journey from Washington to Roe Lake, her information taken from stories and old letters.

The Hansen Journey in 1910 — by Sharon Hansen

Frank and Dovie Hansen, accompanied by their four children (Johnny, age 14; Minnie, age 12; Lee, age 7 $\frac{1}{2}$; and Wesley, age 3 $\frac{1}{2}$) travelled in two covered wagons on their remarkable journey. The family of six went from Hanson's Ferry, Washington to Roe Lake, British Columbia in a trip that lasted between forty-two and forty-four days. Frank's Danish father, Johann (called John), who was 84 years old in 1910, initially joined the family on this adventure. Unfortunately, he became ill when they stopped to visit his stepson, Chris Walter, in Cloverland, Washington. Old John died on April 5, 1910. He was buried in the Walter family plot and the Hansen family continued their trip north towards British Columbia.

Frank took the lead, driving a four-horse team with the heavier items, while Dovie followed, driving a two-horse team. It was a continuously rainy

The Wagner and Hansen families. The Hansens established homesteads at Bridge Lake, Burns Lake, and a few miles south of Bridge Lake on the North Bonaparte Road. Ruth Wagner—said to be a widow, but actually thrice-divorced—lived at Crystal Lake for a few years. From left to right standing: Ruth Wagner, Mabel Hansen, Dovie Hansen, John Hansen, Frank Hansen. Bottom: Calvin and Matt Wagner, Carter Hansen, Vince Johnston (a Hansen ranch hand), and Sharon Hansen. Courtesy Sharon Hansen, Vancouver, BC.

and exhausting ordeal, with many challenging adventures. At one point, Dovie's team ran away when one of the horses was bitten by a rattlesnake. She eventually managed to gain control of the horses and no one was injured. Minnie had a run-in with a black bear near the camp one evening and bravely chased it off with a stick. Young Johnny rode horseback for the entire trip, driving their small herd of twelve cattle and fifteen horses.

Wesley travelled in the wagon with his mother, while the lively and adventurous 7-year-old Lee travelled with his father in the big wagon. Twelve-year-old Minnie also enjoyed riding horseback for brief periods, which gave her a break from sitting in the bumpy wagons with her parents. They stopped on Sundays to rest the horses and to give Dovie the opportunity to wash their clothes and bake bread for the week ahead.

Their route followed the Columbia River up through the British Columbia Okanagan Valley and the town of Princeton, then on to Ashcroft. From Ashcroft, they followed the old gold rush road north, through Clinton to 70 Mile House. At 70 Mile, they turned off the main road onto a very narrow and rough road; in places, there was little more than a path. The further they travelled, the narrower the road became. With the wagons so heavily loaded, progress was extremely slow. Eventually, they came to the Pressey homestead. The horses struggled up the steep and sloping Pressey hills, running adjacent to the homestead and the lake. Although they no doubt stopped at the Pressey place, their goal was to reach the Whitley ranch that day where they would camp again for the night. Frank was anxious to be re-acquainted with Andy Whitley, with whom he had been corresponding since the Whitleys moved from Asotin, Washington.

As they departed from the Whitley place early the next morning, they were cheered by the thought that they were nearing the end of their long journey. Archie MacDonald, along with his sons and some other settlers, had built a rough wagon road from the Pressey place to the MacDonald ranch on Lac des Roches in 1908. However, there were many rocks and stumps and it was slow going for wagons. Frank and family had barely departed the Whitley property when they reached the challenging Graham grade. At this point, the track was very steep, with a treacherous drop to the valley below. The weary teams and livestock slowly ascended the hill. At times the wagons teetered on the very edge. What relief they must have felt when everyone safely made it to the top!

Ten miles further on, they came to the Price homestead, which was situated on a large natural meadow. They introduced themselves to Lyman Price and his many sons and most likely camped there for the night. The next day, as they neared Bridge Lake, they left the main road, heading to their final

The Whitley homestead in North Bonaparte.

destination at Roe Lake. The progress then became so difficult that Frank was often forced to walk ahead of the wagons, wielding an axe to remove bushes, trees, and branches that blocked their way. In places, the trail was almost non-existent. It is estimated that the family arrived in the Roe Lake area on or about the evening of May 20, 1910.

ooooo

Hiram and Lilly Printzhouse, along with their sons Bill and Earnie also came from Washington to Roe Lake about 1910. Preceded into Canada by their son John, who settled in Little Fort, they made their way across the Mt. Olie trail. At Roe Lake, they filed for a pre-emption on Lot 4299 and lived on it for many years, although the paperwork was never completed. Bill married Ada Genier of Little Fort and pre-empted land around Loon Lake, where he operated a sheep ranch. Earnie pre-empted land on Judson Road. About 1926, the family left the area and moved to Oregon.

In 1911, Charlie Potts pre-empted Lot 1486 on the southeast end of Bridge Lake. He had previously filed on the land with a group named Garwin, Potts, and Orr and may also have lived in the North Bonaparte first, since he

The Printzhouses (sometimes spelled Princehouse) were early pioneers at Roe Lake and were the first to homestead at the corner of Judson Road and Bridge Lake North Road. Pictured here are Hiram, Lilly, and their son Earnie. Courtesy Connie (Leavitt) Greenall, Kamloops, BC.

was a friend of the Andrus family and had connections with other people in that area. He seems to have lived part-time in the Vancouver area and by 1918 was back there permanently.

The 1911 census showed that the once-empty countryside from 57 Mile to Bridge Lake now had 115 people living there. The next two years before World War I saw three more families move to Roe Lake, families that had a huge impact on the history of the area: the Hollands and Higgins, both from Oregon, and the Larsons, originally from Norway. The families of the Higgins and Larsons, as well as descendants of the Hollands, still remain in Roe Lake and Bridge Lake today.

The Hollands came to Roe Lake from Lane County, Oregon, in 1912. Bill and Martha had six children ranging in age from 11 to 29: Lawrence, Crate, Ivy, Nellie, Hugh, and Bertha. Their original pre-emption of Lot 1900 was added to by most of the children also pre-empting property, enlarging the farm to about 325 hectares (800 acres). In 1918, Martha became ill, returned to the US, and died there. The family stayed on until Bill too left for the US in 1927 and most of the other children followed. Bertha, who married Ellis Granberg in 1922, was the only one to remain and she and her husband purchased the original Holland homestead.

Ellis Granberg and Bertha Holland on their wedding day in 1922. Ellis was an immigrant from Sweden who came to the Horse Lake area in 1913; Bertha was the daughter of the Roe Lake pioneer family, the Hollands. Their descendants still live in the area today. Courtesy Carla Granberg, Kamloops, BC.

Hilda Larson, with her son Leonard and one of her grandchildren. After her pioneer days in Roe Lake and the death of her husband, Ole, the resilient and remarkable Hilda took a well-deserved retirement in Vancouver. Courtesy Jack and Gail Larson, Bridge Lake, BC.

The next year saw the arrival of the Larsons. Both Ole and Hilda Larson were born in Norway and first lived in North Dakota. Ole heard about the Cariboo and, after much searching, found the land he wanted at Roe Lake in 1913, Lot 4296. By that time, two children had been born, Gunhill and Mary. In November 1914, another son, Karel, was born, the first white child born at Roe Lake. Later, the family was enlarged with the births of Mabel, Jack, May, and Leonard. The Larsons also acquired land at Sheridan Lake, where they lived for a few years. The Larsons ranched, trapped, and ran a tourist operation and a store. Ole died in 1950, and sometime after his death, Hilda turned the ranch over to Karel and moved to the coast. The children all lived and worked in the area for many years. Mabel married a local man, Gardner Boultbee, and Jack married Rita Dougall. Larson descendants still live in Bridge Lake.

Edward and Irene Higgins came from Lane County, Oregon, and pre-empted Lot 4272 at Roe Lake in April 1914, although Ed had been up earlier. They became hugely instrumental in the development of the area, instituting mail service and a school, building roads, and encouraging new settlers. Both Ed and Irene and many of their descendants spent their entire lives in the district. Ed and Irene had eight children: Velma, Marion, Kenneth, Ronald, Noveta, Cecil, Beulah, and Forest, who died as a baby. Five of the children married local people and raised their families in the area: Velma married Ed Malm; Marion married Edna Barnes, and later, Lois Donnelly; Kenneth married Mary McMillan; Noveta married Frank Leavitt; and Beulah married Alex McMillan. The Higgins family, along with the Granbergs, has the greatest number of descendants still living in the South Cariboo.

The family of John and Mary Bundrock settled on Lot 4270 at Roe Lake in May 1914 and stayed for only a few years, while Roy Thompson from Oregon pre-empted Lot 4298 and married Pearl Whitley of the North Bonaparte. James McCracken arrived in 1915 and pre-empted land at Lesser Fish Lake; he too stayed only for a few years.

In the fall of 1914, Calvin and Jessie Smith arrived from Oregon with their family of nine children (one more was born later) and pre-empted a choice chunk of land, Lot 4290, on the southwest shore of Bridge Lake. This land has changed hands many times, most owners operating it as a resort because of the beautiful location. The Smiths became a vital part

Frank and Helen Leavitt moved to Roe Lake during the Depression with their five grown sons. Escaping from the dust bowl of Saskatchewan, the family arrived in an impressive procession: a Model T, grain wagon, lumber wagon, democrat buggy, and another smaller buggy, their livestock trailing along behind. Courtesy Connie (Leavitt) Greenall, Kamloops, BC.

of the community and were known to almost everyone in the area. A man who was always looking for opportunities, Calvin pre-empted Lot 1379 by Pressy Lake in 1918 and established another homestead. Records suggest that he retained the Bridge Lake land as well. During their years in the area, some of their children married local people: Keith had a short marriage to Fanny Scheepbouwer, Emma (Margaret) married Emmit Eakin of Little Fort, and Maude married Dan MacDonald of Lac des Roches. The family raised sheep in both their locations. They left in 1922 and eventually ended up in the Peace River country.

About the same time the Larsons arrived, a new trend developed in the history of the settlement of the region. Including Ole and Hilda Larson, many of the new settlers were Scandinavian or German—most of them bachelors. Except for the Larsons at Roe Lake and Albert Granberg in the North Bonaparte, these new settlers gravitated to Horse Lake or Lone Butte. These included Ellis Granberg, Carl Nath, Victor Furrer, Sig Larum, Ben and Oscar Sneve, and Hartwig Horn. The terrain at Horse Lake was quite different from the land in the 70 Mile-North Bonaparte area and perhaps it was the type of land the Scandinavian and German men were looking for.

The Granberg family originated in Sweden and four sons in the family came to British Columbia, three of them to the Taylor Lake/Roe Lake area: Albert (Frank), Axel, and Ellis. Axel moved away after a short time. Frank farmed on his property and remained in the area for the rest of his life. Ellis married Bertha Holland of Roe Lake in 1922 and they had a family of five children: Helen, Norman, Olga, Harold (Curly), and Janis. About 1926, Ellis purchased his father-in-law James Holland's ranch at Roe Lake. Over the years, the family briefly operated a store at Roe Lake, then another in Lone Butte. As well, they had a cattle and haying operation. In their later years, their son Curly took over the home farm and Ellis and Bertha spent their remaining years in Lone Butte. Some of their children married into families of the area: Helen married Chris Horn; Norman married Anna Nath; and Olga married Charlie Thorsteinson. Many of the Granbergs still live in the area.

The Neal family lived in Bridge Lake in the 1920s and 1930s. Pictured here are some of the Neal children playing at the old Ed Smith place with some of the Higgins children. From left to right: Jonny (Jack) Neal, Ronald and Cecil Higgins, Mary Neal, Noveta and Beulah Higgins, and Edith Neal. Courtesy Connie (Leavitt) Greenall, Kamloops, BC.

The year 1919 saw new settlers in Bridge Lake: partners Ed Malm and John Naff pre-empted adjoining lots around Montana Lake. Ed Malm married a local girl, Velma Higgins, and moved to Roe Lake, where he lived for the rest of his life; the Naffs left in 1927. Jim Case and his wife, Lavena MacDonald, daughter of Archie MacDonald, came up from Washington where the MacDonalds had come from, and finally joined the family at Bridge Lake. They pre-empted Lot 1489 by Crooked (Webb) Lake and stayed until 1938, when they moved to Little Fort.

The Johnston brothers, Ernie, Fred, and Percy, arrived in North Bridge Lake in 1919 and pre-empted land in the Wilson Lake area. Two years later, they were joined by their father, Charles, and another brother, Albert. Percy purchased Lot 4290 on Bridge Lake from Calvin Smith and he, Charles, and Fred settled there. Charles died there in 1924 and was buried on the property; Albert returned to Montana in 1930. About 1934, Fred mysteriously disappeared on a trapping trip and was never found. Percy stayed on but died in 1936. The last Johnston brother, Ernie, left with his family in 1940.

Some important families arrived in 1920: Gordon King, who settled in North Bridge Lake, was born in Manitoba and married Alice Shertenlib, whom he'd met when they were both living in Washington. In 1920, he pre-empted Lot 1455 on the north shore. The couple had two children, Jack and Rita. Gordon ranched and trapped until his death in 1959; Alice died in 1998 at 100 Mile House. Descendants of both Jack and Rita still own the home place on the shores of Bridge Lake.

Fred and Fanny Jowsey, along with their children, John (Jack), Margaret (Maggie), Elizabeth (Betty), and

Alice (Shertenlib) and Gordon King relaxing in front of their log house on the shores of North Bridge Lake. Gordon lost one of his legs in a railway accident as a young man, but he managed to ranch, trap, ride horseback, and carry on normal life despite the disability. Courtesy Ian MacInnes, Duncan, BC.

Fred and Susie Shertenlib and their family moved to Roe Lake in the area now known as the Shertenlib Road. Known as "Old Shertie," Fred was one of the few blacksmiths in the district. Courtesy Ian MacInnes, Duncan, BC.

Members of the Jowsey, Reed, and McNabb families pose at son Jack Jowsey's place. From left to right: Jenny (Jowsey) McNabb; Emma Jowsey (Jack's wife) with Alice, their daughter; Fred, who was the justice of the peace for the area for many years, and Fanny Jowsey; Ronald McNabb; Charlie Reed with his son Jim. Strangely, the driver of the car, Maggie (Jowsey) Reed, cut her face out of the picture. Courtesy Audrey (Reed) Woodman, Merritt, BC.

Jenny, emigrated from England and first lived at Monte Creek. In 1920, they came to Bridge Lake, settling at the southeast corner, with other land towards Montana Lake. Fred was the local justice of the peace, taking on the job from Alexander Burns. In 1924, their daughter Maggie married Charles Reed of Lone Butte and Betty married a local man, Lee Hansen. Fred and Fanny retired to Kamloops in 1935 and turned their ranch over to their children and their spouses.

Harold Webb, who had been a cook with the Downton survey crew in 1920, settled at Bridge Lake and built a store on Crooked Lake. The name of this lake was eventually changed to Webb Lake to honour him.

The years from 1921 to 1929 saw the arrival of many families who were instrumental in the history of Bridge Lake, including the Barnes and Faessler families, the Neals, the Bradfords, the Reichmuths, and the Larners—all of whom pre-empted land in one location or another. During the 1920s, the Mormon family of Elizur Chapman lived in North Bridge Lake, but left in 1926. Settling at Roe Lake during that time period were the lively Shertenlib family from Washington, Martin and Caroline Renshaw, Tom and Nellie Wheeler, Forrest and Cora Bell, and Wilbur Ames and his family.

The family home of Bill and Anna Bradford on the Bridge Lake waterfront. Built to accommodate guests, there were several bedrooms upstairs. The bounty of fish summer guests caught would be packed in ice, put in boxes stuffed with moss, and kept in their icehouse until the guests were ready to leave. Courtesy Lily (Bradford) Ethier, Clearwater, BC.

From 1930 to 1939, over twenty families or single men settled at Bridge Lake and Roe Lake. Only about a third of those stayed for most of their lives: Ernie Ades, Ben Blaisdell, Slim Grosset, the Leavitt family, Lee Roberts, Ernie Hodges, and the Ross family, consisting of John, Peter, and Joyce. Charlie Ashley, William Armstrong, Reginald Chapman, Paul Grauman, Robert Mickle, Albert Morgan, Jim Mulvihill, the Reynolds family, Alan Spickernell, Jack Spratt, Svend Stokstad, Dave Thomas, and Tom Winters all lived in the area, most with families, but they eventually moved on. Most of the new settlers pre-empted land, as Crown grant properties were still available. Those who ended up leaving sold to incoming settlers during the 1940s and 1950s.

The decade from 1940 to 1949 saw an influx of over thirty families and a few single men. Perhaps this was motivated by the end of World War II. Ex-servicemen, jaded by the war, were looking for the dream—independence in the wholesome outdoors and back-to-the-land goodness, not unlike the hippies of the 1960s. Most of them came to Bridge Lake, including the Dougall family (although they had worked in the area in the 1930s), Wilf Bays, Arnold Cornish, and George Spanks. A very important arrival was the Ernie King family. Along with his parents and his wife Olive's parents, two siblings, and three children, they arrived in the winter of 1945 and took over Jack Spratt's Bridge Lake Store. The store wasn't sold until 1981 and most of the family lived in Bridge Lake for the rest of their lives.

Claude and Hannah Dean and their family of four girls ran Braemore Lodge, a hunting and fishing resort on Bridge Lake. No one is quite sure of the identity of all the children piled on the long-suffering horse, but it was likely one or two of the Dean girls and some of the local Bridge Lake children. Courtesy Dorothy (Dean) Smith.

A noteworthy arrival in 1942 was Major Guy Boyer, who purchased Lot 4290 on the west side of Bridge Lake. Perhaps the wealthiest person ever to live in the entire district, Boyer came from a prominent Montreal family. A retired military man, Boyer was a widower and perhaps wished to live an entirely different life. He was popular, employing local people and participating in community affairs. But in 1945, his world fell apart. A Russian spy named Igor Gouzenko defected to Canada and revealed the existence of a spy ring in Ottawa. Among those named was Guy's only son, Raymond Boyer. Code-named "The Professor," the trusted scientist Raymond had been handing over secret information about explosives to the Russians. He was convicted under the Official Secrets Act and spent two years in prison. The case was a huge sensation, splashed over all the newspapers. It had far-reaching consequences and was said to have been the instigation of the Cold War with Russia. The scandal broke patriotic Major Boyer's heart. He sold the resort and moved back to Montreal, where he died a solitary death some years later.

Several newcomers during this time period established or purchased resorts: Norval Craig, Leo Sick, Jack Black and Don Petrie at Twin Lakes;

and Grant Taylor, Mike Graf, and Claude Dean on Bridge Lake. The Deane-Freemans set up a small resort at Knight Lake, the MacLeans established one at Wilson Lake, and Richard Taylor and Mac Thomason purchased Lee Hansen's guest ranch, renaming it the Double T.

Gardner Boultbee purchased the MacDonald ranch and instituted new agricultural practices. In North Bridge Lake, the Law family arrived in 1941: Alan ranched while his wife, Patty, taught school. A few kilometres down the road, the MacLeans, who arrived in 1943, had the same lifestyle: Don MacLean ranched, while his wife, Jean, worked as a teacher. Both Patty Law and Jean MacLean taught at various schools over the years.

Russell Ross, the son of Vi Shertenlib and Norman Ross, spent part of his childhood away from Bridge Lake but never felt happy unless he was in the Cariboo. He returned as a young boy and eventually established his own ranch at North Bridge Lake. Courtesy Ian MacInnes, Duncan, BC.

Russell Ross, who had spent part of his childhood at Roe Lake, purchased land in North Bridge Lake and established a notable ranch. Other newcomers at that time were Jack Adams, Bill Currie, Bert DePutron, Art Fitch, Marvin Hall, Amos Kallock, Phillip Leith, Ruth Wagner, Bill Wilson, Percy W. W. Wilson, and Horace Woodrow. Jack Johnson was located at Roe Lake.

A few people pre-empted land during the 1940s, but most of it had already been taken up. Land prices, however, were still quite reasonable and a working person could easily afford a quarter section, often on a lake. Nevertheless, only half a dozen of the families who came during the 1940s stayed for the rest of their lives. The rest moved on after a number of years, usually locating themselves elsewhere in British Columbia.

From 1950 to 1959, there were only a few people who moved to Bridge Lake: the families of Norm Bonter, Art Brookes, John Conkey, Len Coukell, Bill Greenall, Fred Hart, Jock MacKay, Tom Sprowl, and Stan Williams. Three of those families became long-term residents; others spent five to ten years in the area. A short biography of each of these families can be found in an appendix at the back of the book.

MAKING A LIVING

No matter what the dream, the reality was that some sort of income had to be generated in order for a family to survive. Homesteaders had to be versatile. No one could afford to have just one skill or concentrate on only one occupation. If you had a ranch, you usually also rented cabins and guided hunters. You might also have had a trapline and sold cream on the side from a few dairy cows. Perhaps you cut railroad ties or made shakes during the winter. You fixed your own machinery, doctored your own animals, and grew everything you could.

Those who were flexible, hardy, and inventive had the best chance of success. The Cariboo Plateau was a tough place to live but those who stayed the course and managed to make a living for their families were able to match their wits and succeed against the odds.

Ranching

Most settlers were aspiring ranchers. They might raise from thirty head of cattle to a few hundred. The largest ranches (the numbers fluctuated through the years) were owned by the Clevelands at Eagan Lake and David Hutchison in the North Bonaparte. Several ranches at Roe Lake, Bridge Lake, and down through the valley to 70 Mile House, had 100 or 150 head of cattle, depending on the time of year.

This was in line with statistics in the rest of the Cariboo. A government study done in 1948, *Ranching in the Southern Interior Plateau of British Columbia*, listed 347 ranches in the Cariboo-Chilcotin. The average number of cattle per ranch was 142; most had only 25 to 99 head of cattle. The larger ranches ranged from 900 to 1,200 acres, not including leased land. Smaller ranches might range from 320 acres to as many as 500 acres. These ranches would also utilize leased land or Crown land. The number of acres of open grassland determined how many head of cattle a ranch could support.

According to the government study, 92 per cent of ranches were family undertakings. In the 70 Mile to Bridge Lake area, it was virtually 100 per cent. Everyone in the family, aged from 5 to 85 years old, pitched in to make the enterprise work. Most families had to hire extra helpers during busy times

Arlie Park of Canyon Ranch in the North Bonaparte branding a calf. Courtesy Rose (Park) Scheepbouwer, Vernon, BC.

Fall roundup preparing for beef shipment by the Green Lake Meadows Ranch crew in 1946. From left to right: Frank Haywood-Farmer, Ross Eden, Bert Gammie, and George Haywood-Farmer. Courtesy Frank Haywood-Farmer, Kamloops, BC.

such as haying. Although this might have been a drain on the family income, it did help boost the local economy, providing work for ranch hands and itinerant cowboys.

Lucky families included several older sons and daughters who were able to help with the work of the ranch. In addition to helping with the workload, the children could pre-empt land of their own when they became of age and thus add to the family's holdings. The Burns family, who lived near Bridge Lake, was an example of this: between 1909 and 1916, the family managed to accumulate almost a thousand acres by applying for pre-emptions, one at a time, by each member of the family. However, with this strategy, the problem always arose that sooner or later, the sons and daughters would have to leave and make their own way, since most ranches didn't make enough money to support more than one family. Would they let their land stay in the family unit or would they take it over themselves? Or would they sell it so they could move on to another location, thus reducing the size of the working ranch? Adding to these quandaries was the fact that once the children left, the ranch could not be run without hiring people. Would there be enough income to do that? Every family ranch eventually had to make these kinds of decisions.

Many factors were crucial to success. The availability of water and water rights were of utmost importance. The type of terrain also played a central role. In the areas of lodgepole pine in the 70 Mile to North Bonaparte area, the carrying capacity (number of cows supported per acre of land) was lower than it was around Bridge Lake with its aspen park and fir terrain, which afforded a larger area for grazing. Swamp meadows, more common in the south, helped to correct the difference.

The high elevation of the area meant that summer range readiness was up to six weeks later at the highest elevations, commencing mid-June and continuing to about the end of September. Most ranchers used meadows and valley bottom for fall grazing and utilized Crown land and leased land for the summer range. Most had to feed their stock about six months of the year.

One of the advantages of the 70 Mile and North Bonaparte area was the presence of natural swamp meadows. Many ranchers, such as the Scheepbouwers, strategized to get full advantage of these natural meadows. In the spring, after the snow had melted, the ranchers would dam the meadows to keep the moisture in and the grass lush. About the beginning of June, they'd take down the dams and drain the meadows so they were dry enough to hay around the beginning of July.

In his memoir, Floyd Tompkins described being a cowboy in the North Bonaparte:

> We used to get up at 4 am and never get back to camp until after dark as we were busy ticking cattle... We ticked cattle for six weeks to 2 months. We had 20 miles of spring range and 400 head of cattle to look after... In late summer when it was getting drier and the alkali lakes were drying up and making it dangerous for the cows bogging down, trying to get out for a drink, we had to start riding around the bogs and pulling cows out of the mud, some days we would find one or two cows stuck in the bogs... When I went to work for Dave Hutchinson in 1940 he still had these wild cattle that hadn't been corralled for years. I guess these were probably the wildest ones. There was only 8 or 9 cows that Hutchinson still owned that were wild. They said that they would stay in the thick bush and only come out on the feed grounds at night. My brother [Earl], Dave and I started to catch them one day, it was a few miles from the main ranch. We each ended up with one cow. As soon as we caught up to them they just scattered in singles leaving their calves and scared to death. Earl roped one and so did I, we hollered back and forth as these cows when roped would lay down and wouldn't move. Dave didn't rope his and let it go and came over to where we were with two cows and no calves and four or five miles from the ranch. We had to turn them loose and hope for a better

day and a better place to try and corral them. It was about a month later when my brother and I thought that we would ride out that way, when we found them in front of the wings of a wild horse corral. We headed them into the wings and we really had to ride to keep them together, we were lucky to have found them altogether. After a few minutes of hard riding we had them in the corral and were they ever wild. They were trying to get out but the corral was big and high and we knew we finally had them caught. The next day we went down there and kept the wild ones in the middle of the bunch and got them in corrals at the home ranch. They were put in a small pasture and that fall they went west of the beef drive to the 59 Mile… I believe that these were the last of the wild cattle that was left in the Cariboo country at that time.

Ranching around Bridge Lake was somewhat different. There, south slope aspen meadows predominated and slightly different strategies were used. Russell Ross, who ranched in Bridge Lake for many years, had about 250 head of cattle, depending on the time of year. His cattle grazed on open range land acquired by a grazing permit through the government. Some of his cattle grazed in a natural meadow at Grizzly Lake. When he wanted the cattle to move, he'd move the salt lick he provided for them farther up the mountain. Since the animals craved the essential minerals in the salt lick, they'd follow along to wherever the salt was. Russell raised all his own hay on 160 acres of hay fields. Bridge Lake has more of what he calls "soft grass," which is better for milking and for calves. Around the 70 Mile, they had more of what was called "hard grass."

In the early days, cattle were driven to market at Ashcroft or Kamloops. The trip became much less onerous when the railway terminus reached 59 Mile House and cattle could be loaded there. After the Pacific Great Eastern Railway completed the tracks to Lone Butte, the stockyards at 59 Mile were abandoned and new ones were built at Lone Butte. Ranchers from all over the country drove their herds to the pens at Lone Butte to be loaded onto boxcars. Ranchers in the North Bonaparte sometimes loaded their cattle at Graham's Siding instead.

Most people raised Hereford cattle and, to a lesser degree, Shorthorns. Chosen for their ability to handle the harsh winters and high altitude of the region, they were also able to thrive on wild grass. However, in later years, Aberdeen Angus came to be the preferred breed. Whereas Herefords preferred open range, Angus cattle were more versatile and would forage into the muskeg and graze on grass under trees.

Cowboys rounding up cattle in Bridge Lake. From left to right: Jim Reed, Ernie Faessler, Sid Reynolds, and Fred Reed. Courtesy Audrey (Reed) Woodman, Merritt, BC.

The market for beef went through many highs and lows over the years. When the stock market crashed in October 1929, cattle were selling for $102.00 a head, but by 1934, the price had dropped to $37.00 a head. The hard economic times also caused a decrease in demand. Some years, ranchers only got a few cents per pound for all their work over the year. The only thing a rancher could do was hope that next year the price would be better.

Many difficulties could crop up. Fence boundaries were sometimes disputed and Matt Porter, for one, was elected to be a local "fence viewer." This job dates back centuries, when farmers were settling in the mid-western United States. It became necessary if there was a dispute about a fence between two properties. Issues could include the fence encroaching on someone else's property or the fence being in a bad state of repair. Matt, along with Frank Engema and Isaac Carr of Clinton, covered the District of Lillooet, settling fence disputes and trying to reconcile neighbours feuding over property lines. With his good humour and knowledge of the countryside, Matt was an ideal candidate.

Cattle rustling sometimes occurred, although it wasn't common. Myrtle Bryant Johnson, who worked as a cowgirl for John McGillivray in the North Bonaparte, related one incident:

One time, John McGillivray and I were out riding on the range over Graham Meadows when we heard planes go over and sometimes land. John was spooky about it and told me nothing about it, but apparently, there were rustlers who used planes, landed near a herd, shot and butchered as many cattle as they could, and then took off. John felt it was too dangerous to intervene.

Another time, we were out on the range looking for a particular cow we'd had trouble with. She had too much milk for her calf and John had to milk her himself, as she was a fighter and he didn't want me getting hurt. We came to a fence boundary, close to someone else's place, and we heard that cow bawling her head off—I knew her call. But John said not to go further, as it was obvious that she was calling for her calf, and the calf was in the corral at this person's place. Later, it was said that they'd found an orphaned calf, but John didn't confront them.

No one was more infamous for cattle rustling than John DuBois. The first record of him in the Cariboo occurred in March 1917, and it appears that DuBois had come directly from Alberta, where he'd had major trouble with the law for rustling cattle. It took some genealogical sleuthing to ascertain whether John DuBois of the Cariboo was the same John DuBois whose story appeared in T. W. Paterson's book *Outlaws of Western Canada*. Tracing the family data nailed down the fact that they were one and the same person.

The DuBois (pronounced "Doo-boy" by locals) family consisted of John, his wife, Sarah, and their children, Albert, Basil, Vaughn, and Paloma. They settled on Lot 4637 at 83 Mile Creek, close to Bullock Lake. It became known as the DuBois Place. John ran a large herd of horses there and at his other place across the Bonaparte River above the Mound Ranch, which is now called the Horse Camp Ranch. Floyd Tompkins describes the tortuous route to get there:

> The horse camp was about 25 miles down on the Bonaparte River. You went down the old Cariboo road about 3 miles, where the old DuBois horse trail that you followed [goes] down to Island Lake about 4 miles, then about 15 miles to the Bonaparte River passing through twin creeks and a horse pasture fence of DuBois' and then on down to the river about 3 or 4 miles, then you crossed a narrow saddle horse bridge on up about another mile to the horse camp.

Mae Bryant McConnell, a resident of 70 Mile House since her birth in 1929, remembered the DuBois family well. "Their house was set up on a hill above a meadow," she said, "so John could see people coming. His biffy door even opened inward, so no one could open the door suddenly and surprise him." The Bryant children were fascinated with John and the pearl-handled revolvers he always wore. When John briefly ended up in jail, Matt Porter bought one of the pistols and refused to give it back unless John had the money to re-purchase it. Matt passed the pistol on to the McConnells and eventually Mae ended up with it. "I decided one day I should give it back to one of John's children," she said, "and that's what I did."

Bill Cunningham of 74 Mile House also knew John DuBois. "He either liked you or he didn't," he said, "and I have to admit he did help out the Cunninghams now and then." However, DuBois's neighbour, Bill Bishop, had a different sort of experience. One day in the spring of 1919, he spotted John with a covered wagon. When John wasn't around, Bill took a peek under the canvas. The cargo was slaughtered beef. Together with one of the Pollards, he scouted around for evidence and found buried hides on DuBois's property with the Bishop brand. The hides were seized for evidence and taken to the Clinton jail, along with DuBois.

The Clinton jail, where DuBois and the hides were held, mysteriously burned to the ground a few days later. With no evidence, the charges had to be dropped. One story is that DuBois was out on bail at that time, and another is that his daughter slipped into the jail to free her father. Since Paloma was only a young child at the time, the latter was unlikely. If he'd gone to trial, the jury was to be Jack Maindley, Claud Pigeon, and Henry Atwood.

Interestingly, in 1963, an unidentified person talked to people in Clinton, asking for their opinions on the case. The notebook containing their views is now in the Clinton museum. Six out of seven people considered DuBois guilty, but one sympathizer thought he'd been framed and never stole anything in his life.

Somehow, DuBois led a charmed life. In May 1940, he sold his holdings and moved to Harrison Hot Springs. At the time, John was in his seventies, but he nevertheless ran a riding stable that supplied horses for guests in Harrison and actively worked at it until the moment of his death. His obituary in 1943 matter-of-factly stated: "[Mr. DuBois] had returned with his horses from the Springs and dropped dead shortly after entering the house."

People like DuBois were uncommon. Most neighbours tried to help each other if cattle strayed onto their property. Floyd Tompkins talked about this in his memoir:

> Everybody gathered their cattle along with theirs, nobody's cattle [was] ever left behind, it did not matter how far away they were. If your cattle got in with theirs, they set up a date by mail when they

would meet you halfway and exchange cattle, or you rode over as soon as you heard, if the weather was not too cold, and picked up your cattle.

Ranching was a subsistence way of life, even in the years when prices for beef were high. But ranchers and their families pursued that lifestyle because they loved it and because it was a good way to raise a family. Only reluctantly did most of them give up and sell out. Rose Park Scheepbouwer actively ranched with her husband, Bill, for many years, both in the North Bonaparte and on the Fraser River. When asked if there was anything she missed now that those days were gone, she said wistfully, "I miss the cows—I just loved those cows."

Many who attempted to make a living at ranching, however, were unable to be successful. Over half left the area after less than sixteen years. Of those who moved away, only about a quarter continued to ranch (in the Cariboo-Chilcotin, Kamloops, and the Okanagan). The majority gave up ranching and farming altogether and went on to different work, a telling commentary.

From Gilbert Price to his children in California
Bridge Lake, 22nd Sept 1940

My Dear Children,
…We have had a very rainy summer here. Meadows are still wet. Fairly good hay crops. I will finish this week—about 65 tons. This will give me more hay than I need… I still have some beef I canned at the beginning of haying. My place is litterly [sic] surrounded by moose country. Last year there were nine taken in a 1-1/3 mile radius from my cabin… Autumn is here and in a few days I'll begin getting my garden in. Lots of carrots for the horses and the cow that I milk in the winter. I don't milk in the summer, too much trouble when I'm alone. As it is I can go away from home for a few days but a cow would hold me. Am writing while my bread is baking. 4 big loaves in the oven and 2 more to go in later. Usually bake and wash once a week. Today I've been cleaning house… I try to keep things in order but it is hard to keep house and work outside too and get anything done. Usually get up at 5 and go to bed about 9. Busy at something all the time… Well I'll close hoping this finds you both well and happy. I am feeling good, and am fat.

Love from your Daddy

Horse Ranching

A few ranches concentrated on raising horses. There was a good market for them, since everyone needed horses. Heavy horses were used for ploughing and haying; saddle horses were using for handling cattle. If the ranch also had tourist cabins, horses would be needed for the guests. Dependence on swamp hay meant that a large percentage of ranchers used horses for haying, since this was much more practical than using machinery because of the rough terrain and remote location of many of the wild hay meadows.

The earliest horse dealers were the Graham brothers, Robert and Sam. Listed in *Wrigley's British Columbia Directory* for many years as horse breeders as well as ranchers, the brothers were well known for their outstanding horses. Andy Whitley in the North Bonaparte was also a noted horse breeder. Bringing in aging race horse studs with good credentials from the coast, he bred them with the wild mustangs in the countryside. As well as selling his stock,

The Sprowl children in North Bridge Lake helping to build a hay rack. Farm children played a vital role in the running of any operation and their contribution helped to make them into resourceful adults. Courtesy Carol (Sprowl) Vance, Chilliwack, BC.

he also had saddle horse studs and work horse studs. People around the countryside brought their mares over to be bred. Jack DuBois, despite his failings, had a large herd of what were considered first-rate horses, and kept most of them at Horse Camp Ranch across the Bonaparte.

Another family that raised horses was the Simmons family of Eagan Lake. Arriving in 1907, the Simmons may have raised horses in Washington before they came to Eagan Lake. Ervin MacDonald mentioned them in *The Rainbow Chasers:* "One evening about this time [winter 1907], I had my second visitor, a tall man riding a big bay horse. I had been around saddle horses most of my life so I knew a good one when I saw it, and this was without doubt one of the best. That animal had been ridden about 30 miles across country through 3 feet of snow that day, but he still had plenty of steam left." The rider was Ike Simmons, one of the four Simmons brothers. By 1919, *Wrigley's British Columbia Directory* listed Charles Simmons as a horse breeder and later listed "Simmons brothers" (Charles and Harvey) in the same capacity. The Simmonses were listed as horse breeders until 1929, when the last of the brothers moved from Eagan Lake.

Frank Rossi was also mentioned in *The Rainbow Chasers* as raising high-quality horses. Unfortunately, Frank had a difficult time parting with them. If someone offered to buy one, he would then list the horse's faults and discourage the person from buying it. "He spoiled every sale," Ervin MacDonald wrote. "The truth was he simply could not part with any of his dearly

Fred Reed of Bridge Lake haying. Depending on the size of the ranch, crews were often hired to help out. Courtesy Audrey (Reed) Woodman, Merritt, BC.

beloved animals, though he desperately needed money to pay the taxes on his property and buy grub and clothes."

Some of the horse breeders were listed as "cayuse ranchers" in *Wrigley's British Columbia Directory*. The term cayuse usually referred to a wild or unbroken horse. Herds of wild horses ranged through the area, thought to have originated with Indigenous people who had acquired horses by trading as early as 1740 and also from horses brought in by miners during the Cariboo gold rush. Eventually, the wild horses became so numerous that a bounty was placed on them. Many were shipped to Alberta and other parts of the Prairies and sold to homesteaders. Some sadly ended up as food at fox farms. In the early years, Indigenous people chased and caught the wild horses, utilizing them in their own herds. Later, it became a good way to make money for adventurous young cowboys. The occupation, an exciting and exhilarating pastime, wasn't just for the young fellows—young women such as Mae Bryant McConnell liked to join in the chase too. "I used to go chase wild horses all the time with my brothers Dick and Norman," she said. "We had a great time!" Floyd Tompkins vividly described the process:

> When we corralled the horses we would front foot them and hog tie them down so we could put a strap and a ring on their front foot and a ring tied into their tails, with a short rope that was tied to the ring on their front foot, with their tail put between their hind legs tied to the end of the short rope. You had to make sure of the length of the rope, because if it was too short they couldn't keep up, and if it was too long they could run like hell, and we always had some of them both making them hard to hold together, as these horses were wild. All they wanted to do was get as far away from you as they could and as fast as they could. We had tough days and hard days getting these horses moved from one place to the other. One time Herb's [Matier] horses broke on him at the end of the wings, this took a couple of days getting the horses and getting them down to the big pasture with it snowing so hard that Herb had got mixed up in his directions but luckily we heard Bill Myers hollering at the horses that he was driving down this main trail to where we wanted to go… After corralling a bunch of horses we would take them out of the big pasture and take them over to the stock yards at the railroad to be shipped to Vancouver. We kept the studs separate from one another in the railway cars, this was a big job getting them rounded up and over to the railway at 59 Mile House 8–10 miles away.

Roy Eden related a dramatic story (told to him by his brother Stan Eden) of the Anderson brothers, Axel and Carl, who ran down a herd of wild horses—on skis.

> On that first winter of 1911-12, they [Axel and Carl Anderson] cleaned up on a small band of wild horses that were located at that time on the Watch Lake range. It was, I believe, from this bunch that my brother [Stan] picked his first saddle horse, a black mare that could outrun most any other animal we ever owned. He used to take her to the race meets in Clinton and all other local celebrations where she surprised many of the other race men who ran much bigger horses. During a winter a few years later they skied down another band which used to run in the Lone Butte area.
>
> But here is my brother's story of [Axel and Carl Anderson's] last big roundup and what happened when they were after the wild horse band that used to run on the main Bonaparte River in the vicinity of the Chasm at 61 Mile. They had found out in other winters that it was much better to trail the horses in shifts with one man [skiing] while the other fellow got his sleep in their camp. In this way they kept the horses moving with no chance for them to eat or sleep.
>
> The grandstand seat—on this particular moonlight night on Stan's shift—the weather was clear and mighty cold—around 30 or 40 below zero. "I could feel my feet getting colder and I knew they would soon start to freeze," [Stan told me], "so I started crowding the horses hoping my increased speed would warm my feet. Sweat broke out all over me, and my feet got colder. At last I sighted a lone, dry pine snag about 12 feet in height. Kicking off my skis and using one as a shovel, I cleared away the snow, and with the few dry limbs that were handy, got a fire going. By this time, my moccasins were frozen solid but I managed to get them free from my socks. The bursting flames from the pitchy pine lighted up the surrounding area, and to my surprise I found that the wild horses had camped with me standing just as they had stopped, one behind the other on the trail. Most of them already had their heads down sleeping.
>
> "There were two stallions in the bunch and I could see at a glance that both were cranky, mostly from lack of food and sleep, and they snapped repeatedly at the mares, biting them mercilessly.
>
> "One stallion was a handsomely marked pinto. He had led the band all day but despite the rough trail-breaking that must have

meant, he appeared strong and full of life. The other, a long, gangling bay with a big, ugly head and one leg slightly deformed, had been holding down the rear.

"There was enmity between them, one could sense in the air. Suddenly I heard a vicious squeal and looking over my shoulder, saw the pinto coming full tilt at the bay—running straight at him with ears back and teeth bared. He seized the other in the near foreleg in a vice-like grip, and with a terrific heave threw the bay over on its back. Then began in earnest one of the most awe-inspiring sights I have ever seen.

"Back and forth raged the wild stallions—biting—striking—lashing out with hind feet. The killer-horses paid no more attention to me than as if I hadn't been there at all. One of the most fantastic things of all was that the mares did not bother watching the death battle. Most of them didn't even lift their heads. They were having a sleep while the rivals for the leadership of the band fought each other with all their fury. The fighting drifted farther out into the timber and I did not see the finish. But after a while I knew which stallion had won. The pinto came back alone. His head was high and his neck arched. His heaving sides were glistening with sweat and flecked with blood. Out there in the tall jackpine they had fought to the bitter end. The pinto was victor."

Stan soon got back to their camp and Anderson went out on the horse trail to do his shift. But it was eight days later when they drove the bunch into the horse corral at Watch Lake Ranch. On skis only, they drove these wild horses all the way from the main Bonaparte River area up past what we called the "Curry Place" when I first worked for the Boyds in 1907, and then onto the ice at the west end of Big Green Lake and past the Flying U Ranch to the mouth of Watch Lake where there was only a short portage to the ice trail again on Watch Lake…

"I can remember well the night when I heard them coming up to the Lake to our little bay below the cabin," [Stan said]. "I got out in a hurry and led the mare down to the water hole, and those one-time wild horses followed her right into our horse corral without a bit of trouble. From then on until the Spring came, it was my job to do the bronc-riding, which was much more to my liking than riding snow skis at 60 degrees below!"

Sheep Ranching

Several ranchers raised sheep, to one extent or another, over the years. The earliest was the Price family, who arrived in 1907. *Henderson's Directory* for 1910 states that Port Price, one of the brothers, raised sheep, while Del, another brother, raised goats. This was the only year they were listed with these occupations. Andy Whitley raised sheep in quite large numbers. The *Ashcroft Journal* described his operation in 1915:

> Bounaparte [*sic*] Valley, B.C., April 30, 1915—Sheep raising on a fairly large scale is being successfully carried on in this district by a number of homesteaders and old settlers. One of the finest flocks is owned by Mr. A. Whitley, of the North Bounaparte [*sic*], who has nearly four hundred head on the range. Although engaged in the horse and cattle business when he settled here six years ago, Mr. Whitley later turned his attention almost exclusively to sheep, specializing in Southdowns, Suffolks, and a few Merinos. His returns from fleece average five dollars per sheep, which, with the natural increase of his flock, yield an annual profit of nearly 100 per cent. By careful herding he has escaped serious losses from coyotes but other ranches have suffered more severely. His sheep range on the foothills and are herded by a man and one dog.

Calvin Smith, who lived in both Bridge Lake and later in the North Bonaparte, raised sheep in both locations. The whole family was involved, with his daughters tending the sheep in Bridge Lake. Later, in the North Bonaparte, the operation was listed as "C. Smith and Sons, sheep ranching." Geoffrey Downton, a surveyor of the area in 1920, bought mutton from the Smiths to feed his surveying crew.

In the early years of the Cleveland ranch at Eagan Lake, Carr Cleveland raised a herd of over a thousand sheep. When his eldest son, Robbie, was in his teens, he took over some of the enterprise. In an interview in his later years, Robbie related a few of the challenges involved in protecting the family's herd of 1,300 sheep—including the threat of bears.

"Bears would grab a sheep and flip it right up on their shoulder and trot off with it," he said. "Fending off bears and wolves all year was no picnic." Getting the sheep to market was also a challenge. Each fall, Robbie and his father, Carr, would saddle up their horses and drive the large herd south to Savona, where they'd be loaded onto railway livestock cars. The trip took a whole week, and the pair slept outside under the trees along the way. The last night of the long journey, they usually found welcome shelter at the

Threlkeld ranch—where they bunked down three to a bed.

Eventually, the Clevelands gave up raising sheep, as did many other ranchers. As well as predators being a major problem, the terrain in the area was not ideal for sheep. The market was not as good for mutton as it was for beef, so sheep-raising was only a marginal venture.

DAIRY FARMS

Dairying was an occupation that went back to the early days of settlement. The Saul brothers, John and William, set up a dairy herd at Green Lake to supply the 70 Mile Roadhouse with all the milk, cream, and butter that was needed. Later, Bill Boyd bought the roadhouse and also took over the dairy enterprise.

Many settlers added dairying to their ranching and farming endeavours. With some, it was listed as their main occupation. In *Ranching in the Southern Interior Plateau of British Columbia,* the report commented: "Only near the large centres were dairy herds found." For whatever reason, this was not the case in this district. Those who ran dairying enterprises were far away from any major centre, and in most cases, far from any railway station.

In the early days, the logistics of transporting their products to the market or railhead was mind-boggling. From the remote locations in which many of these dairy operations were located, the cream or butter, usually transported in five-gallon cans, would have to be taken by horseback or by wagon over rudimentary trails. It's hard to imagine how difficult this would have been, especially from Bridge Lake or Bonaparte Forks. Strangely enough, more people operated dairies before 1930, when it was far more difficult. After that date, only a few took on the venture.

In later years, residents shipped their cream and butter from Lone Butte to Quesnel on the Pacific Great Eastern Railway. Before 1921, the railway had not yet reached Quesnel, so their market must have been elsewhere, perhaps Clinton or Kamloops. The last entry in *Wrigley's British Columbia Directory* for anyone listed as a dairy farmer was Chester Provo in 1938. However, there were still many families who produced extra income by sending their cream to Quesnel, where it was distributed to railway camps in the south.

The Faesslers in Bridge Lake was one of these families. Charlie and Margrit Faessler earned a large part of their income by taking their cream to the Roe Lake post office, where it was picked up and transported to Quesnel. With the appalling road conditions even a short outing could be nerve-wracking, as Margrit discovered on one of her first trips to the post office at Wheeler's.

When they first came to Bridge Lake, Margrit was still very much a city person and had never ridden a horse or milked a cow. Nevertheless, she always did her share and when Charlie couldn't drive the can of cream to the Roe Lake post office, Margrit took over. With great trepidation, she climbed on the wagon seat and set about driving the wagon and team to Wheeler's. Pulling hard on the reins, knuckles white with fear, she would yell, "Whoa! Whoa!" over and over, sure that if she didn't, the team would never stop or listen to her. When the trip was over and she arrived home safe and sound, she always heaved a tremendous sigh of relief.

Dude Ranches, Guest Ranches, and Resorts

Gradually, because of the proliferation of lakes available for fishing, the area has become known as the Interlakes region, although this is not a term any old-timers care for. The tourist industry is now one of the mainstays of the district. It wasn't always that way. Early settlers were too busy and too isolated to even think of establishing tourist businesses. But by the 1920s, the idea had filtered into the countryside.

The very first guest ranches were Jack Boyd's Flying U and Lee Hansen's near Bridge Lake, now known as the Double T Ranch. Lee had cabins built, some by Svend Stokstad, and established the place as a hunting and fishing resort sometime after 1924 when he married Betty Jowsey. In the Green Lake area, Jack Boyd transformed his cattle ranch into the Flying U Ranch sometime in the late 1920s, the first dude ranch in the area. The distinction between a dude ranch and a tourist ranch is a fine one, with a dude ranch defined as an establishment where guests can participate in work such as roundups.

The idea caught on. It was another source of revenue for cash-strapped families. Well-heeled American hunters were eager to travel to the Canadian wilderness and go on hunting and fishing expeditions. The Cariboo was the ideal place. Since there were so many lakes in the area, nearly everyone had a lake somewhere on their property, often filled with sport fish. Moose, once non-existent in the area, had moved in about 1918 and were particularly abundant around Sheridan Lake, Needa Lake, English Lake, and Windy Mountain. The North Bonaparte was also an excellent area for wildlife.

Roy Eden, a Watch Lake pioneer, told an amusing story about the return of moose to the countryside. He was riding with Sam Graham on the range about 1912 and noticed that Sam was packing a rifle, something he had never seen him do before. When Roy asked him why, Sam replied, "Well, Roy, my boy, I want you to promise me that you won't say a word to anyone about what I'm going to tell you. I borrowed this gun from a friend of mine in Clinton as

I'm afraid I may see The Beast again." When a puzzled Roy asked him what he meant, Sam described an "awful-looking wild animal with a heavy rack of horns" that had been hanging out with his cows. Roy was soon to find out that Sam's Beast was not a werewolf with horns but a moose. Since moose were virtually unknown in the Cariboo at that time, Sam had never seen one. It was an exciting event for Roy too when the mystery was solved and the identity of the animal revealed.

Floyd Tompkins guided as a young man and vividly described what a sportsman's paradise existed in those days:

> …That fall I started packing game out of the Bonaparte for Dave Hutchinson's [sic] hunters that Earl [Tompkins] was guiding for. I remember having two moose and four deer on one pack trip out to Hutchinson's [sic] with eight horses packed down with game, from the cow camp where we had stayed in that spring. There was lots of game and good hunting on the south side of the Bonaparte River. I also remember packing in fishing parties that summer before hunting season started. This was in 1940 and the fishing and hunting were unbelievable. It was nothing to see 6 or 7 moose in a day's ride and catching your limit of fish within a few hours. We packed in fishing parties to lakes that had hardly ever been fished and they would catch fish that were 3 to 4 pounds.

In 1920, when Geoffrey Downton surveyed in the area with his crew, fish were more than abundant. He wrote on June 27, 1920, "After lunch, Heaney, Burkholder & I went down to 2nd lake on Fly Creek to fish. I caught 21, Heaney 17, H. Burkholder, 14. Returned to camp at 9 PM and had supper. I salted down 42 of the fish in the candy bucket…"

As well as hunting and fishing excursions, resorts usually offered other pastimes: trail rides, boating, campfires, music, and dances. Each of these activities involved additional work for family members and they often had to hire extra help because of the workload. In turn, this helped the local economy. The resort business provided jobs for hunting and fishing guides, ranch hands, and cooks. In fact, several men earned a good part of their yearly income through guiding.

Most operations were small, but a few were quite large, accommodating forty or more guests at a time. One of the problems before 1960 was marketing. With stiff competition for guests (in the 1940s, there were up to twenty different resorts), some resorts didn't do as well as others. Nevertheless, any extra revenue was welcome.

After ten years had passed, many had joined the ranks of Lee Hansen and Jack Boyd. In 1948, *Wrigley's British Columbia Directory* listed at least ten. In the Bridge Lake area, there were the Larsons, Bradfords, Grafs, Deans, and Deane-Freemans. As well, the Black and Petrie families ran the Twin Lakes Tourist Camp. Farther south, there was Don Eden of Moonwinks Resort; Bert Gammie of the G Lazy Q; W. A. (Shorty) Horn; Mobbs Tourist Camp; and Hill & Hubble tourist camp (Hill & Hubble were also mentioned in the *Ashcroft Journal* in 1945 as hauling pulp wood from Bridge Lake).

The Flying U was originally part of a cattle ranch held by the Boyd family of 70 Mile House. About 1921, one of the sons, John George (Jack) Boyd, took over the ranch. It was an ideal life for him. While he ran the enterprise, he lived the quintessential cowboy life. Always a daredevil, he loved competing in rodeos and, in 1923, became a Canadian bronco riding champion, as well as winning many other trophies. In 1929, Jack married local teacher Mary (known as May) Hunter.

The ranch was originally a cattle operation, but after the Great Depression began and depressed beef prices, Jack decided to diversify. Jack and May put their heads together and came up with the idea of turning their cattle ranch into a dude ranch for those wishing to experience an authentic cowboy lifestyle. Histories of the Flying U establish its founding sometime between 1921, when Jack Boyd took over the ranch, and 1931, when *Wrigley's British Columbia Directory* listed him for the first time as "manager of the Flying U Ranch." Jack was thought to have put a two-dollar advertisement in a Vancouver newspaper advertising the dude ranch and, within a short time, began to entertain paying guests. Many of the now-existing cabins were built about that time, some by "Alec the Swede" (surname unknown), a carpenter from the Clinton area.

The name "The Flying U" originated in a series of books written in the early 1900s. A woman writer with the pseudonym of B. M. Bowers wrote this hugely popular series, featuring the imaginary Flying U Ranch in Montana. Several movies—a few starring cowboy superstar Tom Mix—were produced based on the books. It was said that either Tom Mix or William S. Hart, both of whom had once visited Boyd's dude ranch, suggested to Jack that he use this name for his ranch. "The Flying U" it became.

Through the years, guests ranging from the rich and famous to families escaping from the city enjoyed the homespun joys of the outdoors and the cowboy life. Jack was a sociable, charismatic person and he and May instituted trail rides, roundups, nightly dances, campfires, boat rides, and fishing to entertain the guests. Early on, they established the Green Lake Stampede, which became the premier event of the year for everyone from miles around.

For many years, the Flying U was an unqualified success. But regrettably, things began to slip through Jack's fingers. With his gregarious nature, he began spending more time socializing with his moneyed friends than paying attention to business. His marriage to May fell apart and business went downhill. Eventually, Jack sold out. After that time, he went on to other things but never again achieved the success he had once had.

Charlie and Frances Wilkinson from the Vancouver area were the second owners, purchasing the ranch from Jack in 1944. Charlie, a former executive with the Canadian Forestry Association, had a love of the outdoors, and he, with his wife, Frances, and their two small boys, made the Flying U their own. A brochure still in existence from their sojourn as owners from 1944 to 1951 waxes rhapsodic about the joys of their dude ranch:

> A ranch where vacationists may enjoy healthy ranch life at an altitude of 3,500 feet, on the great Cariboo Plateau where zestful air and sparkling water makes one feel the joy of living in the great open spaces of the scenically beautiful and historic Cariboo, where there are no poisonous snakes, insects or ferocious animals to mar this enjoyment.

The Wilkinson family: Frances, Charlie, and sons Billy and Chuck. The Wilkinsons purchased the Flying U Ranch from Jack Boyd in 1944. The venture prospered, but sadly, Frances's ill health forced them to sell out in 1951. Courtesy Chuck Wilkinson, Ashcroft, BC.

The cost for staying at the ranch was stunningly low:

One person in a private cabin $35.00 per week
Two persons or more in cabin $32.00 per week
One or two persons in tent cabin $30.00 per week
Children under 15 years using horses $25.00 per week

The rates included a private horse and saddle, boat rental, nightly dances, trail rides, roundup rides, weekly stampedes and races!

The Wilkinsons thrived in their new venture, but fate took an unkind turn. Frances developed a serious illness and, because of her health, they sold out. In 1951, they sold the ranch to Bert and Ruth Gammie, who were neighbours at Watch Lake. Not long after the Wilkinsons left for Summerland, Frances died and the family was left without a mother.

Bert Gammie met his wife, Ruth Haywood-Farmer, at the Flying U when they both worked there. After their marriage, they bought a place at Watch Lake. Their small ranch burned down in 1951; this happened about the same time that Charlie Wilkinson had decided to sell. It was an easy decision for the Gammies. For the next quarter-century, the family ran the Flying U, everyone involved in the venture: Bert, Ruth, their four children, and Bert's mother from England. At the time, there were sixteen cabins and sometimes as many as sixty guests a week. The Gammies also focused on the cattle operation, expanding their holdings to 3,300 acres and running cattle, horses, and sheep. Around 1975, Bert and Ruth retired and sold the ranch. It has changed hands a few times since then.

As well as providing a living for the families who owned the ranch, the Flying U was a major source of employment for cowboys and young people through the years. Summer jobs were a scarce commodity in the countryside and working at the Flying U was a welcome and exciting experience for young people. One of these was Don Eden, who was interviewed in 2003. The interviewer reported that Eden eventually gave up chasing horses for fun and took a job at the Flying U Ranch at Green Lake. He was paid to wrangle dude horses for the many guests who somehow found their way to that remote part of the Cariboo. It was 1939 and Eden was a 17-year-old. He and head wrangler, Jake Reinertson, were responsible for several jobs around the ranch, one of which included dancing with the guests at their nightly shindigs, held in the log hall which still stands, and serves the same purpose today. He recalled that a good many of the guests were teenaged girls who returned year after year to party with the cowboys and, for a few weeks, enjoy another world. Many of them took home a permanent memento, with a small Flying U symbol branded on the back of their calf. The small branding iron used to mark the girls was normally used to burn the ranch trademark into the back of each saddle, but the girls considered the scar a status symbol. "They all had to have the brand and we branded lots of 'em. They liked it."

Eden and the other wranglers were also responsible for taking the dudes out for Saturday rodeos held at Stampede Hill on North Green Lake. During the evening dance, which would follow, one of the cowboys, known as Hank, would ride his horse into the hall and pass out prizes to winners of the day's events.

Another person who related fond memories in an interview was Joan Dunbar, who came up from Vancouver to work at the Flying U as a teenager. "I have such wonderful memories. Olga (Rust) Cunningham and I were the kitchen help and another

Jake Reinertson was the head wrangler at the Flying U and cut a romantic figure for all the visitors at the dude ranch. Courtesy Robert and Gayle Fremlin, 70 Mile House, BC.

wonderful gal, Ada Smith, played the piano in the evenings and at all the dances. She was really well known for her raunchy Flying U songs, which she taught to everyone."

Local people from all over the area would join the thirty-five or so guests at the twice-weekly dances at the lodge, said Dunbar. "The dances were so great. The old floor was suspended on rubber tires and it literally bounced."

The U was a busy place where spare time wasn't wasted and staff used to spend much of it playing pranks. "We were known for putting chickens in cabins, tying cowbells on bedsprings, and wrapped moose droppings in paper to pass on as candy in the candy dish," said Dunbar.

Head wrangler Jake Reinertson was a legend among the guests as was his sense of humour. According to Dunbar, he was leader of the pack when it came to silent midnight raids on the kitchen. "He had the key to the larder and, in the middle of the night, he'd make bacon and eggs for all of us," said Dunbar. "I wish I could do it all over again. It was such good, clean fun."

Jake Reinertson had worked his way up from being one of the cowboys at the Flying U to the position of ranch foreman and was employed through the years by Jack Boyd, Chuck Wilkinson, and the Gammies. Jake, who had previously been married, was an elusive single man, but his heart was finally won by a visiting German doctor named Ruth Roffman. She came up for a vacation at the Flying U and fell for the handsome head wrangler. They were married in 1963 and eventually retired to a place at 90 Mile. Both were committed people: Ruth didn't retire from being a doctor until she was 70 and Jake finally gave up his cattle operation at the age of 85. However, he continued to ride horseback until he was 90.

Leonard Larson, in his unpublished memoir, also talked about the pranks and fun of the Flying U when he worked there as a young cowboy:

> That spring when I was 16 but looked a lot older, I went to work for the Flying U Guest Ranch on Green Lake, owned by Jack and Mae Boyd. There were a crew of 11 of us men and 11 girls. There were about 75 guests at all times, mostly office girls, nurses, and odd couples with their children. They had a huge dance hall and danced every night until 2 am. Saturday night, we danced until daylight. To entertain the guests we had trail rides and round ups where we could brand and castrate a few calves. That being on a Friday, we would drive about 30 head of steers to the Stampede grounds and every Saturday was rodeo day. They would pass the hat around amongst the guests and the money was then divided amongst us boys that would ride. The guests would stay approximately a week or 10 days. When they would leave they would break down and cry. One special lady from Seattle, Washington, bought all of us an expensive Western shirt… I had a pair of chaps made into the same pattern as Pete Knight's. I had only worn them once, so together we boys gave her those chaps. She was so pleased that she broke down and cried, she said that she was so pleased with those chaps that she felt she could sleep in them.
>
> Our wages were $40 a month and every night we would go down to the lake to the big shower house. The girls were always playing tricks on us and vice versa. One Saturday night, we went down to the shower house with a clean pair of overalls, but the girls that worked there in the laundry had sewn our pant legs back and

forth approximately every inch, so it was quite a performance to try to get on our clean overalls. We ended up wearing our old ones back to the bunk house.

The orchestra consisted of three people—one big Indian by the name of Billy Woods. He had fallen off a bicycle when he was a kid and broke his wrist, so his wrist was bent and he played left-handed. A fellow by the name of Kinik [Howard Reaugh]… played the Hawaiian guitar and a girl by the name of Ada Smith played the piano. People from the 70 Mile House and Watch Lake and as far as Lone Butte and Bridge Lake [all came], so Saturday night was a real wild time.

There was an older man by the name of Alex the Swede who had an old car made into a truck. These dude girls would just go crazy to ride in that old thing. This guy [Kinik] was always playing a trick. One time he hooked the hose from the gas pump over his back bumper. [Alex] was in his glory with all these girls in his jalopy and he took off like a shot out of hell. The glass ball on top of the gas pump went flying up on the road, all in pieces.

Another trick Kinik played on him: two dude girls had gone on a trail ride and had just gone up to their cabins to change clothes. Kinik grabbed a big dipper of cold water and told Alex to run up to Cabin #1, that a girl had passed out. So he ran up there with a dipper of water and barged in the door, finding the two girls… as they were having a sponge bath. If Alex the Swede could have caught Kinik, he would have killed him right there. There were all kinds of other pranks played on each other. It would take hours to tell them all. We had a special taxi to meet these girls at the train in Ashcroft.

Thankfully, the Flying U has survived many years and is still operating as a rustic dude ranch. One hopes the guests still have the time of their lives there, as they did many years ago.

Other major dude ranches in the area were the Watch Lake Lodge, which was owned first by the Mobbs, then by the Edens and Horns; the Double T Ranch in Bridge Lake, which changed hands several times; the Horsehead Ranch, owned by Johnny and Mabel Hansen, just south of Bridge Lake; and the Cleveland ranch at Eagan Lake. Each entertained scores of guests and were busy, thriving places.

The many other tourist facilities of varying sizes that operated through the years had their own share of tourists. In the Bridge Lake area, there were the Twin Lakes Tourist Ranch, Bridge Lake Guest Ranch, Lakeview Resort,

Happy guests at the Bridge Lake Guest Ranch, owned and run by Mike and Paula Graf. Their star guest was a chemist by the name of John Smith. Smith, who concocted a bait whose secret he never revealed, always caught the largest trout in Bridge Lake. Courtesy Pat Tasker, Surrey, BC.

Hart's resort, Bradford fishing resort, Braemore Lodge, Lucky Strike Ranch at Wilson Lake, Knight Lake Ranch, Lesser Fish Lake Resort, and Larson's resort at Roe Lake. Farther down the valley were Tuovila's tourist camp at the east end of Sharpe Lake, the Canyon Ranch, the Scheepbouwer Ranch, the Lost Valley Ranch, the XH Ranch, and the Moonwinks Guest Ranch at Watch Lake. There were few ranches, in fact, that didn't have at least one guest cabin.

Joyce Hodges Ross of Bridge Lake described the small operation she and her husband, Peter, ran:

> So from 1946 until 1988 we were a fixture at Bridge Lake. We had some good memories and some bad. That's what life is all about, I guess. We had a little log cabin on our property that we boarded

The Mobbs family, who originally lived on a remote location on the Bonaparte River, moved to Watch Lake and built a guest lodge and hand-crafted cabins. The Horn and Eden families purchased it from them in 1950 and the Watch Lake Lodge is still operating today. Courtesy Harold Mobbs, Lone Butte, BC.

tourists in and in the process of building it, Peter lost a toe that got in the way of a broad axe. And Peter and John built a cabin at Tobe Lake, on Peter's trapline. He would take them out there and the tourists would stay for several days, enjoying the quiet and fishing, which was very good then. Then he would go back in with his tractor and bring them back out when they were ready. I would always have a pie ready to serve them before they left for their home, mostly to the States.

TRAPPING

Trapping could be one of the most profitable ways to earn a living and certainly helped many settlers add to their yearly income. Even children had small traplines and this provided them with much-needed extra cash.

The foremost trapper in the Cariboo Plateau in the early twentieth century is almost forgotten today except by the very oldest residents. Ed Rioux arrived in the Cariboo from Quebec about 1914 and pre-empted land around Green Lake. He soon started trapping with his partner and neighbour Cassian Postolovski and the two trapped around the 100 Mile House. Cassian left the country and Ed began to trap in the hinterlands above Bridge Lake and east of Canim Lake. Eventually, his trapline extended over a 160 kilometres

(100 miles), right over to the Clearwater area, taking in four major watersheds. For a few years, his headquarters was around Roe Lake. Later he moved his headquarters to Rioux Lake, where he established a large camp (now known as Moose Camp Fishing Resort).

When the trapping season was about to start, Ed got to work. Assembling all the provisions he'd need for an entire winter, he loaded his seasoned pack horses and disappeared into the woods. Once they'd reached the particular cabin he chose, he unpacked the supplies and took the horses back down to winter at Roe Lake. Once the season started, Ed disappeared into the woods on foot or by snowshoe, often accompanied by one adventurous woman or another. Spending the entire winter trapping and moving from cabin to cabin, he snowshoed to all his traps and lived off his provisions. It was rare that he ever came down from the bush.

After each winter was over, Ed snowshoed or walked out, gathered up his pack horses and went back in to load up his cache of furs. The next step was to travel to Vancouver or Clinton to sell them. With the money he'd made, Ed carefully bought all his food and provisions and purchased any new horses he needed. Then and only then would he let loose with his extra money and have a high time for several days. When the mad money ran out, he went back home. During the summers, he fixed up his cabins, keeping things in good repair.

Ed was admired by those who knew him. A short man with a dark French-Canadian look, he always wore jodhpurs and high leather boots. While others might use their own favourite cuss expressions, Ed's preferred expletive was "By gee!" He cut quite a romantic figure, according to Helen Horn (who was a young person at the time), and apparently didn't suffer from loneliness on long winter nights. There was a succession of "housekeepers" who accompanied him into the bush nearly every winter and they would often stay for a few years. One of these was a "Miss Bowers," after whom he named Bowers Lake. Each housekeeper was referred to as "Miss," and possibly these young women were attracted by the idea of an adventurous wilderness experience with a real-live trapper. Later, when Ed spent more time in the Clearwater area, his companions became "Mrs.," although no one ever knew whether a marriage had taken place.

Herbie and Benjie McNeil, who eventually bought Ed's trapline, were sons of Canim Lake pioneer Benjamin McNeil. As young boys, they often went out trapping and exploring together in the wilderness. One winter, they went up Three Mile Creek and got caught in a big snowstorm. They became disoriented and lost their way until they came upon a snowshoe trail. Realizing this must be Ed Rioux's trail, they followed it as best they could through

Hunting
Jean (MacLean) Nelson, North Bridge Lake

Karel Larson (left) with a friend on a hunting trip. Karel often worked as a guide for visiting hunters.

Most residents of the district took advantage of the excellent wild meat that was available to us in the woods and rangelands surrounding our homes. Although we didn't know it at the time, we have since learned that the wild meat we ate through necessity rather than choice was more nutritious and healthy for us than meat from domestic animals.

There are three components to hunting: the anticipation, the pursuit, and the harvest. The anticipation took many forms. It could be the excitement of the first frost and the poplar leaves starting to turn yellow, signaling the start of the season. It could be the arrival of the Eaton's catalogue, which had at least three pages of rifles and shotguns. It could be the awareness that there were only two jars of moose meat left in the larder. It also meant visitors from the city who loved to hunt—ideally, paying guests from the United States who wanted to return home with a set of prize antlers and steaks in the trunk of the car.

The pursuit was my favourite part. My father was an experienced hunter who initially only had a 30-30 Savage and who never took more than the six shells the gun held. I remember him saying once, "If I can't get an animal with six bullets, I don't deserve it." When he bought a used army rifle (a 3.03 British) in the late 1940s, I inherited the old 30-30. Fall is such a beautiful time of year, with the gold and rust colours of the leaves and the air cool and clear. The endless rolling hills of the Cariboo meant that as you topped each hill, there was always the possibility of coming upon a deer or a moose in the next draw. Hunting is best done on foot, where one can move slowly and quietly through the woods, concentrating on your quest.

One always remembers one's first successful hunt and for me, it was a youngish buck lying under a tree chewing his cud. I hit him in the jugular vein and he just lay there and quietly died. I was immediately filled with remorse, but I was excited too.

The harvest requires knowledge that one learns at one's father's knee as well. It is important to bleed the animal quickly and then to gut it cleanly so the meat can cool down as soon as possible. It is then you need to bring in your horses. A deer can be put on the back of the horse whole but a moose must be quartered in order to tie it on to the pack saddle. Not all horses like this job or the smell of fresh meat. When you reach home, the meat needs to be hung for two weeks, weather permitting, before the onerous task of canning begins.

the blinding snow. Finally they came to Ed's cabin, saw a light, and pounded on the door. Ed was home but when he opened the door, the boys were as embarrassed as they were grateful. Ed was completely nude. He urged them to come in and couldn't do enough to warm them up and make them comfortable. But the boys heaved a sigh of relief when he finally pulled on some pants and they could stop looking at the ceiling.

By 1943, Ed was 69, and he decided it was time to sell out, move on, and lead an easier life. His trapline was a coveted one, rich in furs and covering a large territory. Ed was confident about its value, and his asking price was $5,500, a large amount of money in 1943. Herb and Ben McNeil wanted the trapline but hesitated at the asking price. After talking it over, they concluded it was worth it, and they would meet his price. Ed was pleased, but stipulated that he wanted to be paid in small bills—no cheques and no large bills. Herb and Ben went to the bank and withdrew funds in the form he wanted, stuffed their packs with the booty, and made their way by horseback across the country from Canim Lake to Ed's camp on Rioux Lake. Since it was late when the deal was closed, they spent the night. As Herb and Ben drifted off to sleep, they could hear Ed and his lady friend, the current "Mrs. Rioux," counting out the money. Apparently, they spent nearly all night tallying it up. In those days, small bills would have been $1.00 or $2.00, so that would have meant at least 3,000 bills to count!

The Scheepbouwers made part of their living, as many people did, by trapping. Young people in the family also took part in the venture and helped to add to the yearly income. Courtesy Rose Scheepbouwer, Vernon, BC.

No one really knew where Ed and his lady friend went after the sale until research finally uncovered his elusive trail. By 1946, he was in Coalmont in the East Kootenays, running a general store. Somewhere around this time, Ed actually did get married, to a woman named Agnes Otter, who may have been the woman who was with him at Rioux Lake in 1943. In 1952, Ed and Agnes moved to White Rock, where Ed set up another general store. Agnes had a stroke shortly after that and died in November 1952. Ed, who was in his late eighties by then and still running a store, suffered poor health as well and died only two months later.

Ed had done well at his trapping enterprise, and he'd also done well as a storekeeper. In his will, Ed bequeathed over $6,500 to the White Rock Hospital, equivalent to over $57,000 in today's dollars. An article in the paper a week or so later announced that the Hospital Society had decided to name the new hospital's pediatric ward the "Edward Rioux Ward," commemorating their generous benefactor.

Although few in the South Cariboo now remember who he was, Ed Rioux has been commemorated there as well. There is Rioux Lake and Rioux Mountain in the Clearwater area, as well as various lakes named after his lady loves. Ed Rioux was a folkloric figure, and one who deserves to be immortalized in Cariboo history.

Jacob and Catharina Scheepbouwer of the North Bonaparte pose with an impressive bounty of deer. As well as running a working cattle ranch, the family also accommodated visiting hunters, usually from the US. The younger Scheepbouwers served as the hunting guides. Courtesy Rose (Park) Scheepbouwer, Vernon, BC.

Preserving Meat
Jean (MacLean) Nelson, North Bridge Lake

One of the essential buildings on any farm was a place to smoke meat. This was usually ham and bacon from the pigs that most people raised. A smokehouse could be any small building that had an earthen floor and slits or openings near the top to allow the smoke to exit. There needed to be a reasonable amount of air circulation so the meat didn't get too hot.

Ham and bacon first had to be covered with a preservative of salt and sugar. If it was a smaller piece, such as a side of bacon, the mixture could be rubbed in, but larger pieces had to be submerged in a brine of salt, brown sugar, and potassium nitrate. The ham was left in the brine for a number of days calculated by its weight. The pieces of meat were then removed and hung in the smoke house. The fire was made of wood from alder or willows, half of which had to be green. The fire burned for several hours each day.

The smokehouse was also used to preserve moose and venison. If the meat was hung in quarters or large chunks, the fire could be put on once a day to create an hour or so of smoke that formed a "skin" on the meat, which would keep it from spoiling for a long time.

Since no one had a freezer in those days, the excess meat had to be canned so it could keep for a year. A whole moose was a formidable amount of meat to bone, cut up in small pieces, and put into sealer jars. The jars were then boiled on the stove for four hours in the open kettle method or, if you were lucky enough to have a pressure cooker, about one and a half hours.

It has been suggested that Ed's extensive knowledge of the countryside came from Indigenous friends. This could be true and if so, Ed was probably respectful and kept to his part of the bargain. English Decker, said to be a chief in the Canim Lake Band, had a large trapline weaving through the countryside. Sociable and fond of travelling, English would arrive unannounced at many people's doors for a visit. Nearly every memoir of the area, from *The Homesteader's Daughter*, set at Roe Lake, to *Tenderfoot Trail*, set in the Deka Lake area, mention intriguing visits from English Decker. As affable as he was, English did not take kindly to anyone poaching on his territory. Rumours have swirled for years about the consequences of that action.

Disputes could arise, especially in the early days before trapping licences were required. The story is told of a dispute between Keith Smith, son of Calvin Smith, and Gordon King of Bridge Lake. Keith, who had trapped up in the Wavey Lake area, left the country about 1920 and went to Oregon. After Keith left, Gordon King explored the countryside and thought the Wavey Lake country looked like a good area to trap in. Since there were no trapline licences at the time and the custom was to inquire whether anyone else was trapping in the area they were considering, Gordon duly asked around. He was told that Keith Smith had trapped there, but that he'd left the country.

Satisfied by this, Gordon set up his trapline and built cabins and trails. When Keith came back a few years later, he was incensed that Gordon had taken up "his" territory. Gordon informed him that he'd asked around and was told no one was using that territory after Keith had left the country. The dispute festered and one night at a dance at Lone Butte, Keith challenged Gordon to go outside and fight it out. Gordon said, "Okay, I'll just get my boots on." He went outside and as soon as Keith put up his fists, Gordon planted one punch in the face and knocked him out. That was the end of the difference of opinion. The surprise was that, although Gordon had one wooden leg because of a railway accident, he had also been an amateur boxer in his youth. Gordon continued to trap there, and his son Jack took over the trapline from him. Today, two of the lakes in the area, East King Lake and West King Lake, are named after them.

The Johnstons of Bridge Lake were a notable trapping family. Arriving in Bridge Lake in 1919, the family was composed of an aged father, Charles, and his four sons, Percy, Fred, Albert, and Ernest. At least three of them trapped extensively. Ernie trapped around Wilson Lake until 1939. Fred and Percy lived together on the former Calvin Smith property at the west end of Bridge Lake. Sometime in the early spring in the mid-1930s, Fred went out to check his traps and never returned. Search parties never found his body, and to this day, it's not known what happened to him.

Ernie Ades, a former teacher at Bridge Lake, made trapping his principal source of income. The trapping life suited him very well. For twenty-nine years, he ran his traplines and also bought skins from local children who had their own routes. Living alone all winter and travelling between the seven cabins he had in the woods, he averaged $700.00 to $800.00 a year. Content with his life, he said he was never bored or lonely.

Not everyone felt that way. Trapping could be a cold, solitary occupation and if you had a family waiting at home, you could be anxious about them and them about you. Velma Higgins Malm, whose husband, Ed, trapped in the winter, worried about his return from the long cold journeys on the trapline. "The day before he had said he would return," Velma told an interviewer, "I would sit by the window hoping he would arriver sooner. But no, he always returned on the day he said he would."

It was relatively easy to market your furs. In the early days, representatives from the Northwest Fur and Hide Company in Edmonton would arrive twice a year at the Higgins ranch or the Bridge Lake Trading Post to buy furs. Harold Webb was listed in *Wrigley's British Columbia Directory* as a raw fur dealer, and in a pinch, he might let you exchange furs for groceries. Percy Ogden, a descendant of the legendary fur trader Peter Skene Ogden, bought furs for many years from the settlers in the Bridge Lake area. Another market was Pappas and Sons in Vancouver.

Wrigley's British Columbia Directory lists many trappers from 70 Mile House to Roe Lake, some of them unfamiliar names that belonged to trappers who came in for a year or two to see how they'd make out. George Brown, Lee Hansen, Ole Ellingson, Ed Higgins, Ed Malm, Will Whitley, Hugh Holland, and Axel Anderson were some of the trappers listed. There were actually few individuals or families who didn't do some sort of trapping at one time or another. The extra money was always welcome.

Other Sources of Income

Nearly everyone had numerous sets of skills and if they didn't have them, they soon learned. This helped with obtaining extra work when it was available. Many men learned log construction from building their own cabins, and went on to build log houses for others. Producing railway ties and roof shakes was another source of income.

At least eight people over the years were store owners and ran post offices. This usually provided a decent living for the operators and their families and sometimes also provided part-time jobs for other residents.

The Department of Highways at Bridge Lake provided badly needed steady jobs for local people and was a major source of employment. In the 1950s, McMillan's sawmill at Lone Butte was a boon to those looking for work. Russell Ross told an amusing story about travelling from Bridge Lake to work at McMillan's mill—a story that also illustrates the ingenuity required to live in those days of few possessions and little money:

> One year when I worked at McMillan's mill, George Spanks used to hitch a ride with me. He lived at the end of what is now Grosset Road and since he didn't have a tractor to clear the snow from his road, walked four or five miles from there to the North Bridge Lake Hall. I had a borrowed jalopy with a lot of mechanical problems, the worst of which was a leaky radiator. In the morning before work, I would put my makeshift heater under the oil pan of the car, warm the oil up so the car would start in the freezing weather, then fill up the radiator with water. I then drove to the hall to pick up George. Meantime, he had chopped a hole in the ice on the lake and got a couple of buckets of water ready. We poured the water into the radiator and drove to the mill for work. Once there, we drained the radiator so the block wouldn't freeze, then filled it up before we headed for home. We did this every day all winter.

In the 1920s, a few people became involved in soda-making ventures from the raw material found in the many alkaline lakes in the district. *Wrigley's British Columbia Directory* recorded that C. W. Austin and Oren Janes were soda producers in 1925 and 1926. As well, J. Coulson and Sons had an operation at Coulson's Spur at White Elephant Lake. In 1929 and 1930, a company named Dominion Soda Products employed half a dozen people. After 1930, it appeared that the scheme fizzled out, since no one could make enough money at the venture.

There were few people in the country who made more than a subsistence living at anything they did. As long as they managed to generate enough income to support their families, most were satisfied. Those that weren't able to manage eventually had to move away. For some of them, it may have been wrenching to leave; for others, perhaps it was a relief.

HEART OF THE COMMUNITY

Once settlers had become relatively established with essentials such as housing taken care of, the time came for other important considerations. To lead a well-functioning life, people required a way to communicate with the outside world; they needed education for their children; they had to find sources for food and supplies. Last but not least, they needed to connect with other people in the community to socialize, lend each other mutual support, and solve shared problems. Often, it was the more enterprising and assertive individuals who spearheaded supplying these services.

In such a thinly populated place, it was difficult for an actual centre that provided all the needed services to develop. Except for Bridge Lake in the 1950s, which had two schools, a store, a post office, and a community hall in one spot, the heart of every little community—which might comprise of as little as a dozen families—was usually the school. Later, perhaps, it might be a community hall. Wherever it was, this was the place where people gathered, exchanged information, socialized, and did business.

POST OFFICES

The importance of mail service can hardly be overstated. In the days before electronic communication, this was the only way to keep in touch with family and friends, take care of important financial business, and make business transactions.

The first post office was established at the 70 Mile Roadhouse, where mail had been brought up once a week from Ashcroft on the Cariboo Wagon Road. Archival postal records list Mrs. Mary Boyd as a postmistress only in 1908, but no doubt mail service had been established much earlier. Mary resigned in 1911 and her post was taken over, first by her son James, and then by her daughter Tottie. In 1918, the Boyds sold the 70 Mile Roadhouse to the Cummings family and Mrs. Agnes Cummings performed the duties of postmistress until she and her husband also sold out in 1922. Matt Porter, the new owner, then became postmaster, a position he kept until his death in 1954. His stepgrandson, David Porter McConnell, took over the position for part of a year and from 1955 to 1958, various people ran the post office.

70 Mile House was a pivotal point for mail delivery from the earliest days of settlement. Through the years, mail and freight was delivered by packtrain, stagecoach, train, and later, sometimes delivered by bus. Courtesy, Earl Cahill, Clinton, BC.

In the earliest days, residents all the way up to Bridge Lake had to travel to 70 Mile to obtain their mail. In 1908, a new post office at North Bonaparte was set up to reduce the amount of travel. *The Rainbow Chasers* tells the story:

> In the fall of 1908, the MacDonalds wanted to find another way to get their mail, other than riding the 50 miles out to the 70 to collect mail or post a letter, so on one of Archie's trips to Clinton he investigated the possibility of getting a post office closer to home. He talked to Mr. Soues, the government agent, and to Archie Mac-Donald, the MLA. A weekly stage and mail service would be a tremendous help to the settlers who were opening up our district, he told them. As a result of these talks, in the late fall of 1908, the government commissioned the Presseys to operate a post office and weekly stage from their home. Their 18-year-old son Henry took on the task of driving the stage to the 70 Mile, a distance of 22 miles. He would leave home on a Saturday at 8 am with all the mail, express, and any passengers. The road was still very rough with a great many large rocks and stumps that had to be carefully avoided, so the trip was slow and tiresome. It was always with a sigh of relief that the weary driver and his passengers stepped down at the Boyd's roadhouse about 6 pm.

Federal post office records state that J. F. Pressey was appointed as the post-master on January 1, 1909. A little over a year later, the Presseys handed the position over to Andrew Whitley. Although they went out to 70 Mile, collected the mail, and held it at their place, records show that they also used a mail carrier to take the mail from their place to surrounding areas. In 1911, this was Hiram Andrus, who lived a few kilometres east on the present-day Young Lake-Boule Road. Andy Whitley gave up the post office job after three years and the Mawdsley family, who lived between him and Pressy Lake, took it over for four more years. The official postmaster was Mrs. Margaret Mawdsley, but it was likely her husband, Maurice, who picked up the mail from the 70 Mile House and carried letters to various places along the way.

While the Mawdsleys ran the North Bonaparte Post Office, Ed Higgins from Roe Lake established a post office in his area. By 1914, there were about twenty households in the Roe Lake and Bridge Lake district. To receive their mail, residents had to travel an arduous forty kilometres (twenty-four miles) through the bush to the North Bonaparte. Ed was determined to establish a post office in the Roe Lake and Bridge Lake area for the convenience of its residents.

Ed petitioned the government and obtained the job of transporting the mail to Roe Lake. For the magnanimous sum of $3.00 a trip, he travelled the trail winter and summer, bringing mail for local residents to his home. *The Homesteader's Daughter* describes the gruelling trip in winter: "Ed covered that in winter once a week in one day. He used snowshoes and a toboggan to make a trail and would come back with 100 pounds on the toboggan and 100 pounds on his back and be back by 8 or 9 pm." As was the case with the Mawdsleys in the North Bonaparte, the post office was actually a family effort: Ed transported the mail and brought it home, and his wife, Irene, acted as the postmistress. Records state that Mrs. Irene Higgins was appointed "postmaster" on October 6, 1915.

Both Irene Higgins of Roe Lake and Margaret Mawdsley of the North Bonaparte were extremely busy with several small children and in the fall of 1917, both resigned. The position of postmaster at Roe Lake was taken over by Pearl Whitley Thompson, followed later by Lilly Printzhouse. Caroline Renshaw next took it over and carried on until March 1930. A new post office had also been set up in the Lone Butte area in 1916 called "Fawn." This mail was picked up by the postmaster from 100 Mile House instead of 70 Mile House.

In the North Bonaparte, Stewart Haywood-Farmer took over the Mawdsleys' position for a short time, but he too was a busy man and soon gave it up. The post office there was closed until the summer of 1919, when Matt Porter, living at that time in the North Bonaparte, took it on. Pleun Herwynen, who lived not too far away, was listed as a mail carrier in the 1921 census. After Matt purchased the 70 Mile Roadhouse, his brother William Porter took over the North Bonaparte post office and ran it until 1929. On April 15, 1929, it was permanently closed.

In the meantime, Bridge Lake residents finally obtained their own post office at Harold Webb's Bridge Lake Trading Company store. Harold was listed as postmaster from January 1, 1923, until his death on August 31, 1938. Bridge Lake residents, especially from the eastern area, were now able to obtain their mail from a more convenient location. It was also more accessible for people who lived at Eagan Lake and Sharpe Lake, who formerly had to travel to the Porters' place on the Little Green Lake road for their mail.

The Homesteader's Daughter relates that Harold willed everything he had to Beulah Higgins, his young and faithful employee. At the time of Harold's death, Beulah was only 18. Unfortunately, regulations prohibited her from becoming the official postmistress because of her age, so her mother, Irene, took the job. Things were taken out of their hands when Edward (Jack) Spratt arrived in the country and built a store not far away. The postal department awarded him the post office on January 1, 1939, and he ran it until he sold out to Ernie King in 1945. The Kings and succeeding owners ran the post office until 2013. After over ninety years of operation, Bridge Lake lost its post office, replaced by community mailboxes managed more centrally.

At Roe Lake, Mrs. Nellie Wheeler took over the post office from Caroline Renshaw in 1930 and ran it until its closure in August 1938. Ted Leavitt relieved Mrs. Wheeler for several months while she was suffering from an illness. When the Roe Lake post office closed, mail that was formerly addressed to Roe Lake was now handled by the Fawn-Lone Butte post office. Many Roe Lake and North Bridge Lake residents' addresses changed to "R. R. 1, Fawn." A rural route was established and mail was delivered twice a week, first by Robert McMillan and then by Ray Flaherty.

A rural route was also established at 70 Mile House, serviced by the colourful Matt Porter. The mail arrived on Tuesdays via the Pacific Great Eastern Railway. The scheduled time was 1:30 am, but the train could often be two or more hours late. After unloading the mail from the train, Matt made his deliveries along a looping route that ran from 70 Mile House to the North Green Lake road and back on the south side of the lake. Dry weather in summer was the ideal time to travel the roads. In spring and fall, the roads were a morass of mud, and in winter, they were often plugged with snow. Matt used whatever method of transportation worked—a cutter or a Bennett wagon and later a mail truck. One source reports that he had a Pierce-Arrow sedan for some time.

Mail delivery could be a difficult and demanding enterprise. Winter was always a special challenge, whether it was Ed Higgins travelling on snowshoes in 1915 or Matt Porter trying to ram his delivery vehicle through waist-high snowdrifts in the 1930s. It was often so cold that the brakes would freeze in only a few minutes. Adding to the problem was the fact that roads were only ploughed once a week, often at a time inconvenient for the mail carriers. Stallard McConnell, who often helped his grandfather Matt Porter deliver the mail during the 1930s, told of a particularly harrowing trip. The truck was crammed with eagerly awaited Christmas cards and parcels and Stallard knew how important it was to get the mail through. The roads that day were so plugged with snow that he drove the mail truck across the ice on Green Lake as an alternative route. But disaster struck. The truck hit a soft spot and started to go through the ice. Stallard scrambled out and watched in dismay as the truck sank with its load of letters, cards, and parcels. There must have been many sad children around the district that Christmas.

The arrival of the mail was always a highly anticipated event. Opening the mailbox was exciting: there were letters from faraway relatives, correspondence from pen pals, newspapers (especially the *Winnipeg Free Press Weekly*), parcels from Eaton's, and even library books from the Public Library Commission. Today, there are only two post offices in the area, one at Lone Butte and one at 70 Mile. The romance of rural mail delivery is now only a dim memory.

Telephones
Jean (MacLean) Nelson, North Bridge Lake

In the mid-1940s, a member of the Bridge Lake community learned of a set of old telephones being replaced with more modern equipment. The old telephones were available for purchase and people in North Bridge Lake dug deep in their pockets and purchased them. It was then necessary to buy enough small glass insulators to raise the top wire of our barbed wire fences until we reached the fence of the neighbour next to us. This way we were connected with each other even though the line did not extend to any outside areas. The barbed wire fence carried all our chit-chat for the next seven or eight years. Each home had an individual ring (ours was three long and one short), which would ring in every household. This gave us the opportunity to communicate with each other in a way we never had before. In the past, if we had a message for someone, we had to walk, ride a horse, or drive a car, if we had one. What a blessing it was to us at that time!

SCHOOLS

The country schoolhouses that once dotted the landscape in the district were an integral part of local culture. Ebbing and flowing in number over the years, there was a total of at least thirteen schools from Roe Lake to 70 Mile House. These included schools at Roe Lake, Bridge Lake (an early school situated at the present provincial park and a short-lived one at the Double T ranch), the North Bonaparte, Dundon, North Bridge Lake, Watch Lake, Eagan Lake, Taylor Lake, Sharpe Lake, Green Lake, Tin Cup, and 70 Mile House. In the absence of any alternative, these schools were the centres of their particular little communities, providing a gathering place for education and entertainment and a venue for religious services and political meetings. Christmas concerts, plays, sports days, and other school events were attended by everyone for miles around. With little entertainment usually available, these occasions were highlights in everyone's lives. Dances were sometimes held in the schools, and perhaps after a Saturday night dance, a travelling minister might conduct services the next day in the same place. A schoolhouse brought community members together as no other institution did.

North Bridge Lake School, about 1931. Although the children are not named, some are the Faessler children and Neal children. Courtesy Jeannie Creed, Chilliwack, BC.

Reverend Stanley Higgs and his wife, Margaret, who were posted in Clinton, regularly visited the district during 1933 and 1934. In his memoir, Reverend Higgs related the story of an amusing incident that took place while he held a church service in the Roe Lake school:

> At 10:00 the next morning a surprising number of people had assembled at Roe Lake school awaiting our arrival… There was a surprisingly good congregation, especially as far as the men were concerned, the kind of men who worked with animals and worked the land. Some of the women were familiar with a simplified version of morning prayer and I chose hymns which even some of the men knew. Margaret played the piano, as she did when one was available and there was no other pianist. She made no pretense of being accomplished, but so often she made all the difference between a halting, awkward service, and a happy, sometimes even boisterous, worshipping experience. On this occasion, toward the end of the service, even Margaret's aplomb was shaken. While she was leading us in the last hymn, an inquisitive rat ran along the joint between the logs, just above the organ height and stopped to look down at Margaret.

Reverend Higgins didn't mention what his wife's reaction was but we can safely assume that when her eyes met the rat's, Margaret let out a healthy screech.

Establishing a school was never an easy undertaking. The roadhouse families certainly experienced this. Between the 70 Mile House and the 74 Mile House, the Sauls, Boyds, Cunninghams, and Cummings all had school-aged children, beginning in the early 1870s to as late as 1924. Since there were few children in that area along the Cariboo Road, opening a school was not viable. The families coped in several ways: hiring a tutor, home-schooling, or boarding the children in various locations so they could attend school. Two separate photographs show that some of the Cummings children attended the Roe Lake School, which opened in 1914.

The early life of Ira Boyd, the youngest of the Boyd children at 70 Mile House, is an example of the strategies families used to secure an education. At one point, he had to go to school in Clinton. During the school week, he boarded with the Barton family, then came home to work on the farm on the weekends. Just a young boy, he'd ride his horse the thirty-seven kilometres (twenty-three miles) from the 70 Mile to Clinton on Sunday afternoon, then turn around and ride back home again on Friday afternoon. Once he got to high school, his mother sent Ira to Columbia College in New Westminster, but he'd barely graduated before he was called home to help out with the ranch and roadhouse. The Cunningham children at 74 Mile House had a similar struggle: with no local schools, they were forced to employ a tutor or board in Clinton.

Because of the extremely sparse population in the district, establishing schools and keeping them open has been a perennial problem since 1907, when the first settler families arrived, to the present decade, the 2010s, a hundred and ten years later. In fact, obtaining an education for their children was one of the greatest difficulties faced by settlers with families. There were often not enough children to open a school, even with the low requirement of only eight students. And if that requirement was met and a school built, it could be closed in an instant if even one family moved away or if some of the children completed grade 8, the upper limit of most of the schools.

Even though settlers with children began to trickle into the North Bonaparte in 1907, it was years before there were enough children in any one spot to warrant opening a school. In 1910, for instance, there were only three school-aged children in the whole Roe Lake and Bridge Lake district. However, in the Pressy Lake area in the same year, there were seven or eight children, although no records show that a school was established at the time. If one had been, it would have been short-lived, because the Presseys and Nichols moved away within a couple of years and the number of school-aged children dropped to just three or four. It remained at this level until 1920, when the Scheepbouwer family arrived.

Families used a number of strategies to overcome the problem of too few students, although most were far from ideal. Children who were very young could be sent to school before they were ready just to bolster the numbers. Children who were already going to a certain school with a good attendance might be moved to another one that was failing—again to boost the numbers. In that case, the child would have to be separated from his or her family and boarded out.

In fact, many children had to board out if their home was too far from a school. Ideally, it would be with a family they knew, but that wasn't always possible. Sometimes the children were boarded in other towns, such as Clinton, 100 Mile House, or Williams Lake. Both the children and their families often suffered from the separation, but this may have been their only choice. This situation was a serious detriment to the stability of the population. Families who put a high value on their children's education and who objected to their children boarding away from the family home were often forced to move away permanently. This problem continues even today.

Sometimes, families who lived in these remote locations chose not to send their children away from home. In those cases, mothers, often having a scanty education themselves, taught their children the essentials of reading, writing, and math. Correspondence school was also an option, usually in the higher grades. It's amazing how well many of these children did with such a basic education. Later in life, many of these former home-schooled students exhibited lovely handwriting, accurate spelling, and a good grasp of basic math.

The Maddocks family lived between Green Lake and 83 Mile House. When the children became school-aged, their father, Frank, built a small cabin on their property that served as a makeshift school for a while. Frank paid for the teacher out of his own pocket. At other times, classes were held in one of the Cunninghams' cabins at 74 Mile House and Frank paid his share of the teacher's wages. The Maddocks children eventually had to board away from home. To attend school in Clinton, they had to take the train from 83 Mile House on Sunday nights. Once in Clinton, they boarded with Mr. and Mrs. Charlie Robinson, and then turned around on Friday afternoons and took the train back home. Their father either met them at the station or they walked the five kilometres (three miles) home. By 1948, the family decided it was better to move somewhere with more opportunities for education.

Another problem that could arise was the lack of a teacher even if a school was available. Carr Cleveland solved that problem one year when there was no teacher for his children at the Eagan Lake School. Since he had a university education, he got permission from the Department of Education to teach the children himself. Running a ranch and teaching every day must have been quite a challenge. The next year, fortunately, the school was able to find a teacher.

When families such as the Haywood-Farmers at Taylor Lake gave up the struggle and moved away, there was a negative impact on the population base. On the other hand, when a fairly large family moved in, such as the Calvin Smith family at Bridge Lake, they were welcomed with open arms and gave a huge boost to the school and the community as a whole. But there weren't a lot of large families moving into the area or existing settlers who had many children. Of the families with children who lived in the district over the years, only a little over a quarter of them had four or more children who were potentially of school age. The rest had between one and three children.

The children who did go to school were, in common with other children of that era, hardy and resourceful. They had to be. The distances some children travelled to attend school were truly daunting. Sometimes alone, children as young as 5 and 6 walked, rode horses, or rowed boats for miles to reach school. The rule (at least in the 1950s) was that if the temperature dropped below

-20°F, school would be closed. But at any temperature above that, children were expected to attend. An article about the Watch Lake School tells of Stan and Sadie Eden's children and their journey every school day:

> Don and Ross Eden made the journey twice a day from North Watch Lake by Green Lake. This meant a long boat trip across Watch Lake and a still longer walk across Watch Lake Ridge. Even in the best of weather, this was a great distance. But in winter, extreme cold, deep snow, early darkness and treacherous ice made travelling hard…

When Fred Mobbs of Watch Lake turned 13, his mother decided he needed to be trained in a trade. She arranged with Ma Murray in Lillooet to have the boy stay with the Murrays and learn the printing trade. Fred went grudgingly, but it didn't turn out well. He hated the noise of the printing presses and longed to be back in the country and the outdoors. One day, he'd had enough. He walked out the door and made his way home from Lillooet to Watch Lake, a distance of almost 160 kilometres (100 miles). He managed to catch a few rides, but ended up walking most of the way. Marion never attempted to send him back.

Eagan Lake School (c.1940s). Back row (left to right): Eric Cleveland, Pat Larner, Wayne Johnson, Glen Cleveland, Don Larner, Miss Barrett; front row: Lorrein Johnson, Ivy Johnson, Winne Larner, Freda Larner. Courtesy Freda Lamb, Winnipeg, MB.

The first school in the area, as far as we know, was Roe Lake School, built in 1914. Eventually, several other schools sprang up in the district, most surviving about ten to twenty years. The Roe Lake School was followed about 1920 by the original Bridge Lake School. A year or so later, the North Bonaparte School and the first Green Lake School (also known as Dundon School and Taylor Lake School) were built, both small structures. After the first Bridge Lake School closed (or possibly while it was still open), a second school was built in 1927 in North Bridge Lake. This school was open for almost twenty years.

Farther down the valley, the Watch Lake School opened in 1928. The school was set up in a vacant cabin at Watch Lake said to have belonged to a "Lord Elgie." While Alfred Elgie did build the cabin, he hadn't the slightest connection to the aristocracy. He had emigrated from London, England, and may have had a posh accent, so perhaps he invented a new persona for himself in his adopted country. Another school that opened in the early 1920s was the Eagan Lake School. These schools were in use for ten or so years before closing because of the shortage of school-aged children. Between 1951 and 1953, a school was built in Sharpe Lake and a new school in a new location at Green Lake.

Consolidation was in the air. After the Roe Lake School burned down in the late 1940s, a new school was built at the present location in Bridge Lake to serve the entire Bridge Lake and Roe Lake district. This was only possible because the district was able to acquire a school bus that travelled the circuit around the lake. According to local information, the Reynolds family purchased the bus and drove it. Ernie King later purchased the bus from them, although the Reynolds continued to drive it while they lived in the community. In the 1950s, the affable Pat Deane-Freeman was the driver.

The Sharpe Lake School closed in 1964 and the Green Lake School in 1972. In 1957, a school was finally built at 70 Mile House that absorbed the Green Lake children; it served the area for over forty years before closing in 2000. In 2015, the only school left in the district was Bridge Lake School. Sadly, that too closed in 2016. The district is now as it was over a hundred years ago—with no schools at all.

Most of the early schools that were built in the area were one-room log structures; framed schools were built in later years. Community members usually banded together to raise funds and build the schools, although the Department of Education might have helped out in one way or another. A newspaper article from 1928 described the process of establishing a new school and the co-operation among residents that was needed:

Settlers of Watch Lake district, some miles east of the 70 Mile House, Cariboo road, held a meeting and organized a new school district. Application has been made to the department of education for a new school to be called Watch Lake School. A basket social was held at the home of Mr. Porter, North Bonaparte, to raise funds for this purpose. Eighty settlers arrived with several sleigh loads of kiddies to make the occasion a memorable one…

The schoolhouses had only one room, and the source of heat was a barrel heater fed by wood. Students often helped female teachers with the onerous chore of starting the stove and keeping it going during the day, as well as chopping wood. Elbert Johnson, who attended the North Bonaparte School in the 1930s, was one of the older boys who provided wood for the school. Using a crosscut saw, the boys cut logs into manageable pieces, split the wood, and hauled it to the school.

The crackling heater was the heart of the school during the bitterly cold winters, but you had to give it respect. Robbie Cleveland related an amusing incident that occurred when he was going to the Bridge Lake School:

One stern teacher always said, "Think three times before you speak," but one day he was leaning up against the barrel heater, and I saw his big overcoat was beginning to smolder. I just had to say, "I think, I think, I think you're starting to burn." He didn't think it was too funny.

Water had to be packed from a nearby well or creek in every school location and outdoor toilets were the norm, even as late as the 1950s. A September 1933 school inspection report for Roe Lake School remarked: "Water: none. Toilets: 1; poor." It also noted that janitor service was "voluntary." Although there were seventeen desks, there were only seven pupils (three boys, four girls; two in grade 3, one in grade 4, two in grade 5, and two in grade 6). Under "Maps," Mr. Lord, the school inspector, wrote: "Usual maps in poor condition." No mention was made of the number of textbooks available to the children. A few of the schoolhouses did have a piano, a very desirable asset. The children could learn some music and the instrument could be used to provide entertainment for any event that was held in the school. Of course, obtaining a teacher who could play the piano was a big asset.

In the 1950s, Bridge Lake had the good fortune of having community member Myra Deane-Freeman involved with music in the school. Although Myra wasn't a teacher, she was a passionate lover of music and also a poet and a songwriter. Myra loved to sing, and in the mid-1950s, she organized and conducted a children's choir. The school bus took the children to her residence,

All that's left today of the North Bonaparte School is the outhouse sitting in a lonely clearing.

the Knight Lake Ranch, where she conducted practices and rehearsals. The children had a delightful afternoon away from school learning such songs as "In an English Country Garden." Myra took the choir to the Yale-Cariboo Music Festival in Kamloops several years in a row. She also gave piano lessons to several children. Since it was a fair distance to her place at Knight Lake, the children who walked up to her place for lessons usually ended up staying overnight. Not content with all this, she also taught some Sunday school and helped with school events and plays.

The list of teachers in the district illustrates that few stayed more than a year or two—the norm in rural schools across Canada. There were many reasons for the high turnover. The teacher might not be satisfied with her job experience or with the community in general. And, with little job security until modern times, teachers could be dismissed on the slightest excuse. Sometimes these dismissals were warranted because of inefficiency or questionable practices, but they could sometimes be arbitrary.

The wages for a teacher weren't high—just enough to live on. Mrs. Veda Papov, for example, who taught at Roe Lake and Lone Butte, earned $900 a year, according to the school inspector's report in the 1930s. This is worth about $16,000 in today's dollars. A subsistence wage, to be sure, but during the Great Depression, this amount of money would have been coveted.

Teachers earned every cent of their wages. *The Little White Schoolhouse* evocatively outlines the many roles that a rural teacher played:

In addition to their teaching duties they acted as school janitors, stoked fires, diagnosed illnesses and applied first aid. They counselled, scolded, played games, umpired, cut the children's hair, settled disputes, learned to ride horses and drove to school in all types of weather. They… trained the choir, helped at social functions and organized such cultural activities as debates, plays and concerts.

Rural teachers had to teach several grades at the same time, usually from grade 1 to 8, which was challenging. Many of the smaller schools had only the minimum number of students—eight—and most of them would be in different grades. Teachers had to be very organized to make sure that each grade had its work set out, remembering that the youngest pupils needed constant supervision and couldn't work alone. Since there was a shortage of textbooks, which were expensive for both the school and the parents to buy, the teacher often had to copy all the information onto the blackboard for the students to write into their scribblers.

Some skills that are now fading were extremely important in the past: being able to do arithmetic without calculators; map-drawing; legible penmanship; and memorization of historical facts, poetry, and grammar. Maxims that encouraged good character were often written on the blackboard for students to memorize. When Mr. Winston Potter arrived at Bridge Lake School in 1953, the first thing he did was stride to the blackboard and write, "Know thyself: Socrates." Mrs. Jean MacLean, who taught the lower grades at Bridge Lake, had a motto for her students, "Try your hardest, read a book every chance you get, and always have fun."

Physical education, if it existed at all, was usually a very informal affair, mainly games such as baseball or some other simple sport. Since most of the children worked very hard in their daily lives on the farm and often walked a great distance to school, they hardly needed to improve their fitness.

Teachers were sometimes not highly trained, although their education was adequate for the times. The minimum requirement to attend Normal School, as the teacher-training institute was called, was a grade 10 diploma. As a general rule, young, single teachers were preferred right up until the 1950s. This was demonstrated in a letter to Mrs. Veda Papov, who taught at Roe Lake from 1932 to 1934 and in Lone Butte for a few years after that. After applying for a job in another area in 1952, she received a letter from the local school board stating:

> The policy of the Board of School Trustees of this School District
> is that whenever possible, the hiring of married women teachers

can be considered only if suitable unmarried women teachers are not available. In view of this policy, I have been instructed by the Board to inform you that this Board cannot retain your services for the 1952–1953 term.

The basis for this policy was that the school board feared that a married schoolteacher might become pregnant and have to step down before the end of the school year. No doubt the policy was similar in the Cariboo, but since many of the teachers seem to have been married, the community was probably lucky to get whoever applied. Not everyone liked the idea of an outdoor toilet and the lack of running water in both their school and their home.

School inspectors visited once or twice a year and evaluated the level of education, the performance of the teacher, and the standards met by the pupils. Their job was also to evaluate the condition of the school. A. R. Lord, a school inspector, wrote a report on the Roe Lake School in 1933 and noted that the school was "a log building in fair condition; grounds unimproved." He also noted that there was poor lighting and ventilation.

Visits from the school inspector were stressful events for both the teacher and the students. Inspectors could be stern and officious people; everyone felt they were on trial when the inspector visited and breathed a sigh of relief when he left. Mr. Lord, however, apparently approved of Mrs. Papov. His report noted: "Mrs. Papov is doing capable, character-building work in this school." A report from the succeeding year noted: "The influence which Mrs. Papov is exerting in this school is deserving of special praise."

Teachers, however, were not always as exemplary as Mrs. Papov. Leonard Larson, who spoke Norwegian at home, had harsh experiences while attending the Roe Lake School:

My sister Mae and I were milking 18 to 20 cows and then walking to school 3 miles. When I started school, I did speak a lot of Norwegian… It happened we had a young male teacher [and] if I made a slip and spoke Norwegian, he would hit me over the head with a stick approximately 2' long with a knob about 2" thick. If he caught one of us with a pencil or a finger in our mouths he would make us take a bite of Fels Naptha soap. My brother Jack spit his out the window, so the teacher made him take a bigger bite and stood there until my brother Jack couldn't stand it any more because his mouth was burned raw. Another hobby the teacher had was he wanted to play cowboy and he made Norman Granberg and myself to run by him and he would try to rope us, but he hit Norman in the eye… On the way home that day from school, the Granberg kids,

Norman, Helen, Jack and I and Mae were playing on the bridge. Norman's dad was an old seaman and sailed around Cape Horn seven times; he stood a good 6' tall, all muscle and no fat. He came down to the lake for a pail of water and saw Norman's black eye and said, "Oh you kids been fighting." Norman said that the teacher had hit him in the eye with his rope. Lo and behold here came the teacher with a cowboy hat and a weasel skull under his chin hung on a piece of string, wearing chaps and all. Norman told his dad he was using us as guinea pigs. Mr. Granberg just snorted like a bull and reached up and grabbed the teacher by the scruff of the neck. He pulled him off his horse and shook him like a rat. He told him if he wanted to be a cowboy, go and rope a moose, not my kids. The teacher got as white as a ghost when Mr. Granberg let him go and took off like a rabbit.

The school inspection reports from Mrs. Papov's tenure at the Lone Butte School show a bias against children from non-English cultural backgrounds. Several Scandinavian and German children attended school in the Lone Butte and Roe Lake area. Despite giving Mrs. Papov good marks for her teaching skills, Inspector Lord, remarked in May 1935: "The general standing of this school is somewhat below average. The racial and social background of the pupils is a considerable factor." In September 1935, he noted: "The manners of the pupils showed a commendable improvement under [Mrs. Papov's] guidance."

Mrs. Papov may have used kind methods, but discipline was generally strict in the one-room schoolhouses. With students ranging in age from 5 years old to teenaged boys who worked on the family ranch as hard as any man, a teacher could have a difficult time keeping order. Punishments for misbehaviour ranged from writing lines on the blackboard, standing in a corner, writing lines after school, or a ruler or pointer over the knuckles. If all else failed, the dreaded strap was brought out. Although the strap might be considered an antique object these days, until the late twentieth century, it was considered an acceptable way to discipline unruly children. Several inches long and covered with rubber—the rubber coating was to prevent cutting the child and also producing a loud "smack" that served to intimidate the rest of the students—it was used at the discretion of the teacher. Most women teachers went no further than using a ruler over a child's hand, but some male teachers could let themselves be carried away with anger and frustration at their students' antics and inflict the strap too often and in too forceful a manner. Girls usually got off fairly lightly, but there were few boys who didn't have some sort of harrowing tale to tell later in life. Remote schools sometimes had to settle for teachers who weren't acceptable elsewhere because of their erratic behaviour and their students could suffer as a result. However, by and large, most teachers were caring and moderate in their application of discipline.

The ties between teachers and students could be strong, shown in an article about Mrs. Patty Law of North Bridge Lake. When asked what she liked best about teaching, "Without any hesitation [Mrs. Law] stated she liked the companionship of the children. 'I was in with them, it took an awful lot of old age off me, they treated me just like one of themselves, and I loved every one of them just like my own.' "

Ernie Ades felt the same but expressed it differently. He told the following story: "During school, you could hear the wolves howling. How were the kids going to get home? Some had to go more than two miles... Robby Bradford came over with the team and a sleigh and I gave him a 16 gauge shotgun and a box of shells and he took some kids with him. I had the 44-40 rifle and I took three pupils and went the other way. The wolves were howling all around us. It was scary. It took one and a half hours each way."

Myrtle Bryant Johnson, who attended the Dundon School from about 1929 to 1932, said that her three teachers—Miss May Boyd, Miss Grace Cornell, and Miss Lily Wyderet—were young women who had just graduated from teaching school. Although they were all good teachers and kind to the children, Miss Cornell took a special liking to Myrtle. On her Christmas holidays in 1930, she took the young girl with her to Vancouver, escorting her around the city to see all the sights and even taking her to Seattle. It was an eye-opening trip for the young country girl. Miss Cornell only stayed that year, but the ties between them remained strong. Both Myrtle and her mother, Lydia, wrote to Miss Cornell for many years until Miss Cornell finally said she wasn't able to keep up the correspondence anymore because of her advanced age.

In the beginning, most teachers had to board with local families. Several who taught at the original Bridge Lake School boarded with Jim and Lavena Case; in North Bridge Lake, the Morgans and Reynolds vied for the privilege of boarding the teacher. At Eagan Lake, the teachers boarded with the Clevelands; at Roe Lake, it was the Higgins household. At the new Bridge Lake School, Mrs. Jean MacLean occupied a cabin on the Hansen property across the road from the school during the week while she taught. Over the years, North Bridge Lake School, Roe Lake School, and Eagan Lake School built residences specifically for the teachers.

There was a dizzying succession of teachers who lasted only a year or two. Some were young teachers gaining experience and some, perhaps, couldn't get jobs anywhere else. Out of the large number of teachers in the district over the years, only a few made it their permanent home. Among these, Anthony Okon of the North Bonaparte lived there for a few years with his wife and young son. May Hunter, who came from Clinton and taught at the Dundon School, married Jack Boyd of the Flying U. John Livingston, who taught at the Watch Lake School, settled in the area and the family still lives in the district today. The Mobbs lived at Watch Lake and Mrs. Marion Mobbs taught school, both at Watch Lake and in other locations.

In Bridge Lake, Beth Lockyer came to teach school and married Wesley Hansen. After a few years teaching at the North Bridge Lake School, the inimitable Ernie Ades stayed in the community until he left a few years before the end of his life. Patty Law moved to the area with her family in 1941 and taught school until she retired. The MacLean family moved to Wilson Lake in 1943 and Mrs. Jean MacLean taught at both the Roe Lake and Bridge Lake schools until they left in 1953.

At Roe Lake, Veda Papov and her husband, Michael, arrived in 1932. As a young girl, Noveta Higgins Leavitt worked for Mrs. Papov, looking after their small son in the tiny Nellie Holland cabin. Mrs. Papov taught at Roe Lake School until 1934 and in Lone Butte for several years. She and her family moved to Nakusp in the West Kootenays, where she taught there for the remaining years of her life. She died in Nakusp in 1982. There were two more connections with the Arrow Lakes: Mrs. Amy Johnson, who taught at Sharpe Lake School, also ended her teaching career in Nakusp. Miss Bertha Sheill, who hailed from a town near Nakusp, taught school in either Lone Butte or Horse Lake and married Ira Boyd, the youngest son of Bill and Mary Boyd of the 70 Mile House.

Allan MacInnes, who taught at Roe Lake in 1932, just before Mrs. Papov, married Goldi Shertenlib of Roe Lake. They eventually moved to Duncan. Edith Taylor from Bridge Lake served as a teacher for a number of years, first teaching at the Roe Lake School. After her husband Richard's death in 1956, she was persuaded to return to teaching and taught grades 8 to 10 in the Bridge Lake Community Hall.

Today, a few of the old schoolhouses still sit by the road, deserted and forlorn. North Bridge Lake School, Eagan Lake School, Sharpe Lake School, the old outhouse at the North Bonaparte School: they are all slowly decaying reminders of the children who once sat in their desks. Those children are now grandparents, great-grandparents, or have gone from this life.

Berry Picking
Jean (MacLean) Nelson, North Bridge Lake

Picking wild berries was a very important part of our summer activities. The first were wild strawberries in late June, not at all plentiful but delicious beyond belief. We could usually find only a cupful or two at a time so my mother would make cream puffs and fold the strawberries into the whipped cream that filled the puffs. Ambrosia is the only word for it. The next berries to ripen were the raspberries, more plentiful than strawberries; we could usually find enough to can a few pints as well as making jelly. In July and early August, we would walk up our creek that ran between Grizzly and Wilson Lakes and pick all the edible berries that grew there: raspberries, dew berries, red and black currants, and the delicious purple gooseberries. Not enough of any one kind, we mixed them together to make a lovely jam we called Creek Berry, a favourite in our house. Later in the summer came the dwarf blueberry (*Vaccinium cespitosum*), a small cousin to the larger shrubs we see in other localities. I think the elevation and rocky soil of the glacier plateau where the Bridge Lake area is situated influenced the wild fruit that was available. In any case the mat-forming plants hugging the ground were not easy to pick but the more delicious for it; they were at their best in a pie. The flavour of wild fruit is a little more intense than their more anemic cultivated cousins—my preference by far.

STORES

Obtaining supplies was a challenge in the early days of settlement. Although the Boyds took over the 70 Mile Roadhouse in 1886, they appear not to have established a store at that time. By 1900, though, William Boyd was listed in *Henderson's Directory* as the owner of a store as well as a hotel. The facility, however, carried only a limited amount of supplies, necessitating a trip to bigger centres for larger quantities.

Until the 1920s, most settlers drove their teams and wagons to Clinton or even to Ashcroft to buy their annual supplies. The trip to Clinton could be a two-day trip; travelling to Ashcroft added at least another day or two or more. People aimed to buy a year's supply of whatever they regularly used, stocking up on essentials such as sugar, flour, beans, and coffee. Hilda Larson of Roe Lake described her family's trip in an article that appeared in the *100 Mile Free Press*:

> Once a year, usually in the fall, we'd hitch up the wagon and head for Ashcroft to buy provisions. Goods would come by CPR from Vancouver. The trip would take about 10 days, and wouldn't that wagon be loaded! We'd buy 1500 lbs. of flour at $27 per hundred, 1000 lbs. of sugar at $26 per hundred, 25 lbs. of lard, 25 lb. cans of coffee beans, salt, tea, rice, and plenty of dried fruit and beans.

People practically lived on beans in those days. 'Cariboo strawberries', we called them.

Once the general stores at Bridge Lake and Lone Butte opened, it became easier to obtain provisions. But since the stores couldn't carry everything, most people used mail order catalogues for the necessities they couldn't get locally. Leafing through Eaton's or Woodward's catalogues and choosing the items to purchase was an exciting activity, matched only by the arrival of the package on the mail truck. The use of mail-order catalogues continued for many years.

The first store in the district, other than Boyd's at 70 Mile House, was located at Lac des Roches. Jack Demming had a small trading post that he'd established in 1905. Situated close to the Mount Olie Trail, the route between the Canim Lake Band (Tsq'escenemc) to the west and the Chu-Chua Band (Simpcw) to the east, it was an ideal location. Travellers stopped at Demming's store to trade their furs for goods. Once the MacDonalds took over the land in 1907, the store no longer operated.

In late 1920, Harold Webb, who had been working with surveyor Geoffrey Downton's crew as a cook, settled at Bridge Lake and built a store. Situated on Crooked (Webb) Lake, not far from where the present Bridge Lake Store now stands, it was dubbed the Bridge Lake Trading Post. Carrying groceries, hardware, and various household goods, as well as operating as a post office, the store no doubt attracted customers from as far away as the North Bonaparte since it was the only store north of 70 Mile House. (The first listing in *Wrigley's British Columbia Directory* of a store at Lone Butte didn't appear until 1923.)

Harold Webb was a kind-hearted bachelor whose store and clientele became his life and his family. As was the custom at the time, everyone bought on credit and paid up at the end of the month. Harold wasn't a tyrant, though. If you couldn't pay on time, he trusted that you would as soon as possible. He even lent people money for emergencies, again trusting that it would be repaid. When he needed to have his own house separate from the store, local people banded together to build him one, showing their appreciation for his generosity to others.

In the mid-1930s, Reverend Stanley Higgs took a drive over to the Bridge Lake Trading Post from Roe Lake on one of his visits to the area and had a rather harrowing trip:

> At North Bridge Lake, some 7 or 8 miles from the Higgins place
> was a small store and trading house... I decided to drive over to
> the... Bridge Lake Trading Company and buy our guest a bottle

A Christmas card, drawn many years ago by "Diane S.," shows the Bridge Lake Store in the early days. Courtesy Pat Tasker, Surrey, BC.

of oil of citronella, a mosquito repellant, which Titch assured me would be a welcome gift. It was unfortunate that I wasn't warned of a short stretch of road, less than two miles long, which was literally 16" deep in mud. I reached the store much to the surprise of the owner, his store was so far off the beaten track.

By the late 1930s, Harold was suffering from heart problems and beginning to show his age. At the same time, Edward (Jack) Spratt moved from Saskatchewan into the area. At the junction of the Bridge Lake Road, the North Bonaparte Road, and the road leading to Roe Lake, he built a bigger, more modern store. It was an ideal location and unfortunately not far away from Webb's store. Suffering from the competition, Webb's store soon started going downhill in conjunction with his own health. After his death in August 1938, his successors, Beulah and Irene Higgins, tried to keep the store going, but it was a losing battle. The Bridge Lake Trading Post closed in 1944 after serving the community for over twenty years.

The new Bridge Lake Store turned out to be a thriving venture. The post office was moved there from the Bridge Lake Trading Post and a gas pump was installed. In 1949, the new Bridge Lake School was built beside it, and in 1953, a community hall was built just around the corner. This had now become the heart of the community, providing for everyone's needs.

In 1945, Jack Spratt sold out to Ernie King and his family from Vancouver. For thirty-eight years, the King family carried on the tradition of the general store, selling everything from candy to cattle feed. Packed with supplies from floor to ceiling, if the store didn't carry what you wanted, it wasn't worth having. Originally getting supplies by rail at Lone Butte, Ernie bought a truck so he could purchase his provisions in Kamloops. In common with Harold Webb (and no doubt Jack Spratt), business was conducted by credit. Customers bought what they needed during the month and at the end of the month squared up the bill.

On Ernie's weekly freight run to Kamloops, he often took along members of the community who needed to go to the dentist or a doctor, do business of one kind or another, or were on their way to the hospital to have a baby. (Fortunately, though, he was never called upon to deliver one.) Ernie proved to be a generous benefactor to the community in other ways as well. He extended credit to nearly all of his customers and sometimes carried people for an entire winter—or longer. As well as looking after his own family, he helped out anyone who was in need. He was known to take clothes off the store rack for someone who was without warm clothing. If it became obvious that someone couldn't afford to buy what they needed, he sometimes quietly donated food off the shelf.

In a village centre, owning the store, the post office, and the gas pump was equivalent to being the mayor, the banker, and the go-to person for just about everything. So much depended on whether the store had what you needed and whether you could get credit for those purchases. Ernie King and his family generously filled those needs for many years and were an institution in the district. In 1981, Ernie and Olive sold the store and it has passed through several hands since.

There were small, sometimes short-lived stores in other areas of the district. At Roe Lake, the Granbergs opened up a small store in 1929. This ran for a year or two, then Hilda Larson established her own store at the Larsons' on Judson Road. This store operated until the early 1950s.

A 1979 article in the *100 Mile Free Press* tells a little about Hilda and her charms:

> [The Larsons started] a small general store to serve their tourists and surrounding neighbours' needs. They built several cabins plus all the furniture for them and a small store. Hilda was a skilled cook and always set a good table. It was generally known by all the

bachelors that you always came out ahead if you bought a few items at the Larson Store as you were always invited in for a generous meal before you set out for home. Hilda was well known for her famous homemade ice cream which was always served in abundance at haying time, school picnics, and field days.

At Sharpe Lake, Fred Harrison built a small store to service the many workers and their families at his Harrison Forest Products sawmill. That closed about 1956 when Fred moved the mill to 70 Mile. A few years later, local ranchers Robbie and Diane Cleveland built their own store, naming it the South Fork Service. This ran for several years and served the residents and summer visitors.

Ray and Muriel Reinertson operated the Taylor Lake Store for a number of years in the early 1950s. Situated at the location of the former sawmill and settlement at Taylor Lake, the Reinertsons carried the usual assortment of food and supplies and also ran their store as everyone else did—on credit.

These general stores, in common with those in any rural area, did far more than offer merchandise and services. They were and are community centres, places where people met, exchanged news, and discussed common problems. John Ross, a newspaper columnist, often wrote about people he met at the Bridge Lake Store, and he poignantly paints a picture of neighbours meeting and interacting with each other:

Around the Grass Roots, by J. R. Ross (1960)

Olive King and Molly Deane-Freeman were behind the grocery counter, both of them wore spring-like smiles as they waited on us, and exchanged good-natured banter with their patrons. Ernie Ades, who has been in these parts for a quarter of a century, was at the store on business and Bob Hughet, another neighbour, was there too. Jack Black came in, carrying his little daughter Debbie in his arms. The little one refused to exchange her Dad's arms for mine, but when I asked her to smile, her bewitching face lit up radiantly and just looking at the little girl made all of us happy.

In the cornucopia of goods on the shelf, what did people buy in traditional general stores? In rural settings before the 1960s, people generally only bought what they couldn't make or produce themselves. It was considered wasteful and even shameful to buy what you were able to create yourself. Nevertheless, women who knitted and sewed clothes for their family needed supplies: wool, knitting needles, bolts of cloth, thread, lace, ribbon, buttons, needles, pins, patterns, and dyes. With no electricity, people needed barn lanterns, candles, kerosene lamps,

Coleman and Aladdin lamps, along with extra wicks and mantles, kerosene, and naphtha to keep them running. Candy for the children, over-the-counter medications, pens, paper, ink, tobacco, pipes, guns and ammunition, ropes, window glass, hammers and nails—the list goes on and on. Trappers needed trapping supplies; ranchers needed farm supplies. Some of these goods could be obtained a little cheaper from mail-order catalogues, but the convenience of a central store was more important than the little bit of money you could save.

A story about Jack Spratt of the Bridge Lake Store illustrates this. A member of the community once came into the store looking for an axe. He asked Jack what the price was and then informed him that he could get it at Eaton's for the better price of $1.95. Jack agreed to sell him the axe at that price. But when the man reached for the axe, Jack said, "Oh no, when you get something from Eaton's, you have to wait at least a week and a half. So I'm sorry, but you'll have to wait until then to pick it up."

COMMUNITY ORGANIZATIONS

In every small community, there were certain members with vision and energy who spearheaded the formation of beneficial organizations. The first to be established in the region were Farmer's Institutes. Sponsored by the provincial Department of Agriculture, these organizations gave local farmers and ranchers a venue for discussing and solving common problems. The first institute was organized at Roe Lake around 1920. Bridge Lake formed one as well but the two were eventually amalgamated. Watch Lake also had a Farmer's Institute. In the 1940s, a Cattlemen's Association was formed in the North Bonaparte, followed by one at Bridge Lake in the 1950s.

Women's Institutes (WI) weren't far behind. A real boon to the district, a WI supported women who were often isolated and provided a group setting to work on common problems. A uniquely Canadian institution, the Women's Institute was founded in 1897 in Ontario; the movement later expanded to Britain and other parts of the world. The aim of the Women's Institute was to provide companionship and promote education, power, and recognition. The first WI was formed at Watch Lake in 1939, with one appearing in Bridge Lake soon after. A WI was formed at Roe Lake in about 1948 and another in 1960 at 70 Mile House.

A member of the Faessler family wrote about some of the roles of the Farmer's and Women's Institutes:

> Charles Faessler was a charter member of the Farmer's Institute and Margrit of the Women's Institute. Through these they painstakingly raised funds for a pure-bred bull to improve their beef stock.

The North Bridge Lake Hall today is a ghost of what it once was: a vital living part of the community life.

They held annual Field Days at the Faessler Farm. The Dept. of Agriculture would send in speakers. The men trekked around the fields and gardens to show the plot of seeded hay and grains of varieties suitable for the Cariboo climate. The Department of Agriculture provided some seeds and plants to test how it would work. A Home Economics lady would have a talk for the women. The men fared better with their information, but the women had to contain their smiles at the fancy tips the Home Economics lady gave—not too practical for moose meat and fish menus! Or for cooking for threshing crews and stove-wood-sawing crews.

Establishing a community hall was a big project and required the participation of as many residents as possible. A hall was always a boon to an area, providing a location for dances, fairs, weddings, funerals, church services, and other events. Before they were built, people crowded into little one-room schools. Watch Lake constructed its hall in the early 1940s and North Bridge Lake's was completed just before the end of World War II. Bridge Lake's community hall was built by the active Bridge Lake Community Club in the 1950s. The Roe Lake Hall, still in use, was built in 1952.

Today, good roads and better communication have changed everything. It's now unnecessary for each small community to have its own facilities.

The North Bridge Lake Community Hall stood uncompleted for some years until community members decided it must be finished to welcome the soldiers returning from World War II. People pitched together and made it happen. Making lunch for the work crew were, from left to right: Margrit Faessler, Josie Faessler, Maggie Reed, and Jack Spratt. Kneeling in front are Mrs. Barnes and Mrs. Bradford. Courtesy Audrey (Reed) Woodman, Merritt, BC.

Instead of four community halls, there are now just two: Roe Lake and Watch Lake. The Farmer's Institutes faded away, although one still exists in Lone Butte. However, the Cattlemen's Associations at both Bridge Lake and Green Lake are still active as the South Cariboo branches of the BC Cattlemen's Association. The sole surviving Women's Institute is at Watch Lake.

Moose Meat Stew
Catherina Scheepbouwer, North Bonaparte

Cut up moose meat into cubes. Take a Dutch oven and put it on the wood stove, taking out one of the stove lids and replacing it with the Dutch oven. Heat fat very hot and brown moose meat very well, until caramel-coloured. Sprinkle with flour and mix, then add water to make gravy. Simmer until tender.

Contributed by Rose (Park) Scheepbouwer, Vernon, BC, who said, "My mother-in-law, Catherina, made the best, most flavourful moose meat stew that I've ever tasted. This was her method."

THE WORLD OF WOMEN

Women who were wives and daughters of ranchers played an indispensable role in the ranching operations. In fact, the success of these ventures depended as much on them as it did on the men. They were busy, strong women. By and large healthy and long-lived, an amazing percentage of them lived into their seventies, eighties, and even their nineties. It was not a life of leisure that contributed to their health and longevity, but a life of constant activity and work.

Ranching was a hard enough life if you had a husband, but doubly hard if you were a widow. Mary Boyd of 70 Mile House and Margaret Cunningham of 74 Mile House managed their roadhouse businesses after they became widows, but couldn't have done it without the help of their own children. Maggie Reed and Effie Bays of Bridge Lake were in the same position after the deaths of their husbands; with the supportive help of their children, they were able to hang onto their properties.

Possibly the only single woman to try homesteading on her own was Gertrude Boulter, who lived in Bridge Lake in 1924 and 1925, lasting only about a year and a half before leaving. A wealthy English spinster in her mid-forties and who could speak several languages, Gertrude decided to immigrate to Canada, intending to buy land and establish a farm. Whether her family approved of this decision isn't known, but it would be surprising if they didn't regard it as foolhardy. In April 1924, she sailed alone from England on the ship *Canopic* and somehow made her way to the Cariboo. *Wrigley's British Columbia Directory* for 1925 lists "Boulter, G., farming, Bridge Lake." This was the only year she appears in the directory, although it's unknown where she actually lived. Her name is not on the pre-emption records, so she must have purchased her property.

Her new life must have been a tremendous cultural shock to Gertrude. She'd spent her entire life in a wealthy household in London, surrounded by servants. When winter arrived in 1924, it would have been completely unlike anything she'd ever experienced. By the time the next winter rolled around in 1925, it was apparent that Gertrude had had enough of life in Bridge Lake. In November, she crossed the border to Washington, stating that her last permanent address was Bridge Lake, BC, and that she was going to visit a friend in Guadalajara, Mexico. No more Cariboo winters for her!

After warming her bones in Mexico, she returned to England and died in 1932 in London. Somewhere in a collection of family heirlooms, there are no doubt letters from Great-great-aunt Gertrude Boulter, written as she sat in her log cabin in Bridge Lake during the winter of 1924, stoking the fire and trying to keep her fingers from freezing. It would be fascinating to know what she thought of the Cariboo and the people that she met during her brief adventure.

Another unforgettable woman who came to the region was Ellen Mullen. She answered a newspaper ad for a housekeeper placed by Henry Atwood of the North Bonaparte. Roy Eden told the story in a "Cariboo Calling" column in the *100 Mile Free Press* in 1969:

> Late one afternoon, a few weeks later, the regular BX stage pulled up to the 70 Mile House loaded with passengers, mail, and express. I remember well that Fred Peters was the driver, and after handing down the mail bag to Jim Boyd, we heard him say he had a passenger for the 70 Mile "but you will have to give me a hand to help get her out!" The lady's weight must have been at least 225 pounds of fine old happy woman. She was all smiles—and won the hearts of all of us at the 70 before nightfall.
>
> Atwood's ad in the Winnipeg paper had been answered in person. That unforgettable night I looked at her size and wondered if the spring seat in the buckboard would stand her weight. Another problem bothered me a bit, how was I to get her out at "Tin Cup Spring" tomorrow. This was the midday stop for lunch on our way up to the Bonaparte Valley.
>
> I was up early the next morning and loaded my survey supplies. The time of our departure had come. Mrs. Mullen came from I don't know where, but she sure was a cheerful and happy soul, and in high spirits that morning. It was, I'm sure, the trip of a lifetime for her. I had to get a stepladder to get her up to the level of the buckboard seat, but it took a couple of us boys to get her sitting in the proper position. The old springs were sure put to the test! During all this she treated it as a big joke. I climbed up on the driver's side which was a somewhat tight fit, and away we went. She enjoyed every minute of that trip. But long before we arrived at Tin Cup Spring, I wondered what I was going to do if she wanted to get down to attend to her private business enroute… We arrived in good time at the Tin Cup noon stop, and sure enough there was

a big stump just in the right spot alongside the trail. After driving the buckboard up alongside of it, I managed to get Mrs. Mullen, with a lot of her own help, on the stump where she could slide to the ground and find a suitable spot to attend to her chores. After having a good lunch, which had been prepared by the 70 Mile cook, I managed to get Mrs. Mullen back on the stump again and back into the buckboard! By late afternoon we arrived at the Henry Atwood Ranch with no further problems enroute. The unforgettable Mrs. Mullen was a wonderful person, always happy as the birds in May, and ready at all times to help others.

Described in *The Rainbow Chasers* as an "elderly Irish widow," Ellen was much more complicated than that. True, she had been a widow at one time, but she had a new husband, Arthur Mullen, with whom she'd been running a frontier hotel in the now-ghost town Three Forks in the Kootenays. At some point, she and Arthur separated, and he went up north and she came to the Cariboo. She was also not elderly—she was only in her fifties.

Angus Ryder, who wrote an unpublished memoir about his years at the 59 Mile House from 1910 to 1914, recalls a dinner he had with Henry that Ellen had prepared: "One Sunday we were invited to dinner by Henry Atwood. His housekeeper put on a large and tasty spread. After we had finished, Henry asked me how I liked the meat. Of course, I said it was excellent, but was a bit upset when he told me it was from a 'nice young bear cub' he had shot. That was my first bear roast."

Just after Ellen arrived in 1909, she applied for a pre-emption on Lot 1392 on Orren Creek. A few months after gaining title to her land in 1912, she suddenly died. She is buried somewhere close to the site of Henry Atwood's old home in the North Bonaparte; the story of her death and burial has become somewhat a strange legend.

Two respected pioneers, Hilda Larson and Roy Eden, both wrote about the event, but each remembered the story with vivid—but completely different—details. They were both about 80 when they recalled the story, sixty years after the event.

Hilda Larson remembered the story clearly, since it happened when she and her husband, Ole, first came to Roe Lake. She told the story of their journey in an interview with the *100 Mile Free Press* in August 1970:

Well, it wasn't long before we met an old man on a beautiful saddle horse. His name was Henry Atwood, and coming along behind him was a rickety old Democrat with the driver holding on to an old lady who was very sick. The lady was Mr. Atwood's housekeeper, and they were taking her to 70 Mile to phone a doctor. The nearest doctor was in Ashcroft then.

Well, Mr. Atwood told us to spend the night at his place just up the road, and we no sooner got the horses in the barn but the rig came back. The housekeeper was dead. They sent somebody right back to 70 Mile for the priest and my husband said, "I'm a stone mason, not a carpenter, but give me some tools and I'll see what I can do about making a box." So he made it the best he could, and we opened up her trunk and there was a beautiful bedspread she'd been working on for years, real rope silk not quite finished. Well, they laid that in the box, and put her in and wrapped her up real good in it.

By then the priest was there, and Mr. Atwood said, "Boys, you've got to dig a grave." They picked out a nice spot and had a very simple service and then we were all called into the house to eat.

Well, I was crying, and I just couldn't go in there and eat, so my husband set up a tent for me, and when the baby was asleep, I went out into the meadow with a shovel and dug up big clumps of the most beautiful wild flowers, and brought them back and set them into the mound of dirt over the grave and watered them real good. You can't imagine how lovely they were, and I felt a little better.

Roy Eden also clearly remembered the event, but with such conflicting details that one wonders what exactly *did* happen. He related the incident in a "Cariboo Calling" article published in June 1969:

The day came however, not too many years later, when the fine old lady got sick and in the one place she often said she had been so happy. This happened during round-up time in later Fall. Henry had permission from the Government Agent in Clinton to bury her on the ranch which was apparently her wish. We got together with the boys from the 70 Mile House and gave her a cowboy funeral...

He [Henry] made the casket himself in the workshed, and a good neighbour of his helped him dig the grave, close to the cabin and on the east side. As Henry said after it was all over, "She came from the East and I wanted her to be resting in the East."

The pallbearers were Jim Boyd from the 70 Mile House, my brother Stan, and I from Watch Lake Ranch, and the fourth was a cowboy from another area who was on the roundup with us, picking up strays—his name I don't remember. Jim Boyd and I had arrived the night before, as we were rounding up cattle just over the ridge on the Green Lake Range, and my brother came over from our ranch at Watch Lake. We only had to carry the coffin a short distance from the barn. This was fortunate as Mrs. Mullen was a mighty hefty woman.

Old Henry marched in front and on arrival took place at the head of the grave. All of us cowboys had our chaps and spurs on, as we had to ride the range that afternoon after it was all over. At the grave we had placed a couple of jackpine poles to rest the coffin on until we were ready to lower it down with our lariats at each end. Henry had dug out of his old trunk a little old-fashioned bible and he did a fine job of reading what was required, I only wish I could remember the wording now. There were no others present except Henry's good neighbour who had helped him with the grave digging. In those days, the homesteaders were few and far between. I often think now, while sitting in our modern equipped homes looking at a movie of "Virginia City" days, about that day when we buried old Mrs. Mullen, the grandest of the grand.

Perhaps it could be that Roy forgot there was also a woman present—Hilda Larson—and that "Henry's good neighbour" was actually Ole Larson, who was really just passing by? And in Hilda's account, when Henry says, "Boys, you've got to dig the grave," could the "boys" have been the Edens and Jim Boyd, who were actually pallbearers rather than gravediggers? Such are the tricks that memory plays on all of us.

Memorable women were not in short supply in the Cariboo. Sadie Eden often had to take up the slack when her husband, Stan, worked away from the ranch, adding the outside chores to her usual tasks. An article in the *Hundred Mile House News-Herald* in 1966 outlined what that meant:

While [Stan] went to work hacking railroad ties for a living, his newly-married wife [Sadie] took on the responsibility of raising a family in the log house which has remained their home to this day. It wasn't long before there were four children, two boys and twin girls, for Mrs. Eden, "Cariboo style," to look after. However, this little brood was but part of the job.

If Stan was away cutting ties, or working on the Cariboo road, as he often was, there would be the cows to milk first thing. There would be horses, ducks, geese, chickens and other animals to look after, and breakfast for the kids. There'd be a load of hay to fetch with horses and wagon from the other end of the lake, a little trip that might take 2 or 3 hours. One full load of hay would last the Edens' 33 head of cattle for a day.

After a workout like this many modern housewives would probably be retiring pale and limp to their couch, swallowing handfuls of tranquilizer tablets or calling up their doctor. But for Mrs. Eden the day was hardly started. Cattle need water to drink in the winter and the only convenient source of supply was the lake. This meant cutting holes in the ice with an axe, a chore which, just as with fetching the hay, had to be done every day…

With money not being an overly plentiful commodity and in the age before the government became such a generous provider, she used to make all her children's clothes. She even used to make them shoes, cutting soles out of hides and sewing them to felt liners. "I guess their trousers looked a bit baggy, but they didn't know the difference anyway," she says.

Although the main source of income for most families came from raising cattle, many women helped out by earning some income of their own. A few—such as Marion Mobbs, Jean MacLean, Patty Law, and Edith Taylor—were teachers, which brought in a modest yearly income. This was one of the rare paid jobs available, although a few women also worked part-time at the Bridge Lake Store. Some families had a few dairy cattle and it was the woman's role to separate the milk to produce cream and transport it to be sold. A few women made handicrafts and sold them, every penny counting towards the family coffers.

Mabel Hansen of Bridge Lake chose an entirely different way to earn extra money: she became a mystery writer. Mabel wrote and sold many serialized mysteries set in cowboy country. Living on the Horse Head Ranch with her husband, Johnny, and their two children, she had first-hand knowledge of ranch life. A surviving page from one of her stories written in the 1940s shows that it was entitled "The Hoodoo Ranch: Beginning an absorbing, thrilling murder mystery for 'who-dun-it' fans…"

Women called on their strength when they had to. In Bridge Lake in 1944, Ben Blaisdell became ill, eventually developing gangrene in his right leg. At certain times of the year, men in the area had to take their turn working on the road, and Ben was worried because he wasn't able to do his share. His wife, Bernice, took charge of the situation. Donning a pair of overalls, she marched out and took Ben's place, wielding pick and shovel along with the best of them.

Sometimes, women might show a different kind of strength when it came to ranching duties. Hilda Firrell of Watch Lake believed in the power of faith. Reverend Higgs and his wife witnessed this first-hand:

> After Communion we returned to the Ferrals [Firrells], and on the way I spotted a young steer almost up to its neck in a small slough. We hurried back to tell Mr. Ferral. However, he was out, and would not be back until noon. Mrs. Ferral told us not to worry: things would be alright. It turned out that she was an ardent Christian Scientist. First she sat us down to breakfast, which was all ready. Then, armed with "Science and Health, with Key to the Scriptures" by Mary Baker Eddy, and a small camp stool, she made for the slough, sat herself down, and proceeded to read to the young steer. Either the floor of the slough was solid, or the treatment worked, for he managed to keep his head above water until Jim arrived with a block and tackle, hitched it to a convenient tree, and pulled the creature out to dry land, at which achievement Mrs. Ferral commented, "You see!"

Lamps and Lanterns
Jean (MacLean) Nelson, North Bridge Lake

Before the advent of electricity, people managed well enough with the use of kerosene and coal oil lamps and lanterns. The lamps that burned kerosene had a fibre wick that allowed the oil to be drawn up from the bowl of the lamp to the metal burner. For going to the barn after dark, there was a coal oil lantern made of metal with a glass globe enclosed in a wire cage to prevent breakage. The light it gave was rather poor but quite adequate for milking the cow or feeding the horses.

Most of the light for reading or working in the house came from a lamp equipped with mantles and using white gas as fuel. The gas was put into a metal base that contained a pump: this was used to pump air into the base to put the gas under pressure. The gas then turned into vapour and travelled up the tubes to the mantles where it burned nicely. The mantle was a little bag made of cotton fibre treated with thorium dioxide. The bottom burned away, leaving the thorium to carry the light, as it had a very high melting point.

Taking care of these lanterns was a daily task, making sure the receptacles were full of fuel and cleaning the glass of soot so the light was as bright as possible. The globes were very fragile so you had to be careful.

Mildred Haywood-Farmer showing her grandchildren how to churn butter, a chore she'd undoubtedly performed countless times in the past. Courtesy Frank Haywood-Farmer, Kamloops, BC.

It would be a fallacy to say that every woman thrived and loved the challenge of country life. Some were unprepared for the hard life. Emily Stokstad of Bridge Lake came from Alberta to join her husband, Svend, and her sister Mabel Grauman, but the life didn't suit her. In a short memoir she talked about the difficulties she experienced:

> The next day we continued on three miles to our destination—the farm belonging to Charlie Reid [Reed] where we were to live and operate the farm for him. The farm had been the homestead of the Johsey's [Jowseys], Charlie's in-laws. There was an old log house with kitchen, living room and two bedrooms. For the first time in my life, I had running water in the house—it was piped from a spring on the hill behind the house. This was just cold water so we still had to heat water on the stove for all purposes. This was the only convenience. Everything else was strictly primitive. We didn't have a cookstove at first, just a flat topped wood heater, so for the first few weeks I had to do all the cooking on it. We bought bread from Mrs. Hansen twice a week, and since I couldn't bake anything, I made big batches of raised donuts. The batches had to be big because the word spread and every cowboy in the country stopped by to sample my donuts. Even after I acquired a proper stove, I had to continue making donuts by popular demand...

I didn't adapt very well to this new experience. I was used to near neighbors whom I'd known all my life. Here, our nearest neighbors were over a mile away through bush and rough road, and were not overly friendly when we did meet. There were no social events, as we were used to in Alberta. I was very lonely and hoped we wouldn't have to live in this isolation too long. We had a team of horses and a few cows on the farm and Svend managed to tame one cow enough to milk her.

The store and post office were three miles away and the mail came in once a week from Lone Butte—about 20 miles away. A trip to the store on mail day was the highlight of the week and about our only contact with other people…

Svend learned to hunt wild game, deer and moose and thus supplied us with all the meat we needed. All else had to be bought at the store—very little fresh vegetables and fruit. I worried about the children's diet, but they seemed to thrive on what we could get for them…

Somehow, the winter passed and late in April, signs of spring began to appear. Life was a little easier and there was work to keep us busy, but I was not happy. I didn't have the pioneering spirit of my parents and wanted only to return to some form of civilization. There was no school near enough for our children to attend and I vowed to myself that somehow we'd get out of there before Elsa was six. Children in the area were taking classes by correspondence with what help their mothers could give them. I was determined to make other arrangements before my children were ready for school.

Women and girls who were strong and capable were admired, especially by the older generation. Bill Scheepbouwer, the youngest son in his family, had other ideas. In 1950, he announced he was going to marry petite Rose Park, whom he'd had his eye on for some time. His father wasn't altogether approving.

"She's pretty little and she doesn't look very strong," Jacob observed.

"I'm marrying a wife, not a workhorse!" Bill retorted. It turned out that Rose was the ideal partner. Having grown up on a ranch herself, she thrived on the challenge.

Girls in every family did both inside and outside work from the time they were quite young. Some, as they grew up, took on the more demanding ranch chores of rounding up cattle, haying, branding, and other work usually done by men. Anne Scheepbouwer was known as "Cattle Annie" because of her skills; Jenny Jowsey in Bridge Lake did most of the ranch work at her

Rose Park as a young girl, herding cattle along the North Bonaparte Road. Wives and daughters played an essential role in any ranching operation, adding ranch chores to their usual round of household work. Courtesy Rose (Park) Scheepbouwer, Vernon, BC.

parents' place; Jean MacLean of North Bridge Lake hayed, sheared sheep, and helped her father with every aspect of the operation. Some went on to work as cowgirls for other ranchers who were in need of help, especially during World War II, when many farm labourers went off to war. Some of these were Anna Chabara, Retia Cunningham, Mae Bryant, and her sister Myrtle Bryant. For many years, Retia Cunningham of 74 Mile stated her profession as "cowgirl" in *Wrigley's British Columbia Directory*. Andy Whitley also had an unnamed cowgirl working for him, although she incurred his wrath when she caused a wagon accident in which Andy broke his hip.

Although there weren't a great number of jobs to be had other than being a cowgirl or working at tourist ranches, local girls appeared to not be in a rush to get married. The few eligible women in the earliest years of settlement took their time about choosing who and when they would marry. This may have reflected the fact that it was more difficult during those years for their prospective partners to become economically established enough to take on a family. Later, among the group of families who stayed the longest in the district, the average age at marriage was 22.

Nevertheless, there was always pressure on a young woman to marry. Annie Rodman, the stepdaughter of Hiram Andrus who lived in the North Bonaparte, was a victim of this pressure. The Andruses had become acquainted with a young man up at Eagan Lake named Fred O'Toole. He was Leon Borleske's stepson and liked to visit the Andrus household with its pretty

Hazel Park of the North Bonaparte poses on her horse with her friend Joyce Walker from Vancouver. The two went bird-hunting together every fall . The horse on the left is Blaze, a wild horse caught by Jack DuBois and sold to Jack Park. Courtesy Gene Park, Langley, BC.

young daughters. He particularly had his eye on 17-year-old Annie.

"I liked Fred," Annie wrote some years later to one of her sisters. "He was good looking, clean, and [a] willing worker, didn't smoke, chew or drink, nor was he from town." Nevertheless, Annie, an independent-minded girl, wasn't interested in marriage at that point.

But whether she liked it or not, that was what fate had in store for her. Hiram decided that the family had had enough of the Cariboo and were going to move to California. The plan was to take the train from Ashcroft. Money was tight, and he had to buy several tickets for his family. But there was one ticket he wouldn't have to buy if Annie agreed to marry her suitor, Fred O'Toole. Hiram felt Fred would be a good husband, and since Fred's mother had been good to Annie, she owed it to her. Annie, not persuaded, argued that she wanted to go with the family to California. But Hiram refused to pay for her fare. With no choice left to her, Annie and Fred were married at St. Alban's Church in Ashcroft on June 16, 1916. After the wedding, her family boarded the train, bound for California, and Fred and Annie headed

The women of North Bridge Lake pose at a community gathering about 1944. From left to right: Dorothy Reynolds, Margarit Faessler, Rosa King, unidentified, unidentified—but could be Florence Boultbee, Mable Boultbee (with her baby, Helen), Josie Faessler, Maria Reichmuth, Bernice Blaisdell, Lizzy Barnes, Rosa Ross, Goldi (Shertenlib), Alice King, Nellie Wheeler, Edna Grosset, Jean MacLean. Courtesy Audrey (Reed) Woodman, Merritt, BC.

back to Eagan Lake. Fred and Annie did later get to California, but their marriage was a chaotic one, and they eventually divorced. Annie suffered a mental breakdown and no one in the family knows to this day what actually happened to her.

Despite the hardships, many women who spent their entire life in the region wouldn't have it any other way. Mae Bryant McConnell, who was born in 1929 and spent her entire life around 70 Mile House, passed away in 2016 at the age of 86. She grew up far from any amenities and never went to school, learning everything from her mother. Her journey through life was not without many challenges and setbacks, but she loved living in the Cariboo. A year before her death, she said, "I've had such a wonderful life—if only I could live it all over again!"

BIRTH, DEATH,
AND LIFE IN BETWEEN

Miles from civilization, far from hospitals, clinics, and doctors, settlers on the Cariboo Plateau were forced to be resourceful and quick-thinking. When accidents happened or illness set in, it was usually the woman of the household who administered healing. Every woman was expected to know at least the basics of how to deal with sickness and accidents. She might have learned these from her mother or older relatives, from her friends and neighbours, from the advice pages in farm magazines, or from medical manuals such as *Dr. Chase's New Receipt Book.*

As well as being required to treat ailments, most women were assumed to have a natural skill at helping with childbirth. In many cases, this was true. Most had given birth to their own children and had often helped someone else with theirs. This was a fortunate thing before 1940, since a mother about to give birth could be in an isolated spot far from medical help. Stories survive about various midwives around the area: Edith Edall of Sheridan Lake delivered several babies; Caroline Renshaw, Dovie Hansen, Irene Higgins, Anna Bradford, and Josie Faessler, all from Roe Lake and Bridge Lake, often assisted with childbirth. Farther south, Sadie Eden and Elma Johnson acted as midwives and brought many babies into the world. Perhaps the youngest midwife on record was Francis Mobbs. At the age of 3, she helped her mother deliver her youngest brother, Fred, while they lived in the remote Bonaparte River region.

If they had the funds and opportunity, some expectant mothers preferred to go to a large centre and have their babies in a hospital. They would generally go and stay with a friend or at a boarding house near the end of their pregnancy, rather than being caught by surprise and forced to have a home birth. These mothers were in the minority, however. Of the approximately seventy children born to settlers before 1940, over three-quarters were home births. The statistics were impressive: all the babies survived, and so did their mothers. The only possible case of a death during childbirth was that of Robert Jamieson's wife, who died in 1900. Most home births were unrecorded, which no doubt caused problems when people went to apply for their old age pensions later in life. After 1940, most babies were born in the hospital, either at Ashcroft, Kamloops, or Williams Lake.

Although most women had cures they depended on, it was often a frightening event when their young children became ill. Penicillin had been discovered in 1928, but it wasn't widely available until the mid-1940s. Before this, the death toll from unidentified fevers and illnesses was high. Serious childhood diseases such as pneumonia, scarlet fever, meningitis, croup, whooping cough, polio, and diphtheria were often fatal. Although the population in the district was low and contact with strangers infrequent, children could still contract these diseases.

The children who lived at the roadhouses and were in constant contact with travellers were especially at risk. Two of Isaac and Sarah Saul's young children died while they lived at 70 Mile House, both of diarrhea caused by an unknown fever. Two of the Boyd children at the 70 Mile House died in 1903, one of complications from strep throat and the other from influenza and pneumonia. The Cunninghams at 74 Mile were struck seven years later: John and Margaret's son Kenneth died from peritonitis, said (perhaps erroneously) to be brought on by a case of the measles; two weeks later, John also died, of pneumonia. Farther into the interior, children were safer, but deaths still happened.

Hugh and Bertha Holland, along with the younger Higgins, Bundrock and Cummings children. Before the 1940s, the lack of immunization and antibiotics meant children were at risk. Fortunately, most children were healthy, despite bouts of measles, mumps, scarlet fever, and the like. Courtesy Carla Granberg, Kamloops, BC.

In 1911, the Andrus family of the North Bonaparte was stricken: their two young daughters died five days apart, both from an unknown fever and pneumonia. In the 1920s, the Haywood-Farmer's young daughter Mabel died of an unidentified fever. A few years later, Stanley Horn, son of Hartwig and Anna Horn, died of croup.

With little knowledge of disease, and immunization years away, families were struck with terror when one of these illnesses presented itself. They did everything they could, but many times it wasn't enough. Doctors may have been far away, but even if they were present, they would have been unable to save those who were extremely ill with contagious diseases. The strain of this must have been tremendous. Eva Andrus, the mother who lost two daughters within five days, later had what was known then as a "nervous breakdown." She had to be sent to an institution to recover. Eventually, the family left, never again to live that far from civilization. Eva never completely recovered from the tragic loss of her daughters.

Though there might have been the threat of infectious diseases, children in the countryside had surprisingly few accidents. They also had an extraordinary amount of freedom. Most children explored and played in the bush for hours at a time without anyone having any idea where they were. They walked long distances alone to school, sometimes in below-zero winter weather. Working on the family farm, usually performing chores from pre-school age, they were often in risky circumstances. They learned to ride horses as soon as they could, helped to hay, rounded up cattle, drove machinery, split wood with sharp axes, and stoked roaring wood stoves.

Astonishingly, hardly anything unfortunate ever happened. Despite the fact that nearly every child in the countryside lived beside a creek or lake and often went out in rowboats with no life jackets, there was only one known drowning. Even one drowning is too many, nevertheless. In 1918, William and Clara Kearton's young son fell into Fawn Creek while they were visiting and was swept away. The devastation they felt over his death lasted for years.

From a very young age, the Scheepbouwer boys were expected to help out when it came to bringing meat to the table. Though this could involve what would be considered scandalous risk today, it was normal at the time. The three boys were often sent out to bag ducks and geese, and their father, Jacob, would give each of the boys two shells, with instructions to bring home one bird for each shell. The boys would find a good spot by a lakeshore and then build a fire. After they shot their bird, they'd strip off, dive into the lake, and retrieve it. Back on shore, they dried off, got dressed, and warmed themselves by the fire before taking their booty home. A boy who brought in his two birds got a pat on the head; those who didn't succeed got a frown of disapproval.

Young Bill Scheepbouwer was a great shot and adept at bagging ducks to fill the family larder. Children played an important part in the economy of the family and every child contributed in some way. Courtesy Rose Scheepbouwer, Vernon, BC.

Children at Bridge Lake were no less intrepid. The Bradford children led adventurous lives, described in *Exploring Our Roots: North Thompson Valley, McLure to Little Fort, 1763–1959*:

> The boys were kept very busy with chores as they were growing up but loved to fish and skate on the lake in winter. They were resourceful too. They would make up skateboards by fastening old skates to the bottom of a board, make a sail and come "just hallo-whooping" the mile and a half across the lake. One time Victor skated off the ice into the water. The older boys pulled him out and all was well. On the way to school the boys would set out a trap line and check it on the way home. They got ten cents for a squirrel and hide and twenty cents for a weasel. During the war squirrels went up to $1.10 each. Jimmy did very well selling the winter's catch in the spring. When they were boys haying with a crew at Crooked Lake, Albert shot a deer with a .22, wounding it so that it swam out into the lake. The younger boys, Jimmy and Victor, rowed out to it and pulled it into their boat, stunned it with an oar, and cut its throat. The deer was then butchered, some packed in brine and some canned in bottles, and all shared with the crew. When there were community picnics, they would pack a huge picnic lunch, pile into an old car or ride horseback to travel ten or twenty miles to the spot.

Sadie Eden of Watch Lake eloquently described how things were in the pioneer days. She had four children who were close in age, and life was different in a way that is hard to imagine now. In 1966, the *100 Mile News-Herald* interviewed Sadie Eden about "the good old days." One thing she said was that there was no problem with babysitters—there were none. If she had to be out of the house, doing chores outside or answering a call for help from neighbours, the children had to look after themselves, no matter what their age.

Sadie had myriad outdoor chores that were her responsibility if her husband was away working. Some of these tasks could take hours and the children had to stay in the house and look after themselves. But they'd been taught well: they knew what could be touched and what couldn't; they knew they couldn't squabble or there'd be trouble; they knew they had to do as they were told. When she returned from her chores, she'd often find the four of them watching out the window for her return.

"I used to worry about it sometimes," Sadie told the reporter, "but there was nothing else I could do. They never got into any trouble though." From these early experiences, the Eden children (and other country children) learned invaluable lessons of resourcefulness and independence. They were also good at making their own entertainment. Their favourite activity—when their parents weren't around—was roping and riding whichever of the livestock would tolerate it. The girls would chase the lambs and the boys would rope them; the long-suffering milk cows were ridden so often, they got used to it.

But accidents do happen and when one did, it was the parent who had to step up to the plate. Mothers (and fathers) set broken limbs, stitched up serious wounds, and did anything else that was demanded by the occasion. Mary Haines in the North Bonaparte had to take needle and thread and sew her daughter Marge's ear back on. It had been severed after a bad fall against a piece of furniture. George Spanks in Bridge Lake also had to do an emergency stitching job when his daughter Barbara was hit in the forehead by a baseball bat during a community picnic. Her skull was cracked open, but George called on his army experience and stitched up the wound himself. At Sharpe Lake, Elma Johnson had to do some quick thinking. Her son Zale had picked up a crosscut saw and accidentally put it on his shoulder with the sharp teeth down. He cut himself badly and nicked a jugular vein. With blood spurting everywhere, Elma yelled at her 5-year-old daughter Ivy to press on the wound while she burnt some flour on the stove. When her mother said the word, Ivy let go and her mother slapped on the flour. It staunched the wound and Elma was able to stitch it up. There were many households with similar stories.

Families did the best they could when sickness and accidents struck. Every household had a medicine chest or shelf with the essentials to cover most emergencies. The materials were usually readily available and reasonable in price. Most could be ordered through Eaton's catalogue. Other cures came from women's pantries and gardens. One well-known cure for a chest cold was to rub the area with warm goose grease. Mustard plasters were also a very common remedy for a cold. Everyone used onion poultices, turpentine, and sometimes kerosene for a number of purposes. One of the most common cure-alls was whiskey or brandy. Considered a panacea for just about everything, it was used as a cure, a preventative, and even as a tonic. Many patent medicines were heavily laced with alcohol: Lydia Pinkham's Vegetable Compound was an example of this. Other patent medicines commonly used (some of which are still available) were Dr. Fowler's Extract of Wild Strawberry, Dodd's Kidney Pills, Carter's Little Liver Pills, Minard's Liniment, Vicks VapoRub, and Phillip's Milk of Magnesia.

Della Sneve, Will Whitley's wife, had particular ideas from her Norwegian background on how to stay healthy. Her granddaughter, Betty Wishart, related one of her grandmother's health edicts:

In the winters at the ranch, Granny and Granddad had us run around the house outside in the snow barefooted and sometimes we ran out to the road and back. I was even convinced to take a snow bath. The snow was soft and easy to stick into my bathing suit, but when the cold hit, in the house I'd go as fast as possible. The boys at the ranch had to do the same thing.

Della's sister, Mabel Sneve Sandburg, also had knowledge of health cures. She once cured her neighbor Hilda Larson of the Spanish influenza.

"It was during the First World War, and the Spanish flu was so bad, we didn't know what to do," Hilda told an interviewer. "My husband had to go on his trap line and he told me, 'Now Mum, don't you go anywhere and you won't catch the flu,' but it travelled through the mails, and I got it, and didn't I get it good. I don't know what would have happened if Mr. Holland hadn't come by and seen the little ones sitting outside, quite dirty." Mr. Holland, alarmed, alerted Ed Higgins, another neighbour, who went quickly to find Hilda's husband, Ole. On his journey, Ed killed a coyote, and this turned out to be a lucky circumstance.

By the time Ed and Ole got back, Mabel Sandberg had arrived on the scene to nurse Hilda. "She wanted some kind of animal fat," Hilda said. "She cut up some of the [coyote] fat and rendered it out in a pan and mixed in some turpentine. Then she took one of my husband's heavy wool undershirts and cut strips of wool and soaked them in the fat. They kept that fat warm on the stove and kept changing cloths whenever they cooled off. They had me propped up all night, with my legs hung over the bed and my feet in strong mustard water, and they kept that hot. I'll tell you, if it wasn't for Mrs. Sandberg, I never would have made it."

Sometimes you just had to go it alone. Blanche Neal, who lived in Bridge Lake in the 1920s and 1930s, became ill and needed to go to the hospital far away in Kamloops. The circumstances are unclear, but her husband, Roy, may have been away at the time. Blanche, undaunted, made her way alone to medical aid. A granddaughter told the following story that was part of their family lore: "Granny needed an operation and had to get to Kamloops for the surgery. She went alone on horseback on the trail from Bridge Lake down to Little Fort, and had to camp overnight on the trail. When she got to Little Fort she was helped by the store owners, the Jims. He got her across the river to catch the train, took care of her horse and sent it back on the trail for home. Granny was a tiny little woman, but tough!"

Another person who had to go it alone out of necessity was John Scheepbouwer, up on Grant's Mountain. John and his wife, Enid, were living in this remote, isolated location but they were both up for the challenge at the time. They had a small cabin, about thirty head of cattle, and John guided game hunters. Unfortunately, John developed lung problems and became extremely ill. He made it through the winter, but in spring, he needed to get down the mountain for medical help as soon as possible. He was in poor shape, but Enid had to stay home to look after the livestock.

"I put him on his saddle horse in the spring," Enid said, "waved goodbye, sending him off about eighteen miles, and hoped the horse wouldn't come back again. I knew if he fell off, the horse would come home." John made it to his parents' ranch. They were able to take him to a hospital, where he convalesced for several months. When he came home, the couple realized their days on Grant's Mountain were over.

Bill Anderson of the North Bonaparte was from Finland and had quite a broken accent and unique expressions. He once got himself into a dangerous situation and wondered if he would ever be rescued. He'd been putting up a pole gate and it fell on him, injuring him and pinning him down so he was unable to move. He lay there for hours until he saw his neighbour Jack Park riding in his direction. Jack leaped down and in a short time freed Bill and helped him home. Old Bill said in gratefulness, "I t'ot I'd have to lefty-lay there 'til I died."

The travelling minister, Stanley Higgs, had little medical training, but he was often called upon to help in all sorts of medical situations. He, his wife, and a friend attended the Green Lake Stampede in 1933. "It was a real lively show, with good riding and some fine cattle ponies from the great Chilcotin cattle country," he wrote. "There were Brahma bulls from somewhere, and plenty of ornery horses to test the riders." During the performances, a Clinton policeman, Constable Morley Green, approached him and asked if he could help one of the riders out. "I said I would," Higgs continued. "There upon a ground sheet, lying face down, was a cowboy in severe pain. I knelt down beside him, and very gently laid a hand on the length of each collar bone. I didn't think it was a fractured clavicle."

Once he was certain there were no broken bones, he approached Constable Green and asked if there was any liniment available. Green had no idea, but Higgs had an inspiration. " 'I bet there's lots of gin about,' I said, and Morley said he was sure there was. The refreshment tent was just a stone's throw away. Morley and I collected some butter, a large thermos of boiling water, a wash basin and a towel and Morley went off to raise a mickey of gin." Higgs massaged the painful knotted shoulder with the hot water, gin, and butter mixture and it seemed to be bringing relief. But then he accidentally dropped a little on the young man's face.

"Suddenly he was no longer the recumbent hero," the amazed Higgs wrote. "He had tasted the gin, and without ceremony, he bucked me off his back, seized the jug, and declared, 'I've never had this—stuff wasted on the outside of me before.' And without a pause he put the jug to his lips and took a long draft." Higgs found out that the man who had suddenly recovered was actually no ordinary cowboy. He had won the world championship for his specialty, bulldogging steers, at the Wembley International Exhibition in England in 1925. Unfortunately, Higgs never recorded his patient's name.

Toothaches were a major problem since families were far away from dental care. For many years, the closest dentist was in Kamloops, or possibly Ashcroft, and residents were forced to travel there if the pain became unbearable. In a newspaper interview, Robbie Cleveland of Eagan Lake told a story about one trip to the dentist.

"The only time I ever got to go [to Ashcroft]," he said, "was when I had a run-in with a horse's hoof and it knocked out my tooth. I had to go get the stub pulled." While Robbie's dental work was left to a professional on that occasion, there was at least one other time when he turned to his own brand of dentistry. When he was 12 years old, the young boy experienced an unbearable toothache and tried to remedy it himself with a smearing of battery acid. "When you're in pain, you'll try anything," he laughed, as he hinted it wasn't the last time he'd tried the unconventional cure. Self-doctoring didn't stop there. Years later, a severe case of strep throat had him thinking a shot of pink eye spray might do the trick. "I sure danced around after that, but they brought me to Doctor Fischer and he said he couldn't do any better."

Another hazard of life—a very real one because of wood stoves—was house fires. Stovepipes and chimneys were often of poor quality and many fires started with a chimney fire. Nevertheless, the percentage of people who lost their home to a house fire was relatively small. The earliest recorded fire occurred in 1907, when the Graham brothers, Sam and Robert, lost their first cabin to fire. The brothers wasted no time in rebuilding, but they had lost everything they had. The same happened to Alfred Anderson, a Swedish settler in the Chasm area. Unfortunately, one of his sons was burned as he fled the fire, but the rest of the family escaped unharmed. Ellis and Bertha Granberg of Roe Lake lost their home in the 1920s and narrowly averted losing members of their family but for the quick thinking of Bertha, who spotted the fire and whisked her children to safety. The home of the Cunningham family at 74 Mile House burned down twice: once in 1923 and again in 2010. The Gammies, who went on to own the Flying U for many years, lost their home and buildings at their original G Lazy 2 at Watch Lake in 1951. Like others

Fire, a constant hazard in wood-burning days, struck the 74 Mile House and consumed everything within a short time. The Cunninghams set to work rebuilding as soon as they could. Courtesy Earl Cahill, Clinton, BC.

who'd had the same experience, they regrouped and went on to make the best of it.

Until modern times, few, if any, had fire insurance, or indeed, any other kind of insurance. That kind of protection was expensive and sometimes unattainable. Allen Furrer of Lone Butte was quoted in a newspaper article on the subject of insurance: "You made your own insurance," he wisely stated. "Use common sense; think; and use caution." A good maxim at any time.

Life expectancy was surprisingly high among the families who remained in the district for most of their lives. Considering the lack of medical care and the hard, demanding life people led, their vital statistics stack up well against the provincial standard. *Becoming British Columbia: A Population History*, by John Belshaw, shows the average age of death between 1961 and 1981 in British Columbia was 70 for men and 78 for women. In contrast, people who lived in the area from 70 Mile House to Bridge Lake exceeded that. In a study of almost sixty families who had been among the original settlers and lived in the area most of their lives, the average life span for men was 76 and for women, 84—six years above the BC average for both sexes. Among the women, none died younger than 60 and over a third lived into their nineties. They outlived their husbands by eight years, also above the provincial average.

What accounted for the remarkable longevity of the adult population? In the days before advanced technology, nearly everyone worked hard and was active and fit; the people of the Cariboo Plateau were no exception. The high longevity could possibly have been a result of people moving away from areas with no medical care when they began to suffer ill health, leaving behind only the relatively healthy.

If someone died at home, neighbours often acted as undertakers, preparing the body and building a coffin for the bereaved family. Some people had a natural ability to help in this role. Noveta Leavitt was one such person, as related in *The Homesteader's Daughter*. Other people named as "undertakers" on death certificates included Forrest Bell, Lilly Printzhouse, Fred Jowsey, Stanley Eden, and Pleun Herwynen. Marvin Hall had been an undertaker before he came to Bridge Lake and he often offered his services without asking for payment. Sometimes, a death certificate would simply state "neighbours" or "friends and neighbours." Their help and support must have been a source of immense comfort to bereaved families.

Sadie Eden of Watch Lake talked about her experiences to an interviewer:

> But just as like as not, just when [Sadie] would be comfortably settled in front of the stove there would come a call for help in some way from a neighbour. With no doctors in the area, she found herself helping out on a number of occasions with births… "I'd ride miles and miles at night over the hills and lakes and trails," she says. "In those days you had to do these things. There was nobody else to help. My mother had been a nurse and I had learned a lot from her, as well as from my father, who was a veterinary surgeon. Here again, it always seemed to work out alright, although I had my worries at the time. I used to just pick up and go when someone came and called for me. But I always asked the Lord to be with me—that's what I lived by, faith and prayer."
>
> Once, she sat up all night with a neighbour who was dying of TB while back home her children, none of them more than four years old, minded themselves. "There was no one else to do it. Someone had to do it. I was there when she died," says Mrs. Eden simply…

Death certificates record unadorned facts, but a great deal can be surmised from them. When the Andrus girls died in the North Bonaparte in 1911, both their death certificates listed under "Name of Physician, if any" the names of Charles Potts and Emma Whitley. Charlie was a friend of the Andrus family and Emma was a neighbour, although not their closest one. They would have done everything within their power to help the Andrus family. They would have helped the exhausted mother minister to the sick girls, meanwhile trying all the remedies that they knew of. Emma would have made meals for the rest of the frantically worried family, trying to soothe them as much as she could. When Jessie died on April 10, followed by Jane on April 15, Emma and Charlie would have been the ones to prepare the girls' bodies for burial. Will Whitley, Emma's son, built the caskets for the girls, poignantly recorded on the back of a photo in the possession of one of the Andrus descendants. "Mr. William Whitley, North Bonaparte, Cariboo," the handwriting reads, "the man who helped build the caskets and took them to the North Bonaparte Homestead where Mom lived. Then they buried Mom's 2 small daughters who died." No doubt he and Charlie Potts dug the graves close to the house, where they lie today.

Jack Park of the North Bonaparte had a death that perhaps would be the sort men in that country would prefer to have, if they had a choice. Jack, then 73, had developed a bad heart and had to take medication. On October 5, 1962, the cook who worked on the ranch said to Jack, "I'll make a nice meal if you get me a moose." Jack saddled up one of the horses and went out alone to go moose hunting in the back country. He was doing just fine until suddenly he felt an attack coming on and reached for his medication. It wasn't there. The attack staggered him, but mustering all his strength to stay on the horse, he managed to ride back home. The cook heard him calling out for her, and as she rushed out of the house, Jack collapsed and fell off his horse. She carried him into the house and laid him on a couch, but it was obvious he didn't have long to live. With his dying breath, he struggled to tell her where he had left the moose he'd shot. He wanted to make sure it wouldn't go to waste. Later, Anna Chabara, his cowhand, and his neighbour Bill Scheepbouwer rode out and found the dead moose, right where Jack had described it, and they brought in the carcass. Jack was buried in Clinton.

There were few mysterious deaths in the countryside, but Joseph Reinhold's was perhaps one of them. Joe was born in Texas in 1905 but had come to Canada when he was very young. He came to the North Bonaparte in 1922, when he was only 17 years old. Reinhold lived on the Boule ranch and probably worked for the Boules. One day in 1932, ten years after he'd arrived, Joe's life ended tragically. The young man hadn't shown up when he was expected and was found dead on the Boule property. The coroner from Clinton ruled that Joe had been thrown from a horse, hit his head, and died instantly, but rumours surfaced. Dan Puckett, who lived near Young Lake at that time, stated that Reinhold had owed money to John DuBois, who came and claimed the young man's horse, saddle, and equipment after his death. The unfortunate young man was buried in Clinton.

Eventually, a cemetery was established in the district. A tragic event in 1933 prompted the residents of Roe Lake to create a place for burials. Hope Ashley, a 12-year-old girl, had been the victim of an accidental, fatal gunshot wound. Everyone in the countryside was horrified and shocked. No one wanted to see the young girl buried in a strange place, so the community gathered together to see what they could do. Kind-hearted Ole Ellingson donated some of his land at Roe Lake to establish the cemetery, and together, friends and neighbours prepared Hope's body for burial.

In the 1940s, a cemetery committee was set up at Roe Lake to deal with burials, and no doubt the committee was made up of the same compassionate neighbours. Most of the pioneers and residents of the area lie at rest in the Roe Lake Cemetery, the Clinton Cemetery, or the 100 Mile House Cemetery. A few, however, are buried on their own properties.

In birth, death, and life in between, neighbours were incredibly important to each other's lives. They provided companionship and entertainment; they helped out during haying, house-building, and anything else that was needed. They provided comfort when life was difficult. They helped with illnesses and accidents, delivered their neighbours' babies, and buried their neighbours' dead. There were no doctors to provide health care and rarely a minister to provide comfort and words of wisdom. Neighbours and family were everything.

Life was sad for those who isolated themselves and didn't have neighbours to check on them. The *Ashcroft Journal* reported in 1943 on the lonely death of Charles Simmons, who once lived in the North Bonaparte:

> Charles Simmons, aged 79, who had been prospecting in the Scotty Creek region for several years, was brought into hospital here a fortnight ago suffering malnutrition and appeared to be improving when he suddenly passed away Thursday of last week. The funeral was held Saturday and internment took place in Ashcroft cemetery, Rev. E. R. Bartlett officiating. Little is known of the man's past and apparently [he] had no relatives in this country. According to a local citizen, Simmons along with a brother, William [should be Harvey], came to this province from the United States some 35 years go and went ranching in the North Bonaparte section. It is said they had a "pretty fair spread" and went in for raising pure-bred horses. They were doing quite well when William [Harvey] Simmons died. Charles then left the ranch and went cowboying and prospecting until he "holed

up" on Scotty Creek where he was found by the police and doctor to be living in terrible circumstances.

According to the doctor he was unable to walk when he entered hospital and in a week had improved considerably but collapsed Thursday of last week and passed away shortly after.

From Eva Andrus of the North Bonaparte to her daughter, Ethel Rodman Ryder
North Bonaparte, Canada
May 31st, 1912

Dear Ethel and Jack and tiny baby,

I thought I would drop you a few lines asking you if you would like me to send down a few things. You pay the charges. I will send them for the baby. Would you accept some nightgowns for her made out of flour sacks. In the fall, if we should leave here, do you want my sewing machine—will sell it to you cheaper than anyone else. I now have 15 hens—they have laid lots of eggs—are doing fairly well now. I have made Annie 1 white silk waist, trimmed it with white silk lace. I will send you a sample—she has a blue silk—it is not made yet. She has lisle silk hose and tan lace for best—to go with tan shoes. Last mail I got ten yards of gingham for Vivian—Annie has 15 yards coming in the next mail. While I have a $60.00 order made out to send for their summer things—new hats, gingham and underwear, stockings and other things they need. Is your baby a good baby—like mine was?

…This mail I went out with Hite to the 70 Mile House. Mrs. Chisholm has left the 59 Mile House. I heard she was fired but did not know the cause. Mr. Sargent has broke his leg—Hite was up to see him last Monday—they have 5 children—all are younger than Inez—they now live where Cora and Port did—above Maudsleys.

Our mare Sylvia has a mare colt—1 month old—10th of June. It is lighter coloured than Black Bess was. Hite named it Susie. We still have Baldy and Dick and a wild horse—a stallion (Dexter) and Silvia—that is all now. Hite has just got home from a fishing trip last evening—got some 25 lbs.—they had quit running before he got up there so he had to use a line and hook—wish you were near enough so that I could do your sewing and give you a mess of fish. The weather is cool today but the long meadow is going to be better than last season. I heard not long ago that Angus [Ryder] was trying to claim our Daisy cow that strayed down to the 20—we have sold her to Furguson [Ferguson] for cash. It was our cow—just because Hite gave Mr. Chisholm fifty dollars for her—and I would like to see him claim her by law…

There are several Pansies in the little Yard—the grass is 8 inches high there now—but what a sad and lonely spot for parents can never forget—but that is the way with this world—but hope you will never see such trials as these days were. Mr. [Charlie] Potts said he was coming here for about a month, coming the last of June. I may tire you but you can read this and hold baby too—tell me what clothes you have so I won't be making too many of one kind.

Yours as ever,
Mother—write soon

Neighbours were generally kind to the single men in the countryside, and in response, many bachelors made it a habit to visit friends—often at mealtime. A hot, tasty meal with a woman's touch was irresistible. In *The Homesteader's Daughter*, Noveta Leavitt painted a charming picture of several of the old bachelors, such as Bruce Craddock and Will Wilson. In fact, there was more than one Bill, Will, or William Wilson in the countryside. It was a major challenge to untangle who was who: one had long, thin fingers (W. W. W. Wilson); one kept snakes for company (Bill Wilson); one was a Scotsman who was a farm labourer around Eagan Lake (William Wilson); another was the tall, lanky man from Washington that the MacDonalds met on the trail (Will Wilson).

Perhaps the most well-loved of the bachelors were Henry Atwood and Ole Ellingson. They had both arrived in the area early and are remembered to this day as interesting, quirky characters who were lively members of their communities. Bridge Lake bachelor Bill Wilson, a quiet, unassuming fellow, was sometimes visited by John and Mabel Hansen's children, Sharon and Carter, when they were riding through the neighbourhood. Bill, who had become a recluse by that time, was very welcoming, although it seemed he didn't really expect many visitors: he had a chemical toilet set up on his porch just so he could survey the scenery while using his facilities. Carter once accepted Bill's invitation to come inside and see his cabin and later reported to Sharon that Bill had some house companions: garter snakes, at least ten of them. Nothing would persuade her to go into the cabin after that, although they never failed to stop and say hello if they were passing that way. "I'm not sure that he was that lonely," Sharon said. "I think he rather thrived on solitude. Besides, he had his snakes."

Remains of Henry Atwood's house still standing today. Henry, an American rancher, was one of the very earliest pioneers in the district. Courtesy Helen Matson, Prince George, BC.

Many bachelors, rather than trying to go farther afield to find a wife, stayed where they were and instead led a single life. The friendliness of their neighbours made it possible to lead a relatively social life. And without a doubt, there was a certain percentage who had no interest in marriage to begin with.

Of course, with neighbours, it wasn't all roses. People in small places gossip and get into each other's hair. They can be unkind and they can have quarrels, some of them never resolved. But even if a family eventually moved away, no matter how far they went or how many years had passed, they would never forget those people who had played such an intimate part in their life. Floyd Tompkins wrote eloquently about the ties among neighbours:

> We all worked hard to make a go of life, we knew everyone for miles and they were good people and good friends. Their doors were always open to any passerby. If they were bad people, thieves, liars, or mean to horses, no one had much time for them... Word travelled fast. Most neighbours were good to one another and always glad to see their neighbours if they were good people and went all the way out to help them. Most ranches were 20 to 25 miles apart, and some were a lot further, but they always seemed to keep in contact, either by rodeos, funerals, or weddings although most were hard to get to when riding horseback.

WHEN THE WORK'S ALL DONE

The culture of the district between 70 Mile House and Bridge Lake wasn't much different from other ranching and farming communities across North America. Everyone was fully occupied keeping their ranches and farms going. Yet, when the work was all done, settlers could play just as hard as they could work. They created and attended events that were enjoyed by the whole family. Once a year, there were exciting affairs such as rodeos, fairs, school concerts and picnics, amateur concerts, and sports days. Dances happened as often as residents could find an excuse to hold one. In between these occasions, neighbours visited each other as often as they could.

The Scheepbouwer family, along with a few friends, enjoy an impromptu jam session. Perhaps they were serenading their pet moose, who declined to turn to face the camera. Courtesy Jackie Scheepbouwer, Surrey, BC.

In a letter to her uncle, Muriel Powell Morris of Sheridan Lake expressed the pleasure of visiting friends and neighbours, especially after a long winter:

> Another thing I would like to mention is when I was young, there was no such thing as snowplows so when there was three feet of snow on the ground, there weren't many people moving around especially till someone broke out the road with a team & sleigh (oftentimes using an extra team to spell the first team off). So every spring when I got old enough Dad [Carl Nath] would have me go with Mother [Hilda Nath] & [my sister] Anna in our democrat (two-horse buggy) to visit with people she knew at Roe Lake & Bridge Lake which is over 20 miles away. We would be gone about a week, staying overnight at the different people's places. This was a nice treat for mother which she enjoyed very much.

Winter didn't always deter people from visiting each other or attending events. Up to the 1940s, nearly everyone had a horse-drawn sleigh. A sleigh was actually more efficient than travelling by car, since horses were able to manage much deeper snow. Families often stayed overnight when they visited, because it might be too long a trip to return home in the dark. The children would be put to bed while the parents stayed up until all hours of the night, talking, laughing, playing cards, and sometimes playing music. In the North Bonaparte, neighbours—usually the men—got together and played poker during long winter nights.

Ian MacInnes, a nephew of Gordon King of Bridge Lake, wrote of family get-togethers, eloquently describing his uncle and aunt's house (which could have described almost any house in the area):

> The location at Bridge Lake chosen by Uncle Gordon for his homestead is arguably the finest on the north shore. It looks out on a bay sheltered by a small island, and all around the land slopes gently to the water's edge... A second house was built, which still stands today (1998) and the family moved into it in 1936. Built of logs and with a steep-pitched shake roof, it was larger than the original and a little further from the lake. Nearly half its floor area was devoted to kitchen and pantry and the remainder divided into a living room and two bedrooms. Aunt Alice's kitchen was dominated by an old-fashioned wood-burning range, complete with warming oven and hot water reservoir. A good-sized, substantially built table, surrounded by chairs, stood before the windows, and a

buffet rested against the wall nearby. Because the house lacked a bathroom, a washstand and mirror were conveniently placed near the door, where those coming in from work could clean up before eating. Years later, a cream separator, securely bolted to the floor, left no one in doubt where the kitchen ended and the pantry began. A doorway beside the kitchen range led into the room that was in every sense a "living" room. Besides the commonplace soft furniture, it contained a wood burning heater, an upright piano, and my uncle's favourite chair. On a tall chair-side table sat the family's only year-round contact with the outside world, a battery-powered radio. This apparatus was reverently regarded, providing as it did all the daily news and weather report. But to spare its complement of batteries it otherwise remained silent. The living room walls were adorned with the mounted horns of deer, moose, and mountain goat, the larger of them used as racks for guns and other hunting gear. A banjo resting in its well-worn case neatly evidenced another of my uncle's interests. He loved his music, and when my dad was there the two played often, Uncle Gordon picking away on the banjo and Dad strumming accompaniment on guitar. Later, when Russ [Ross] had also taken up the guitar, the three played together, both there in that cozy living room at King's and at the Saturday night dances held at the Double T Guest Ranch.

Once in a while, there were unusual visitors to the countryside. Olga Prydatok, who grew up at Green Lake, vividly remembers a travelling missionary who visited a few times. Olga recalled that she was called "Deaconess" and she might possibly have been a member of the Anglican Deaconess Association. The Deaconess would arrive in a swirl of dust with her car, picking up many of the young girls from around the area. Together, they went on memorable outings—to marshmallow roasts and campfire singsongs and on other excursions. If they were singing, the Deaconess made sure they had accompaniment. With a flourish, she would whip open the back of the car, reveal her portable organ, and begin playing with enthusiasm. To children whose lives included few exciting events, these occasions were never forgotten.

Since hardly anyone had a telephone before the 1960s, few people made pre-arranged visits. Visitors just arrived, perhaps to stay for hours, perhaps to stay overnight or even for a few days. Meals were flexible and it was easy to throw a few more potatoes in the pot. Everyone was welcome, anytime. Visits were often punctuated with jam sessions and singing. With such a thriving social life, it could be disorienting for people who left the area and went to the city. When Edna and Slim Grosset of Bridge Lake finally retired, they moved to an apartment in White Rock. Life was easier, but Edna was lonely. In a letter she wrote to a friend, she lamented, "I sure miss it up there, those were the good old days… I wish people here would mix better. Nobody goes visiting or plays cards here. I liked it when people up there would drop in any old time to have tea & meals."

Dances

Music and dancing: these were the lifeblood of entertainment for all the local communities. Quite a large percentage of the population, from young to old, could play a musical instrument. In some families, such as the Scheepbouwers in the North Bonaparte and the Faesslers in Bridge Lake, several members of the family had musical skills.

Dances were held in schools, halls, and sometimes in people's homes. Music was provided by local bands made up of musically inclined neighbours. Dances were often held to provide funds for some worthy cause or for a special occasion, such as a fall fair, a rodeo, or a wedding. Everyone turned up for the occasion: old, young, married, or single.

Even the virtuous Reverend Higgs and his wife, Margaret, got into the action:

> Now the social evening got under way. Dancing was announced, and the chairs were placed around the walls of the hall. A little 4-piece orchestra took up their positions and proceeded to motivate the oddly assorted members of this party to dance. The results were quite remarkable. Some of the older ones had obviously danced in the days before the Bonaparte, others had probably never danced, but were brave enough to try, while some of the younger people present had learned such skills as they possessed in dances such as this one. All of this made Margaret and me feel like Fred and Adele Astaire. I met several people of Lone Butte and the Lakes whom I had not met previously. Several of them expressed their regrets that we were leaving the Bonaparte. Some said they felt this way for the young people's sake, and added their appreciation that someone had tried to do something about bootlegging to the children. About two in the morning the last dance was announced, and when it ended a spokesman for the people thanked us for having worked among them, and regretted our leaving after so short a time when so much could have been done. Then pointing to Margaret

Square dancing, as well as the polka, schottische, and foxtrot were among the favourites at the many dances held at the Flying U and throughout the region. Here, a square dance caller sings out his instructions at the Flying U dance hall during the 1950s. Courtesy Robert and Gayle Fremlin, 70 Mile House, BC.

and me, he led in the singing of "For they are jolly good fellows." "And now your train will be here in less than ten minutes," he said, and addressing the whole party, "I think it would be a good idea to see our friends safely onto the train." It must have been an unusual happening for the Butte: the parson and his wife being escorted to the train by about 50 people, all singing at the top of their voices at nearly 3:00 in the morning.

In the time he spent ministering to the people of the region, Reverend Higgs had developed a great affection for them, even if he did seem to consider their area to be somewhat uncivilized backwoods country. The fact that a few people had stills hidden back in the woods and that they were not averse to selling their products to underage children didn't improve his opinion.

No one was left at home the night of the dance. Small children were put to bed on benches that lined the walls; the older children stayed up as long as they could and danced along with the adults. There were usually refreshments offered, as well as liquid refreshment outside for the men. Dances usually started about 9:00 pm and didn't end until daylight. People who had danced the entire night went home afterwards and had to feed their stock and do their daily chores before they could even think of having a nap.

The Eden twins of Watch Lake, Minnie and Alice, loved to dance and thought nothing of riding miles to go to an event. Minnie told an interviewer: "Alice and I went to a dance once at Lone Butte; we were about 16. We danced all night long, came home and changed, and rode to Roe Lake to another dance. We were so tired coming home, we hadn't slept for two nights. Alice fell asleep on her horse and fell off."

Dancing was energetic and enthusiastic. Square dances were part of the evening's entertainment, as well as foxtrots, polkas, waltzes, and the schottische. Several different people, including Ed Higgins, acted as the caller for the square dances.

The Rainbow Chasers recorded that as soon as the population of Bridge Lake finally got large enough to warrant it, people got together and held dances. The year wasn't recorded, but it must have been before 1915: "The women brought enough food for a midnight supper and for breakfast," Ervin MacDonald wrote. "Music was provided by the guests themselves; often Dan [Ervin's brother] played his violin and, though he had never had a lesson, he did very well. The people who didn't care to dance just sat around and gossiped."

The earliest dance recorded in the North Bonaparte was mentioned by Eva Andrus in a letter she wrote to one of her daughters in 1913. The Andrus family was moving from their location on what is now the Young Lake-

Boule Road to property at Chasm. People in the area organized a farewell dance for them. Eva mentioned that one of the Wilson brothers from Eagan Lake played the violin at the dance. No doubt there had been dances before 1913, however, considering that many of the settlers had already been there for around five years.

Among those who played at dances in the 1920s and 1930s was Johnny Hansen on the guitar and his brother Wes on the violin and mandolin. It was not unusual for them to ride forty kilometres (twenty-five miles) on horseback to Lone Butte, play all night, and then ride back home in the morning. After Johnny purchased his ranch, dances were frequently held at his place. The large upstairs had no partitions at the time and was ideal for a party. "Neighbours would come from miles around on horseback, and by wagon or sled, depending on the season," his daughter Sharon Hansen said. "The guests would bring food and stay for two or three days."

Another Hansen brother, Lee, held parties at his ranch by Burns Lake (later known as the Double T Ranch) in the Hoedown Hall. Dances were held every Saturday night during the summer. A group calling themselves The Bridge Lake Ramblers provided the music. This band was made of up Sid Reynolds on the drums, his brother Cy Reynolds on the accordion, Russell Ross on the banjo or guitar, Jack Black on the guitar, Lloyd Woodman and Dave Law on the violin, and Dave's mother, Patty Law, on the piano. Stan Williams, with his guitar, sometimes played with the band as well. There were no stories of anyone singing with the bands, but sometimes, after a fall fair, the Faesslers would do some Swiss yodelling.

In the North Bridge Lake area, dances were held at the school and later at the community hall. There, the band was usually composed of Gordon King on the banjo, Charlie Faessler on the coronet, his brother Ernie Faessler on the trombone, and Patty Law on the piano. Peter Ross played the accordion, fiddle, banjo, and mouth organ and joined with a few others in a local band. While the Neals lived in the area in the 1920s and 1930s, Blanche Neal played her harmonica at events. Ernie Ades talked about the parties in North Bridge Lake and said, "People would ride for two days, dance all night, then ride back two days. One dance, Tom Winters played his mouth organ all night."

One unnamed woman who lived at Bridge Lake for several years had reason to remember a New Year's dance at the North Bridge Lake Community Hall. She wore a red knit dress for the occasion. At midnight, while everyone was kissing everyone else and wishing them a happy new year, Ernie Ades came over to give her a kiss. As he bent over, his pants suddenly caught on fire. He had a bunch of matches in his back pocket and they'd gotten warm from all the dancing and gyrations. People rushed him out of the hall and rolled him in the snow to put the fire out. Later, Ernie told everyone it was dangerous to kiss Mrs. X, since her red dress made her so hot, you'd burst into flames. Mrs. X, mortified, never wore the dress again.

Roe Lake residents also held dances, usually at the school or at people's homes. One group that played together in the 1920s and 1930s was Charlie Ashley on the fiddle, his wife, Ethelyne, on the washboard, and Ole Larsen on the button accordion. Frank Leavitt played the fiddle and his brother Chester played the piano at informal gatherings. Ole Ellingson, in his younger days, was one of the people at Roe Lake who attended every dance he could. Whirling all the ladies around the floor, his fancy footwork was impressive. If there were any prizes to be won, Ole and his partner usually captured them.

At Eagan Lake and Sharpe Lake, parties were often held, either at people's homes or in the schoolhouse. Jack Dyer and Claude Johnson both played the violin and Ben Francis played the button accordion. Ben was a talented musician, able to play both the violin and the button accordion. Tor Tuovila played the fiddle and they often had jam sessions in a friendly competition to see who the better player was. Together with a few others, Ben and Tor played at local dances, usually until far into the morning. Ben often played Irish jigs on the violin and his youngest daughter, Sheila, would join him by tapdancing to the tune, even though she'd never been taught a step. Robbie Cleveland wrote in a letter to his parents about a dance that had been held at Zale Johnson's house and suggested the next one be held at one of the Cleveland's cabins. For their last shindig, Jack Dyer and Claude Johnson had played the violin, while Harry Leavitt and Robbie played the guitar. "My fingers are still sore from the strings," Robbie declared.

Everyone in the countryside was enthusiastic about dances. The time of year and the state of the weather didn't make much difference. A memorable event was held in the dead of winter in 1928, when a party was held at the Porter brothers' place in the North Bonaparte to raise funds to build a school at Watch Lake. A basket social was held in the late afternoon, ending with a dance that lasted until breakfast. According to a newspaper article, eighty settlers (including children) attended, arriving in their horse-drawn sleighs. This must have accounted for nearly every person in that part of the country. Everyone ate breakfast, then harnessed their teams and saddled up their horses and made their way home through a howling snow storm. No doubt they all considered it a small price to pay for all the fun they'd had.

Other musicians who were well known in the Green Lake and Watch Lake area were Billy Davies, who played the guitar; Howard (Kinik) Reaugh on the Hawaiian guitar; Don Eden on the fiddle; Eddy Dougherty on drums; Ashley McConnell on the sax; Charlie Prest on the violin; and Katy Prydatok and Ada Smith on the piano. Perhaps the most notable musicians in that area, however, were the Scheepbouwer family. Nearly all the siblings in the family were musical: Bill played the accordion, John played the accordion and banjo, Anne played the banjo and guitar, and Jake played the violin. The family performed at dances in Clinton, Watch Lake, Lone Butte, 70 Mile House, and Green Lake.

Many of the events were enhanced by the Scheepbouwer's famous potato champagne. A recipe brought to North America by many European immigrants, potato champagne was made by fermenting potatoes for about six weeks with water, sugar, yeast, and such ingredients as raisins, pearl barley, and lemon juice. For a money-shy economy, it was a socially acceptable alternative to expensive whiskey.

From Robbie Cleveland to his parents, Carr and Minnie Cleveland

Eagan Lake Ranch, March 8, 1943
Dearest Dad and Mother,

Hope you and Mama are fine, and that you have a good job. We are all fine and getting along well. Weston and I helped Zale [Johnson] get in four loads of wood today. He is going to help us tomorrow. Golly, I wish that I had the woodsaw fixed up. I probably will be going up Friday to see the cattle and leave the mare up there as the roads are getting too icy to chance her on, it would be pretty dangerous on having the horses at Young Lake on the frozen hillsides and I don't think that there would be much picking anyway. They are up in the far end of the meadow now, there is lots of rustling there if the crust isn't too bad. John Morris is leaving Tuesday, has sold everything but his team and harness, don't know if he has sold them yet, Marion [Higgins] & [Art] Fitch might buy them, I didn't know until Claude [Johnson] came over that he wanted to sell them. If he didn't sell them at Bridge Lake, he is leaving them with Claude at North Fork he said. Morris said he thought we would take them. Hope he hasn't sold them...

They have been talking about having another dance and card party somewhere, said Zale's place was too small. So I told them that we could have one in the No. 2 cabin, something to have a little fun in the Valley. If it would be as good as the one at Sherman [Davis's] it would be fine. Harry L. [Leavitt], Jack D. [Dyer], Claude played the violin, Harry [Leavitt] and I played on the guitar, my fingers are still sore from the strings... Old Elma [Johnson] had a black dress on this morning that could of fit a rail perfectly and a couple fat short stockings rolled down to her knees, I never seen anything before that was so funny that I could of busted laughing... I'll have to close for now as I'm getting short of material. With lots of love,
Robt. C.

The Scheepbouwers usually had a batch on the go and this had disastrous results for a pet they once had. Despite being crack hunters and trappers, the Scheepbouwers had a soft spot for wild animals. As well as once having a pet bear, the family rescued an orphaned moose calf and brought it home. The moose grew up and lived at the ranch for years, affectionately bonded to the family—although she hated most women and would chase any that came around. Unfortunately, she tangled with another Scheepbouwer specialty, the potato champagne. After the boys had finished one particular batch, they dumped the mash outside the yard. The moose, curious, ambled over and thought it smelled like tasty food. It didn't take long before the family saw her staggering around the yard and realized that the poor moose

Kinik Reaugh was a well-known cowboy in the area and often played his guitar at Flying U dances. His unforgettable high spirits and hi-jinks were recounted in both Floyd Tompkins's and Leonard Larson's memoirs. Courtesy BC Cowboy Hall of Fame.

was drunk. Not unlike her human friends, she ended up with a terrible hangover and for a day or two, she dragged around, a pitiful-looking animal. But that was the end of it. In the future, whenever she saw a batch of dumped mash, nothing on earth would make her go near it.

STAMPEDES

No event during the year created as much excitement as the prospect of a stampede. Not only was it a wonderful event to watch, but young (and old) cowboys had an opportunity to try out their skills and compete against each other.

Leonard Larson, who participated in many rodeos, told an amusing but slightly alarming story about one of those cowboys:

> A friend of mine by the name of Eddie Bontor was going to try his luck at being a cowboy. He came to me and said, "I understand

The Green Lake Stampede and the Bridge Lake Stampede were exciting annual events, anticipated by everyone. Jack and May Boyd instituted the Green Lake Stampede at the Flying U and Jack was himself one of the star participants. Courtesy Connie (Leavitt) Greenall, Kamloops, BC.

that this horse that I have drawn is not a good bucker." There was a little sorrel horse just behind us and Eddie asked me to talk to the chute judge whether he could get that horse. I told him that he was crazy as it was not a saddle horse and that she was too small and too fast, strictly a bareback. But I did go over and talk to the chute judge and said if Eddie was damn fool enough to want her, that he should let him have her. The second jump, Eddie landed face first in the dirt and she jumped on his back with all four feet and she was going after him again, but I plowed my horse Scooter into her and drove her away while Don Eden and a few others packed Eddie out, as he was out cold. Walter Horn, being the taxi in case someone got hurt, wanted to take him to Williams Lake Hospital, but Eddie refused to go. He just wandered around as if he were in a daze. My sister Gunhill and my brother-in-law Charlie also talked to him about going to the hospital, but he would not go. Meanwhile I broke a stirrup and I went over to Eddie and he said, "Leonard, I have not seen you for six months" and shook my hand. I did check on him in his cabin about a month later and he still was not making sense, so I was quite concerned about him. I asked him to take off his shirt to look at his back and you could see all the four markings of the hooves, his back all colours of the rainbow. I tried again to take him up to the doctor's but he again refused; I do believe that it was his religion. But in time he did come out of it.

Leonard related the story of another rodeo cowboy, Ray Reinertson:

In the next two years, Don Eden and I would make the rounds of the rodeos, starting in the summer, we would go as pickup men. One of the best riders that I ever knew was Ray [Reinertson], but the damn fool would be right in the final rides when he had had one too many. One instance at Lac la Hache, by the time they had a proper corral when his bareback horse started bucking and started to run, I was right along side of him, being 12' from the fence. I yelled at him, do not jump for the fence, but the darn fool hit for the fence and his riding boot hit the bottom post and broke his ankle. When we got to him, he said, "Muriel, bring me the whiskey!" Walter Horn, better known as Shorty, took him to Williams Lake in his taxi. According to the way Shorty tells it, it was quite a ride. The doctor asked him if it was broken and Ray, in his squeaky voice, said that you ought to know, you are the doctor. The doctor examined his foot and twisted him and asked Ray if it hurt. Ray let out a screech and said, "What do you think?!" It did leave one of the best bronco rider friend[s] of mine a bit crippled on that foot.

The Green Lake Stampede was created by Jack Boyd, who had turned his working ranch into the Flying U Ranch. It isn't known exactly when the rodeo first began, but one of Noveta Leavitt's photographs is marked "Stampede Green Lake, June 29 & 30, 1928." Usually held in the first week of July, it was the event of the year for people from all over the South Cariboo. People arrived in swarms, including a big contingent of people from the Canim Lake Band. Everyone camped out in canvas tents for the two-day affair.

The Homesteader's Daughter paints an indelible picture of the colourful rodeo. The two-day stampede started with a parade. Indigenous people in full regalia rode by, followed by cowboys in brilliant outfits, everyone cheering them on. Next would come any special guests and a clown or two (Steve Prydatok played the clown on more than one occasion). Jack Boyd himself was usually the highlight of the exciting rodeo; he would swoop in with perfect timing and rope up the calf that no one else could capture or save the day when someone was thrown from the saddle. After the rodeo was over, the horse races began. Besides the standard horse race, there was also the Roman race, where each competitor stood astride two horses, hanging onto the reins for dear life while trying to keep his balance. And there was the horse swimming race, which according to Noveta Leavitt was the most exciting event of the whole stampede. Spectators watched while horses and their riders raced into the waters of Green Lake. Splashing and churning, they had to reach a marker anchored in the lake bottom, go around the marker, and swim back to shore. The competition was fierce as spectators cheered on their favourites, identified by a large number hanging on the side of the horse.

Dances were held on both nights of the stampede and musicians from around the area played for these events. For some years, Russell (Ginger)

Coote, a pilot and member of the BC Aviation Hall of Fame, would fly a seaplane to the stampede. For $3.00 a head, he would take people for a ride over Green Lake and the surrounding area.

Many people packed their own food to eat in their tents, but there was holiday fare available as well. Ed and Irene Higgins sold homemade ice cream, packed with ice from the Bridge Lake ice caves, a local spot where ice and snow remained all year round in small, deep caves. Stan and Sadie Eden ran a concession stand offering a whole range of tasty treats. As well as attending all the events, people visited with each other and caught up with friends they hadn't seen for months. The rodeo over, exhausted and happy revellers made their way back home again. With travel time counted, it was a rare three- to four-day holiday for everyone.

Although the Green Lake Stampede was instituted in the late 1920s, the first stampede in the area was held at Bridge Lake. In 1920, when the Jowsey family arrived at their property near the southeast end of Bridge Lake, they were surprised to find that a stampede was being held right on their property. And in 1926, when the Barnes and Faessler families arrived, a rodeo was being held at the Hansen farm. Whatever the circumstances, there was a stampede held in Bridge Lake for several years during the 1920s. After that, when people started going to the Green Lake Stampede, the Bridge Lake event died out.

In the late 1940s, interest in the idea of holding a local stampede at Bridge Lake arose again. In 1948, the Bridge Lake Community Club purchased several acres of land from Frank Hansen and laid out a proper stampede ground. Previously this land had been used as a picnic ground and ball field. Wasting no time, the first stampede was held that year. Events over the years included bronco and bareback riding, steer riding, wild cow milking, barrel racing, and pole bending. There were prizes for the best-dressed cowboy and cowgirl. North Bonaparte people often did very well at winning this contest. Bill Scheepbouwer won as "best-dressed cowboy" so many times, officials asked if he would bow out next time and let someone else have a chance. Anna Chabara, a glamorous girl who worked as a ranch hand for Jack Park, won several years in a row for "best-dressed cowgirl."

Sharon Hansen, who participated in the contest during the 1950s, said that "Anna Chabara usually deserved to win because she was such an authentic cowgirl and had better equipment than the rest of us." She went on, "We usually just rode around the arena to compete, but on a couple of occasions they made us do some things to show that we could handle our horses in different situations. We always had to wear spurs to complete our cowgirl/cowboy outfits."

Johnny Hansen and Will Whitley were the event judges for many years, beginning in the late 1940s. Taking over for them in later years were Howard Malm and Shorty Horn. The judges in those days weren't up in a booth, but were always out in the arena on horseback. "Pickup riders" were part of the action in the arena too. Sharon shared her memories of these:

> I always admired the pick-up riders who would go right beside the bucking horses as the ride was ending, put their arm around the rider and take them briefly onto their horse until they were out of danger. Sometimes the competing riders were already on the ground, so it didn't always work. I recall being amazed when the Reed twins, Linda and Louise, who were only about sixteen years of age, were the pick-up riders at the rodeo. Both girls were super riders but not very big, and normally the pick-up riders were strong men. Both girls did the job well, as I recall.

For a number of years, the first aid station was at the Grauman house by the stampede grounds. A member of the family recalls a wounded cowboy being carried in with a horseshoe-shaped indent in his forehead!

The Bridge Lake Stampede gradually became more and more popular. At the height of its fame during the 1970s and 1980s, as many as 3,500 people attended the event. And, of course, there was always a dance afterwards.

John R. Ross, a resident who wrote a column for the *100 Mile Free Press,* colourfully painted a picture of Bridge Lake during the July 1 rodeo weekend in the mid-1950s:

> Roe Lake Avenue and Little Fort Boulevard were busy on July 1st. All forenoon the traffic was headed for the Bridge Lake Community Club's stampede grounds. Shortly after noon, broncos and cowboys were already in the arena and the grandstand was packed with a thrilled audience. The grandstand was presided over by Jack McKay. Under the spacious grandstand was the soft drink and confectionary mart. Miss Molly Deane-Freeman was in charge there, assisted by Mrs. Olive King and Mrs. Rita Larson. The hot dog stand did a roaring business all day and kept Mrs. Thomason, Mrs. E. Whalley and Mrs. Joyce Ross busy. The midway. Ah! the brassy jaunty splendor of it all with such magniloquent barkers as Frenchy, Jack Larson, Bill Greenall, Peter Ross, Bill Bonter [this was likely Norm Bonter] and others to give a big time touch to the show. Between the arena and the midway was a good place to meet old friends and new ones. I saw a Mountie there, I don't think he was

looking for me, at any rate I was not molested, besides I was escorted by my six-year-old granddaughter at the time. One old timer
whom I had not met for years was Bill Haines... Mrs. Georgina Bradford and Mrs. Audrey Woodman were among the visitors
from the North Thompson valley, and from around home I was glad
to see Charlie Faessler senior and Pat Deane-Freeman who has
been teaching school at Eagle Creek. The annual stampede was a
financial success, and as usual, it was a social success. A great place
to contact the people I like to meet.

As a celebration of the fiftieth anniversary of the stampede in 1999, a cattle
drive was organized, something no one had seen for many decades. It was a
four-day cattle drive of about forty cattle on a fifty- to sixty-kilometre trail
from 70 Mile House to Bridge Lake. Participants herded the cattle, camped
at night, ate trail food that cowboys in the past had never dreamed about, and
partied with music every night. Although it rained almost the entire journey,
the trail ride was an unforgettable experience.

Today, the Bridge Lake Stampede carries on, nearing its seventieth anniversary.

PICNICS, BALL GAMES, SPORTS DAYS, AND FALL FAIRS

Picnics were wonderful, happy events that everyone looked forward to. These
were usually held in conjunction with a sports day or a ball game or the end
of the school year—and sometimes all three. At Roe Lake, near the end of
the school year, a gala picnic was usually held, often followed by a ball game.
It was a huge event in the children's lives, as well as their parents'. Everyone
packed hampers with delicious food and watched the children participate in
entertaining races. Seated on a blanket on the ground, often by the shores
of a lake, people could catch up with each other and enjoy the holiday food.
This was one of the highlights of the year for children, and if they missed it,
they were devastated. Leonard Larson told of one such occasion, which was
indelible in his mind years later:

> [I told my dad a lie] and for punishment, my dad would not allow
> me off the property for a month. It was at the same time as the
> school picnic would be on. Our own school picnic was only three
> days away. My mother tried talking my dad into letting me go but
> he just refused. He said that I would have to finish out the month.
> I believe that was the saddest part of my life. It was a treat we all
> looked forward to. The Malms and the Higgins would make the

best potato salad and ice cream, plus we could make a few cents in the races such as the sack race and the 3-legged race, plus a lot of other entertainment. I swore that I would never lie again. That was the worst punishment that I ever had.

Freda Larner, now Freda Lamb, related that the school picnic, held at Major Boyer's place at the west end of Bridge Lake, was one of the fondest memories of her childhood years. "We children tasted watermelon for the very first time," she said.

At Watch Lake, an annual picnic was held, attended by everyone. Eva Wrigley wrote about one of the picnics in her memoir, *To Follow a Cowboy*: "[This] reminds me of the time when everyone attended the Annual Watch Lake picnic. This, of course, included a ball game and dance afterwards, with everyone heading for home in the early hours. Several people, including Jack Dyer, stopped in at our ranch for coffee and pancakes." A welcome respite from unending work, the picnic provided a venue for people to relax and visit with friends and neighbours.

Ball games were a bright spot in the summer, with teams competing from the many little communities in the area. When Japanese internees were housed at Taylor Lake during the 1940s, they had an enthusiastic team as well.

During the 1940s, Frank Haywood-Farmer belonged to the Lone Butte team. Before the team travelled to Bridge Lake for a game, he would always get hold of Ernie King, just to find out what condition the road was in and how many potholes they'd have to fight their way through.

Making Skis and Toboggans
Leonard Larson, Roe Lake

My dad [Ole Larson] made all us kids skis and toboggans. The way he would do this, he would pick out birch trees about a foot through. He would run the log through the sawmill, cutting them in a square timber... He then stored these square timbers in a shed where they could dry out slowly for about two years before he could cut them into boards. Then he would proceed to shape them into skis. He made a wooden block with the end shaped like the end of a ski. He would tie the ends of the skis to the block, put them in a boiler with boiling water and boil them approximately an hour. Then he would gradually bend the boards closer to the block. When he got the boards secured together, he would boil them for another hour to make sure that they would not crack. He would then take them out and put them on the drying rack, leaving them there for a good six months. He also did likewise with the toboggans. The next winter he would have at least a dozen sets of skis, plus a couple of toboggans, so that we were very well equipped for winter sports.

Picnics and ball games were held at Sharpe Lake during the summer, usually once a month. The community would gather at a meadow close to Robbie and Diane Cleveland's place and enjoy ice cream and all the good food that the women carried out to the site. Those that didn't play in the ball game sat and cheered the players on.

Robbie Cleveland talked about the fun of the baseball games when he was interviewed for a newspaper article: "There were quite a few of them around, and we'd all travel in the team wagon to games. Sometimes the trip could take three hours or so, [and] everyone would be half asleep when we'd hit a rock. It sure woke you up fast." Matches were played on fields and pastures while parents and friends pitched in to officiate. He went on, "I still remember John Scheepbouwer sitting on a gallon jug of wine, umping the games." According to Robbie, Mrs. Elma Johnson from Sharpe Lake could always be counted on to churn them up a pail of ice cream after a game, but that soured when a mother of one of the players accused the kind lady of using bear fat in her recipe. "There was no more after that," Robbie said. Elma, who took pride in her ice cream, took it as an insult that her bear fat was considered less than socially acceptable.

In 1940, the Bridge Lake Farmer's Institute organized a fall fair that continues to this day. Held in the North Bridge Lake School, the 1940 event was a huge success. Three-quarters of the population in the countryside attended, arriving by horse and wagons stocked with crafts and produce. The fair was later moved to the North Bridge Lake Community Hall and grew to include activities that would involve the men, such as a calf show and outdoor

The first known photograph of a fair at Bridge Lake, taken in the 1920s. It appears that teams of horses are about to be judged and this rare photo could have been taken at the present stampede grounds. Courtesy Connie (Leavitt) Greenall, Kamloops, BC.

competitions of rowing and nail driving. During the 1950s, Watch Lake also had a fall fair. These fairs provided a chance to show off your prize dill pickles or your huckleberry jam and enter your best squashes and choicest potatoes. You could also enter your handiwork in many different crafts and show off your paintings and perhaps even your poems. Women were justly proud of their homemaking skills and it was a chance to see just how well you could do. Competitions to see who had the best canning, breads, cakes, pies, quilts, embroidery, butter, eggs, flowers, and many other items may have been friendly enough, but everyone wanted to win that first prize.

The highlight of the winter was the annual Christmas concert, an exciting event for children, their parents, and the entire community in which they were held. Every small school had its own Christmas concert. Ivy Johnson attended both Eagan Lake School and Sharpe Lake School and remembers concerts and potluck dinners being held at both schools every Christmas. And, of course, there was always a dance afterwards.

At Bridge Lake, Amateur Night concerts were held for a number of years. At the local hall, people would sing, play musical instruments, dance, and put on plays. In the 1950s, the Bridge Lake Community Club purchased a projector and brought in movies that were shown once a week during the summer at the community hall. Most of the movies were four or more years old, but moviegoers were riveted nevertheless.

During the long, cold winters, many of the residents skied, snowshoed, and skated on the ice on the many lakes. The Double T Ranch had an ice rink on Burns Lake and had skating parties and hockey games.

Although the district's pioneer families worked very hard, when it came time for playing, they could play with as much gusto as they could work. Looking at the statistics for how long-lived and healthy they were as a group, that lifestyle served them well. The vitality they had was astonishing and it's something that is in shorter supply in modern times.

Social change in the area was slow during the time period between 1907 and 1959. Telephones were installed in the 1950s but few people had them until the 1960s. Power also did not arrive until later, nor television services. Throughout the years, there were no medical services, other than a public health nurse at Lone Butte towards the end of the period. Roads, though they had gradually improved, weren't paved for years. By the 1950s, most people had a vehicle of one sort or another, and some had mechanized farm machinery. But life wasn't dramatically different than it had been fifty years earlier: hard work interspersed with enjoyable community events and fellowship with friends and neighbours.

Although the winters were long, many people took advantage of the cold and snow by snowshoeing, skiing, and skating. The Double T Ranch had an ice rink on Burns Lake and had skating parties and hockey games. This photograph of a hockey game was probably taken at the Double T during World War II. Courtesy Audrey (Reed) Woodman, Merritt, BC.

Once power, telephone, good roads, and television arrived, everyday life began to catch up with social changes that had already occurred in larger centres. Children and grandchildren of pioneers who had been satisfied with a subsistence lifestyle with little money and few possessions no longer felt the same way as their predecessors had. They too had their dreams, but they were likely to be different dreams. Many moved away and the result was homesteads that were abandoned or carved up into smaller lots. In fact, there are now very few properties that remain as they were fifty years ago.

There were some descendants, though, who still felt a strong attachment to the land. They too had to make changes, along with the developments that were happening in society at large. They had to invent new ways to make a living, to make their dreams work.

For many who were forced to leave, the landscape of the Cariboo Plateau still holds a magnetic pull. It's hard to shake the images of those crisp cold nights with a full moon overhead, the sound of poplar leaves rustling in the wind, the meadows with grazing cattle, and a silence so pure that, as one visitor said in 1954, "If you dropped a handkerchief here, you could hear it in Vancouver." Many return for holidays and some have summer homes. But the essence of life as it was before the 1960s has gone and will never return.

SETTLERS OF 70 MILE HOUSE TO BRIDGE LAKE 1871–1959

70 Mile House, 74 Mile House, and 83 Mile House

Boyd Family: The Boyd family ran the 70 Mile Roadhouse from 1886 to 1918 and had a dairy operation at Green Lake. Bill and Mary Boyd had a family of seven: James (Jim), Catherine, Sarah (Tottie), William (Bill), John (Jack), Ira, and Herbert. Bill died in 1905 and his widow, Mary, and their children carried on for many more years. In 1918, the 70 Mile Roadhouse was sold to Fred and Agnes Cummings. Part of the Boyd family property at Green Lake was Jack's, and this became the Flying U Ranch. Mary eventually moved to Vancouver and died in 1948.

Cummings, Fred and Agnes: Fred D. Cummings and his wife, Agnes, were born in Nova Scotia and came to the Cariboo about 1914. In 1918, they took over the 70 Mile Roadhouse from the Boyds and ran the enterprise until 1923, when they sold it to Matt Porter. The Cummings had eight children: Margaret, John, Robert, Doris, Elizabeth, Velda, Gladys, and Joan. After the sale, Fred ranched for a while on Lot 4967 in the North Bonaparte. They moved to California in 1924, where most of the family remained.

Cunningham Family: The Cunningham family of 74 Mile House is unique because five generations of the family have worked and ranched in this same location. From the time of John Cunningham's pre-emption in 1896 to the present family in 2017, the Cunninghams and the 74 Mile House have been synonymous.

McConnell, David and Isabelle: David McConnell was born in Ontario and moved to Montana as a young man. There he met and married Isabelle McDaniel. They had a family of three sons: David (Sonny), Mitchell (died young), and Ashley. In 1908, the family came to the Cariboo, where David worked in various places, mostly as a freighter. Around 1919, David, who was then in ill health, went to join his brother in Manitoba. Isabelle took a job working for Matt and Bill Porter in the North Bonaparte. When Matt purchased the 70 Mile House, Isabelle worked for him as a cook. After David's death, they married in 1931.

Molson, William McAndrew (Andy): Andy Molson was the only son of prominent businessman William Hobart Molson, part of the Molson Breweries family. He first worked at 74 Mile House and later lived in the 70 Mile area. He died in 1966.

Porter Family: Charles (Matt) Porter and his brother Bill came from Ontario to the North Bonaparte in 1914, pre-empting Lots 4469 and 4470. They established a cattle ranch and added the job of North Bonaparte postmaster in 1919. A year later, Matt moved to 70 Mile House and Bill stayed on at the ranch for some years. In 1922, Matt purchased the 70 Mile Roadhouse; in 1931 he married Isabelle McConnell, who had been working for him. The couple ran the roadhouse until Matt's death in 1954. Isabelle died in 1968.

Saul, Isaac and Sarah: Isaac was the youngest of the four Saul brothers who came to the Cariboo. He married Sarah Quinn in 1865 in Ontario and the couple had seven children. In 1871 or 1872, Isaac and his family moved to the Cariboo to join his brothers, John and William, and ran the 70 Mile House that they had recently purchased. Isaac and Sarah remained at the 70 Mile House for fifteen or sixteen years and returned to Ontario in 1886.

Walsh Family: Frank, his wife, Annie Cruickshanks, and their children, Francis (Fran) and Monica, came from Vancouver and purchased the 83 Mile House in 1933. The family ran the roadhouse until they sold it in 1946. They retained much of their property in the area.

Green Lake, Watch Lake, and North Bonaparte

Anderson, Andrew William (Bill): Bill Anderson was born in Finland and arrived in Canada in 1901 after living in the US. He pre-empted part of Lot 1913 in the North Bonaparte in 1914, and when the Andrus family left their ranch on Young Lake Road, he purchased it from the next owner, J. K. McLean of Clinton. This is now known as "the Buck Place." Bill ran a small ranch until 1947, then sold to Buck and Eva Wrigley and moved to Vancouver.

Anderson, Axel and Ethel: Axel Anderson came from Norway to the US and from there to BC. In 1912, he pre-empted Lot 3804 near Taylor Lake. A few months later, his brother Carl joined him and pre-empted land at Horse

Lake. Axel married Ethel Alais of Vernon when he was 41; after her death, he moved to Matsqui in 1956.

Andrews, Bert and William: Bert and William were brothers born in England who had immigrated to Vancouver. In 1914, they came to the Cariboo and pre-empted adjoining lots at Bonaparte Forks, Lots 3848 and 3849. They set up a dairy operation they called the Andrews Brothers Dairy. Bert and his wife, Elizabeth, had four children born while they lived there: George, Alden, William, and Theresa. William Sr. returned to the coast and Bert and his family continued to farm until 1926, when they too returned.

Andrus, Hiram Wayne (Hite) and Eva: The Andrus family arrived from Idaho in 1908, pre-empting Lot 1385 on what would become the Young Lake Road. The family was composed of Hite and his wife, Eva, her three daughters from a previous marriage, Ethel, Inez, and Annie, as well as their baby, Jane. Jessie Harriet, Fred, and Eleazer were born after they arrived. After losing two of their children, the Andruses moved to another quarter section near 57 Mile Creek. Life in the Cariboo proved too arduous and, in 1915, they moved to California.

Atwood, Olney Henry: Henry Atwood arrived from Washington in 1904, already in his fifties. He pre-empted Lot 1316 in the North Bonaparte but, in 1911, sold his ranch and pre-empted land at Horse Lake. Henry died in 1933.

Bellew, E. Donald: Donald Bellew pre-empted Lot 3388 in the North Bonaparte and ranched there from 1926 to 1932.

Bentley, Thomas and Hunter, Archibald Dunlop: Bentley and Hunter were partners who pre-empted Lots 3858 and 3859 on Young Lake Road in 1914. In February 1918, Archibald died suddenly at the age of 48, apparently of heart failure. He was buried on the property on March 1, probably by Thomas Bentley, and the grave is still there today. Bentley left soon after, but that area is still called the Hunter-Bentley range.

Boule, Harvey and Orpha: Both Harvey and Orpha Boule were born in Oregon and came to Canada in 1913. In 1920, they arrived in the North Bonaparte and established the Oxbow Ranch on Lot 4964 on the Young Lake-Boule Road (named for them). They had no children and together ran the ranch and drove cattle to market. About 1948, they sold out and moved to Yahk, BC.

Bowden, Harry and Adriana: Harry and Adriana moved up to Watch Lake from the Fraser Valley around 1939. Harry had two sons from a previous marriage and two more sons were born to him and Adriana while they lived at Watch Lake. The family had a ranch and also tourist cabins. They left around 1947 and moved to Clinton.

Brennan, Peter and Phillip: The Brennan brothers were born in Minnesota and came to Watch Lake in 1913, pre-empting Lots 4380 and 4381. Both brothers enlisted in World War I, but sadly, Peter was killed by "friendly fire." On his deathbed, he willed his share of the land to his brother. Phillip briefly returned to their land after the war, after which he moved to Phoenix, Arizona, although he owned the land until at least 1928.

Bryant, Havelock and Lydia: The Bryant family came from Greenwood in 1921 to take up a job at the Flying U. Later, they moved to a homestead they called Willow Flats close to the 83 Mile House. Havelock worked at many jobs and the family grew to include eight children: Leona, Vera, Jean, Myrtle, Gertrude, Norman, Dick, and Mae. Havelock died at 70 Mile House in 1960 and Lydia in Kelowna in 1974. Two of their daughters married local boys: Mae married David McConnell, son of Isabelle "Ma" Porter, and Myrtle married Elbert Johnson of Sharpe Lake.

Campeau, Fred: Born in Quebec, Campeau came to the Cariboo from Ymir, BC, in 1914. He pre-empted Lot 3879 in the Young Lake area on a lake that now bears his name. He left sometime after 1921.

Chisholm, John and Adelia: Although the Chisholms are remembered as living at Roe Lake, their first home was in the North Bonaparte. John and Adelia, who both had had previous marriages, came from Idaho in 1908 with Adelia's son, Everett Manor. Chisholm pre-empted Lot 1383 on the present Young Lake-Boule Road, but eventually decided he liked the Roe Lake area better. In 1915, he pre-empted Lot 4280 at Roe Lake and established a place there. Records show the family in both Roe Lake and the North Bonaparte. In 1920, the family left Canada and moved to Spokane County, Washington.

Coulson Family: John Coulson moved to Green Lake in 1923 at age 65 with his wife, Jane, and their sons, John and Ernest. He pre-empted Lot 1507 and set up a soda processing plant at what became known as "Coulson's Spur." In 1931, he and Jane moved to Louis Creek. Their son John Jr. married Florence Kearton of Watch Lake and they remained in the area, later moving to 100 Mile House.

Currie, John and Florence: As far as is known, the second settlers in the North Bonaparte, John and Florence Currie pre-empted Lot 656 in 1896 on the old Brigade Trail between the Bonaparte River and Green Lake. Four children were born to them there: Mary, John, Charles, and Harold. They established a cattle and dairy operation and stayed about fourteen years. The family left about 1910 and moved to Prince Rupert.

Davies, John (Jack) and Mary (Minnie): Both Jack and Minnie were born in Wales and had immigrated to Canada by 1911. The Davies family with their children, Gwen, Harriet, Bill, Cecilia, and Helen, lived first in Lone Butte, about 1925. Jack then pre-empted Lot 3811, NE ¼ on the road to Watch Lake, where the family lived for another twenty years. In 1946, they moved to Kamloops.

Dospital, John and Madeline: Dospital, born in France, came from California with his wife, Madeline, in 1929. He filed for a pre-emption on Lot 1635 on the southeast side of Green Lake and this is presumably where they lived. Listed as cattle ranchers, the Dospitals left before 1945 and moved to the Fraser Valley.

DuBois, John and Sarah: John was born in Alabama, married Sara Burgess in Utah, and later moved to Alberta. John had one son, Albert, from a previous marriage and he and Sara had three children: John Vaughn, Basil, and Paloma. After being run out of Alberta, DuBois arrived in the Cariboo by 1917, where he pre-empted Lot 4637 around 83 Mile. He and his sons ranched and raised horses until 1940, when they moved to Harrison Hot Springs.

Dyer, Herman (Jack): Jack Dyer was born in Wyoming and came to the Cariboo around 1934. He lived in various places in the North Bonaparte and was a well-known, interesting character. His last years were spent in a cabin on the Robbie Cleveland property.

Eden Family: The Edens were the original settlers at Watch Lake. Roy Eden, whose family was in Vancouver, first came up as a young man in 1907 and returned to pre-empt Lot 2083 at Watch Lake in 1910. He was followed by his brother Stanley, who pre-empted Lot 1919 in 1911. In 1916, their oldest brother, Frank, pre-empted Lot 4477. Frank married Hylda Parker and remained on his Watch Lake property until his death in New Westminster in 1932. Roy left in 1920 and moved to Quesnel where he worked as a forest ranger. Stan married Sadie McMillan of Clinton and members of the family have lived at Watch Lake ever since. Stan and Sadie had four children: Ross,

Don, and twins Enid (Minnie) and Alice. The twins married local boys: Minnie married John Scheepbouwer, and Alice married Walter "Shorty" Horn.

Elgie, Alfred: Alfred Elgie, born in London, England, filed for a pre-emption on Lot 1919, NE ¼ at Watch Lake in 1914, built a cabin, and lived there for a couple of years. He eventually settled in Vancouver.

Evans, Edward: Although Edward lived in the district for at least twelve years, there is little record of him aside from land records and a business directory listing. He first lived at Horse Lake, then Roe Lake, and then in the North Bonaparte on Lot 1389. He was listed through the years as raising sheep.

Firrell, James: Jim Firrell, born in England, came to Watch Lake in 1915 and pre-empted Lot 1918. He and his wife, Bessie, had a dairying and ranching operation. Unfortunately, Bessie died from tuberculosis in 1918. Some years later, Jim was remarried to Hilda Hughes, and they lived in their comfortable, well-furnished house until they retired to White Rock about 1950.

Gammie, Hubert (Bert) and Ruth: Bert Gammie first came out from England about 1936 and briefly worked for the Flying U. He loved the life so much that shortly after, he and his widowed mother, Jessie, emigrated from England to the Cariboo. In 1939, he married Ruth Haywood-Farmer and established the G Lazy 2 Ranch at Watch Lake. The couple had four children: Donna, George, Lynn, and later, Mardi. In 1951, their house burned to the ground and at the same time, the Flying U went up for sale. The Gammies bought it and operated it until the 1980s, when they retired to Savona.

Goetjen Family: The Goetjens were friends of the Eakins who settled in Little Fort, both families coming from Oregon to the North Thompson. Albert and his wife, Viola Eakins, lived in Little Fort until 1920, at which time they moved up to the North Bonaparte and pre-empted Lot 3875, S ½. Albert's older brother Henry joined them, and they ran a dairy operation as well as raising horses. Albert and Viola returned to Oregon in 1925, but Henry stayed on until 1932, when he too left and moved to Washington.

Graham, Robert and Sam: Robert and Sam Graham, bachelor brothers from Scotland, homesteaded around Kelly Lake for years after coming from Scotland and moved to the Green Lake area in 1901. They pre-empted Lots 1389 and 728 and had a well-run cattle operation as well as raising fine horses. The brothers continued to ranch until their deaths in the 1930s.

Grant, Charles and Benjamin: Charles and Benjamin Grant, for whom Grant's Mountain is named, filed for a pre-emption on Lot 4909 in the North Bonaparte on September 7, 1916. They appeared to be in the area until about 1920.

Haines, William and Mary Jane: The Haines family, along with Mary Jane's brother, Robert Ritchie, arrived in the North Bonaparte about 1920 from the coast. Bill ranched on three pieces of land during his almost thirty years in the North Bonaparte. The first piece was Lot 3792, NE ¼, which was just north of Green Lake, the next (as far as is known) was on "Haines Island" on Green Lake, and the last was Lot 4966. The couple had six children: Bill, Bessie, Jack, Marjorie, Olwin, and Yvonne. Jack married Nina Bell of Roe Lake and Marge married Alan Spickernell. Bill and Mary Jane parted ways, and Mary Jane moved to Kamloops. Bill remained on the homestead until about 1940, when he moved to Kelowna.

Haywood-Farmer, Stewart and Mildred: Stewart Haywood-Farmer was born in England and settled in BC in 1903. In 1915, he and his wife, Mildred, and their family filed for a pre-emption on Lot 1379 at Pressy Lake. Two years later, they moved to Lot 3785, NW ¼, on the north side of Taylor Lake, where they ranched until 1929. By this time, they had had eight children: Muriel, Ruth, Edward, George, Mabel (who died young), Robert, Frank, and Betty. The children needed to have an education, so the family moved to Kamloops. In 1932, they purchased Indian Gardens Ranch at Savona. Frank returned and lived at Green Lake with his wife, Betty Wilkinson, and their family until 1961. Ruth married a local man, Bert Gammie, and Muriel's first marriage was to Herb Matier.

Herwynen, Pleun and Bessie: Both Pleun and Bessie were born in the Netherlands. Pleun came to Canada in 1903 and in 1919 pre-empted Lot 1401 in the North Bonaparte. He married Bessie Okon, the daughter of a local schoolteacher, Anthony Okon, and set up a dairying operation. In 1928, the couple moved to Merritt, along with their only son, Leonard.

Hutchison, David and Helen (Nellie): Dave Hutchison, originally from North Dakota, came to the North Bonaparte in 1914 and pre-empted Lots 3863 and 3864, along with a partner who was killed in action in World War I. Dave's brother Allan also pre-empted property, but eventually left. In 1924, Dave married Helen Baxter from North Dakota and they had one son, Baxter. In 1960, the Hutchisons sold out and moved to Salmon Arm.

Innis, Alexander (Sandy) and Jamieson, Robert: Alexander Innis and partner Robert Jamieson have the distinction of being the first settlers in the North Bonaparte area, or at least the first for whom records were found. They were both living in Clinton when Sandy pre-empted Lot 786 in 1891, 320 acres on the Bonaparte River. Robert, along with his family, ran the homestead while Sandy worked as an itinerant carpenter. Robert died in 1902 in Ashcroft. Sandy gained title to the land in 1905, but may have abandoned it after that. He died in 1919 in Ashcroft.

Kearton Family: William Shaw Kearton was born in Scotland and immigrated to Vancouver, BC. He married Clara Clark, and in 1914, they pre-empted Lot 4510 at Watch Lake, acquiring other parcels later. They had two sons, William and Tom. In 1929, they were joined by William's sister Florence Kearton, who married John Coulson that year. William died an untimely death in 1940, and Clara and her son Tom carried on with the farm, despite Clara's ill health. Clara died in 1950 and Tom in 1965. The Kearton farm was taken over by Florence and John Coulson, then later sold.

Livingston Family: John and Bernice Livingston came from Vancouver and pre-empted Lot 4176 at Green Lake about 1924. They had a family of seven children—Jean, Donald, Margaret, Maud, Eleanor, Neil, and Catherine— although they didn't all relocate with their parents. John, who had been a lawyer, taught school at Watch Lake, as did his daughter Margaret. Descendants of Neil, who married Margery Davey, still live in the area.

Maddocks, Frank and Gladys: Frank Maddocks emigrated from England to Canada and ended up in the Cariboo shortly thereafter. He married Gladys Couper and they pre-empted Lot 3422 between Green Lake and 83 Mile House. Frank built log houses and ranched. The couple had four children: Raymond, Lois, Bruce, and Frances. In 1948, they moved to Summerland.

Maindley, Jack: Jack Maindley came from England and pre-empted Lot 4379 at Green Lake in 1914. After a few years of ranching, he moved to Alexis Creek.

Marsden Family: In 1914, William Marsden, born in England, came from Port Coquitlam to the North Bonaparte with his sons, Fred and Gladstone, and possibly his wife, Elizabeth. The Marsdens pre-empted Lot 3861 near the forks of the Bonaparte River and farmed until about 1919, when William returned to the coast. Fred and Gladstone spent time on the pre-emption, the last record being in 1926.

Marshall, Benson: Marshall ranched in the North Bonaparte from about 1926 to 1936, but other than that, little is known about him.

Mawdsley, Maurice and Margaret: The Mawdsley family came from the Kootenays in 1908 and first pre-empted Lot 1396 in the North Bonaparte. Maurice and his wife, Margaret McLellan, had five children: Stanley, Margaret, Gladys, Frances, and Maurice Jr. Through the years, Maurice added several other parcels of property; Margaret was the postmistress for the area. The family left in 1920 and moved to Alberta.

McGillivray Family: John McGillivray emigrated from Scotland in 1911; his children, William, John, and Elsie, followed in subsequent years. The family arrived in the North Bonaparte in 1915, when John pre-empted Lot 1395. Between them, the family pre-empted parcels of land and established a ranch. William married Sharlet Turney of Lone Butte, and Elsie married Deloy Cleveland of Eagan Lake (they later divorced). In 1935, John Sr. married Dora Graham and they had a daughter, Shirley. John, Dora, and Shirley moved to Armstrong in 1946.

Millard Family: The Millards arrived in the North Bonaparte in 1914 and had a place near the forks of the Bonaparte River, where the Andrews and Marsden families also settled. Gus Millard and his sons, Tom and Bert (Albert Stallard), came from Port Coquitlam, where Gus had been a successful merchant. For over ten years, the Millards ran a mixed farm, alternately going and coming between the Cariboo and the coast. Gus's daughter Mary Alice joined them and ended up marrying David McConnell Jr. Most of the family had returned to Port Coquitlam by 1925.

Mobbs, Edward and Marion: Edward and Marion Mobbs arrived in 1920 and took up Lot 4906 near the Bonaparte River. Four children were born there: Frances, Walter, Fred, and Ben. They moved to Watch Lake in 1928, and Marion became the teacher at Watch Lake School. They developed their property into the Lake View Ranch, a tourist lodge, and after selling to the Horns and Edens in 1950, Edward and Marion moved to Kamloops.

Morris, John De Bohun: John Morris first came to Roe Lake in 1934, possibly from Saskatchewan, then pre-empted Lot 4920 on the Young Lake Road. He established a homestead but left in 1943 and moved to Clinton.

Morrison, Daniel: Morrison was born in PEI and arrived in the North Bonaparte about 1910, pre-empting Lot 3843 near the Bonaparte forks. After serving in World War I, he returned sometime in the 1920s and permanently left after 1926.

Morton, Jesse and Bert: The Mortons were brothers born in England who pre-empted Lots 3781 and 4091 in the Watch Lake area in 1914. They both served in World War I and obtained title to their land, but by 1921, they had moved to Alexis Creek.

Nichols, James and Sarah: The Nichols arrived from Idaho in 1908 with the Chisholms and Andruses and pre-empted Lot 1394 in the North Bonaparte. Nichols, with his wife, Sarah, and their children, Cora, Hazel, and Willis (daughter Laura was born in the North Bonaparte), worked hard on setting up a homestead but in November 1911, one month after obtaining title for their parcel, they left the country and moved to California.

Okon, Anthony and Cornelius: The Okons were originally from the Netherlands and were probably friends of Pleun Herwynen (who married their daughter Bessie) and the Scheepbouwers, two other Dutch families that had settled in the same area. By 1920, they were living on Lot 4920, quite a remote spot. Anthony Okon was apparently highly educated and spoke several languages. He was listed as a teacher for a few years and taught or tutored somewhere in the North Bonaparte. With their son Leonard, who was born while they lived in the North Bonaparte, the family left about 1922 and moved to Vancouver.

Park, Overton and Mattie: The Park family came from Chloe, Missouri, to the North Bonaparte in 1920 with an entourage that included three generations of the family. Settling on Lot 1383, they left within a year and returned to Missouri. In 1932, one of the sons, Jack, with his wife, Hazel, permanently returned to the Cariboo, (their four sons: Monty, Gene, Bob, and David were born after their arrival). Jack's brother, Arlie, and his family followed in 1940. Arlie, along with his wife Theresa and children Donald, Rose, and Jerry, settled on Lot 1631, the Canyon Ranch. Members of the Park family still own Lot 1383, called the Lost Valley Ranch.

Postolovski, Cassian: In 1917, Cassian Postolovski, originally from the Ukraine, pre-empted land around Green Lake. He established a farm and was part of a successful trapping partnership with his neighbour Ed Rioux. After serving in World War I, he farmed and trapped for a few more years, then moved to Alberta in 1919.

Pressey, Frank and Harriet: Frank and Harriet Pressey came from Yakima County, Washington, in 1907 and settled at the lake that now bears their name. The Presseys had nine children and the younger six came with them: Ethel (who married a neighbour, Albert McGregor), Henry, Agnes, Lucy, Christa, and Bernard. In 1911, the family left and moved to Saskatchewan to find better farmland. Eventually, they all returned to Washington.

Prest Family: Prest family members lived around Green Lake for about thirty years, arriving around 1924 and leaving sometime after 1953. After the death of Thomas Prest Sr. in 1928, most of the family left and returned to Chilliwack, except for two sons, Thomas Jr. and Charles (Pinky), who lived and worked off and on in the district. Tom Jr. married Kathleen Boyd, daughter of Sam Boyd and Emma French in Clinton.

Price Family: The Prices from Addy, Washington, arrived in 1907 and the last family members left in 1922. A tightly knit family of six grown sons and one daughter, they moved back and forth between the Cariboo, the North Thompson, and Washington over the years. Lyman Sr., Curtis, Dell, and Eugene lived out their lives in British Columbia; Lyman's wife, Linda, daughter, Lindette, and sons Levi and Lyman Jr. returned to Washington; one son, Port, ended his days in California. The original pre-emption of Lot 1494 was eventually purchased by Johnny Hansen and became the Horsehead Ranch.

Price, Gilbert: Gilbert Price came from California in 1929 when he was in his forties and eventually settled on Lot 4967. Well-known throughout the whole district, he had a small ranch and did odd jobs. He married Annie Larner in 1955 and when they could no longer run the property, the couple moved to Lone Butte.

Provo, Chester and Sarah: Hailing from Washington, Chester and Sarah Provo first moved to Trapp Lake in BC, then around 1928, they pre-empted Lot 1631 by Pressy Lake. They were joined by Chester's parents, Leonard and Emma. They ranched until sometime between 1935 and 1938, when they moved to the Big Bar area, selling their North Bonaparte place to Arlie and Theresa Park.

Prydatok Family: The Prydatok brothers—Bill, Harry, and Steve—came from Galacia, in Poland, to Canada in 1910. About 1914, they settled around Green Lake and Watch Lake. Bill ranched with his brothers for a while, then worked for the Pacific Great Eastern Railway and moved to Clinton. Harry established the Graham Dundun Ranch, as well as working for the railroad. He and his family also retired to Clinton. Steve married Doris Lopachuk of Lone Butte and established the VT Ranch. They sold out in 1948 and moved to the Cache Creek area.

Puckett, Daniel: A bachelor from California, Puckett came to the Cariboo in 1911 and was the first to pre-empt land on Young Lake, Lot 3878. He lived in the area until about 1918 and then moved to Tatlayoko Lake, where he spent the rest of his life.

Reaugh, Howard (Kinik): Kinik Reaugh was a well-known cowboy who worked for many of the ranches in the district, including the Flying U. Because of his musical talent and high spirits, he was inducted into the BC Cowboy Hall of Fame. After getting married, Kinik bought his own place at 16 Mile in 1971, and in 1972, became the provincial brand inspector.

Reinertson Family: The Reinertson brothers—Jake, Chester, Clarence, and Reinert (Ray)—came to the Cariboo from the Peace River District in the mid-1930s. Chester married and settled at Davis Lake; Clarence worked in the area and then moved to Vanderhoof. Ray married Muriel Turney of Lone Butte and they ranched at 90 Mile, eventually retiring to Chase, BC. Jake worked for the Flying U Ranch for thirty years as their head wrangler and foreman. At the age of 63, he married Dr. Ruth Roffman, and they also settled at 90 Mile; Ruth worked at the 100 Mile Hospital for many years.

Scheepbouwer Family: Jacob and Catharina Scheepbouwer were originally from the Netherlands. They had farmed in Alberta and after they came to the North Bonaparte, in 1920 they pre-empted Lot 1387 and established a successful cattle ranch that supported them and their children: Frances (Fanny), Nellie, Jacob (Jake), John, and William (Bill). The family became an integral part of the region and ranched until 1964.

Tompkins, Earl and Floyd: The Tompkins brothers came from the Fraser Valley to the Cariboo as young men and worked as cowboys and general ranch hands. In 1943, they applied for pre-emptions so they could try homesteading. "… You could homestead on 160 acres for $2," Floyd wrote. "Earl and I had both pre-empted 160 acres each, on his place we built a cabin and broke up 10 acres of land and fenced it by hand the first year. The cabin was 18' x 24'." The brothers gave it up and left after a few years, Earl turning to logging in the Fraser Valley and Floyd continuing to work as a cowboy and big game outfitter in the Kamloops area.

Whitley Family: Andrew and Emma Whitley, along with their children, Bill and Pearl, arrived in the North Bonaparte in 1909 from Washington. Andy first pre-empted Lot 1382 on the North Bonaparte road and ran a mixed farm of cattle, sheep, and horses through the years. Emma, Bill, and Pearl also had properties. After Andy's death in 1945, Bill and his wife, Della Sneve, took over the ranch. Emma eventually moved to Oregon to live with Pearl and her husband, Roy Thompson, and died there in 1956. Bill and Della sold the property in 1962 and moved to Kamloops.

Wilkinson, Charlie and Frances: Charlie and Frances Wilkinson, along with their young sons, William (Bill) and Charles (Chuck), lived in Vancouver and purchased the Flying U Ranch from Jack Boyd in 1944. They were later joined by Charlie's daughter from his first marriage, Betty. The family ran the Flying U for seven years, during which time Betty married Frank Haywood-Farmer. Frances became seriously ill and the Wilkinsons moved to Summerland in 1951. Frances died a year later. Charlie later built and ran the 20 Mile Store near Cache Creek.

Wrigley, Edward (Buck) and Eva: The Wrigleys were the third or fourth owners of Lot 1385 on the Young Lake-Boule Road. After serving in World War II, Buck and Eva and their children, Bill and Jim, purchased the ranch from Bill Anderson in 1946 and ran a cattle and sheep operation. Two more children were born—daughters Elaine and Lynne—and the family moved to Green Lake in 1955 so the children could go to school. Buck started a new career as a forest ranger so they sold the ranch in 1958 and moved to Chase. Eva later wrote a memoir about their lives called *To Follow a Cowboy*.

EAGAN LAKE AND SHARPE LAKE

Barter, John (Jack) and Phyllis: The Barter family lived at Sharpe Lake, arriving about 1949. Jack ranched for a living, and he and his wife, Phyllis, had three children: Sharon, Marvin, and Diane. They left the area about 1953.

Borleske, Leon and May: Leon Borleske and his wife May, along with May's children, Eddie and Fred O'Toole, came from Washington in 1913 and settled in the Eagan Lake area on Lot 1409. Fred filed for a pre-emption on Lot 1408. They lived there only four or five years and by 1918 had moved to California.

Brown, George Edward: George Brown was born in Oklahoma and made his way through the United States to Iowa. From there, he immigrated to Canada and arrived in the Eagan Lake area in 1909. In 1910, he found a piece of land that suited him and pre-empted Lot 3876 on Red Creek, later adding Lot 4914 on Brown's Creek. He died in 1945.

Cleveland Family: Carr Cleveland travelled from California to the Cariboo in 1912, pre-empting land at Eagan Lake. He married Minnie Belle Hansen and they raised six children: Robert (Robbie), Evelyn, Jamie, Weston, Eric, and Gary, each of whom established their own ranching operations of varying sizes. The home ranch by Eagan Lake is still in Cleveland family hands.

Francis, Ben: Ben Francis came to Sharpe Lake from Alberta in 1936 with his six children: Edna, Louis, Roy, Ellen, Shirley, and Sheila. They lived on Lot 1408 between Sharpe Lake and Eagan Lake, where Ben ranched a little and also worked as a mechanic. In 1941, the family moved to Kelowna.

Harrison, Fred and Jennie: Fred and Jennie Harrison came from Alberta to BC, and in 1951 Fred established a large sawmill at Sharpe Lake called Harrison Forest Products. Employing as many as twenty workers, Fred also instigated the building of a school for the local children as well as a small store. He moved on to 70 Mile House in 1956 and from there to Little Fort in 1960, working in the same business. Sadly, Fred was the victim of a homicide in the Kamloops area in 1967.

Hollanbeck, William (Bill): Bill was born in Michigan and came to the North Bonaparte by 1906 and worked for the Boyds at their Green Lake property. In 1908, he pre-empted Lot 1432 by Eagan Lake, where he built up a homestead. By 1918, when *Wrigley's British Columbia Directory* first started, there were no records of Bill, although he did cancel a pre-emption he'd filed for in 1922. No records were found for him anywhere after that year.

Johnson Family: Orren and Claude Johnson were brothers who came from Washington. Orren arrived in the district in 1921 and married Elma Janes, daughter of Oren and Nettie Janes, who lived in the Big Bar area (Oren also worked in the soda industry around 70 Mile House). Orren and Elma had a family of six: Zale, Elbert, Nettie (who died as an infant), Wayne, Lorrein, and Ivy. The family later moved to property in the North Bonaparte. In 1935, Orren's younger brother Claude came from Alberta to pre-empt Lot 1421 at Sharpe Lake. After the breakdown of Orren and Elma's marriage, Claude took care of the family at his place at Sharpe Lake. Orren moved to his property on the road to Little Green Lake, where he died in 1966. Claude, Elma, and the girls moved to Kelowna in 1955, and Zale, who had married a local schoolteacher, Amy Robertson, took over the property. Elbert married Myrtle Bryant of the 70 Mile area.

Richards, Bernard and Margaret: Coming directly from England to Sharpe Lake in 1949, the Richards and their children, Stephen and Anne, resided on a 320-acre property. Bernard worked for Harrison's sawmill and had a few cattle. They left in 1966 and moved to Williams Lake.

Simmons Family: The Simmons family arrived from Idaho in 1908. The group was made up of a widowed mother, Susan, and her children, Isaac (Ike), Charles, William and his young family, Harvey (Harry), and widowed daughter, Susan (Wilson). Between them, they pre-empted four parcels of land around Sharpe Lake, Lots 1404, 1406, 1407, and 1425. Eventually, they moved away, one by one, until there were only two left in 1920, Charles and Harry. Records show them as the Simmons Bros., raising horses. Neither married and both died in the Cariboo.

Tuovila, Tor and Svea: The Tuovilas emigrated from Sweden in 1929 and came to the Cariboo in 1935 from Alberta. Settling at Sharpe Lake, they built up a tourist camp and Tor built log cabins. In 1942, the family moved to Kelowna.

Bridge Lake and Roe Lake

Adams, John (Jack) and Winnifred (Winnie): Jack and Winnie Adams came to Bridge Lake in 1943 to join Winnie's brother, Wilf Bays. They occupied Lot 4918, and in 1954 moved to Mahood Falls. All three of their daughters—Mary, Penny, and Jackie—now live in the Bulkley Valley area.

Ades, Ernest Harold (Ernie): Ernie Ades came to Bridge Lake from Vancouver in 1936 and taught for a few years at the North Bridge Lake School. After his teaching stint, Ernie toured the world with the navy. Eventually, he returned to Bridge Lake and spent the rest of his life there as a trapper. His last few years were spent at 100 Mile House.

Alexander, William Paul and Julia: Paul Alexander and his wife, Julia, immigrated to Bridge Lake from Colorado in 1919 and settled on Lot 1459 at Muddy Lake. They and their sons, Harold and William (who was born in Bridge Lake in 1921), lived in the area for about six years and moved to Oregon about 1925.

Ames, Wilbur and Elizabeth: The Ames family came from Oregon to settle at Roe Lake on Lot 4279 in 1921. The couple had four children: Evelyn, Florence, Irene, and Ernest, some of whom attended the Roe Lake School. They only lasted a few years and moved several times before they finally settled again in Oregon.

Armstrong, William (Bill) and Iva: The Armstrongs lived in the Bridge Lake area for five or six years at Montana Lake between about 1932 and 1939, although no pre-emption record was found for them. They had four children, two of them born in Bridge Lake: Virginia and William. Bill was said to have run a large herd of horses. They eventually moved to Alberta.

Ashley, Charles and Ethelyne: Charlie Ashley and his second wife, Ethelyne, originally from Michigan, arrived at Roe Lake about 1932. With their four children, Richard, Vernon, Robert, and Hope, they settled down at the former John Chisholm place at Roe Lake. Sometime in the 1940s, the Ashleys moved to Chasm, then to Clinton, and finally to Williams Lake.

Bailey, Charles and Marie: Early settlers in the Eagan Lake area, Charles and Marie Bailey had come from Michigan, possibly about 1910. Two years later, they left the Cariboo and moved to Washington.

Bannon, William (Bill): Bill Bannon arrived from Michigan in 1908. He pre-empted Lot 1449 and left sometime after 1911 (although he was missed on the 1911 census). Very little information could be found about him.

Barnes, Arthur and Elizabeth: Arthur and Lizzy Barnes were among the wave of settlers who arrived in the 1920s. Both Arthur and Lizzy were born in England, as were Lizzy's daughter, Edna, and their son, Arthur Jr. By 1920, the family had immigrated to Canada. Along with the Faessler family, they pre-empted land in North Bridge Lake in 1926 and established the ranch that is now owned by Russell Ross. When Arthur Jr. was a young boy, he was disabled after being injured while he was playing with dynamite. Edna married Marion Higgins and later, Slim Grosset. In 1949, Arthur, Lizzy, and Arthur Jr. sold out and moved to Vancouver Island.

Bays Family: Wilfred Bays, a returning soldier from Vancouver who served in World War II, purchased Lot 1483 in Bridge Lake in 1941 and brought up his bride, Effie McKay, as well as his parents, Bill and Mary. The Bays established a dairy operation and had two children over the years, Bill and Kathie. Wilf died in 1959 and the family carried on with the farm. Their son, Bill, took over the running of the place until his death in 2015 and Kathie now lives there, carrying on her father's dream of the property remaining in the family.

Bell, Forrest and Cora: Forrest Bell was born in Michigan and immigrated to Saskatchewan in 1905. There, he married Cora Wells. Around 1923, they settled at Roe Lake, pre-empting Lots 4273 and 4279. The Bells' daughters all married local men: Bernice married Sig Larum, and after Sig's death, she married Len Litke; Helen married Ted Leavitt; Nina married Jack Haines; and Pat married Jim Reed. Forrest and Cora retired in Prince Rupert. Several of the Bell descendants still live in the Interlakes area.

Black, Jack and Polly: The Black family, John Sr., his wife, Gladys, and their son, John (Jack), moved up to Bridge Lake from Ioco, BC, in 1946, along with the Don Petrie family. The group bought the old Hugh (Paddy) Boyle place at Twin Lakes from the Craigs and developed it into the Twin Lake Tourist Ranch. In 1958, Jack Jr. married Polly King, a daughter of Ernie King, who owned the Bridge Lake store. They bought Forrest Bell's old place and developed it into a ranch where they raised a herd of prize-winning Charolais cattle.

Blaisdell, Ben and Bernice: Ben and Bernice (Forrest Bell's sister) arrived at Roe Lake in 1931. They eventually settled on part of Lot 4228, and during that time, had a son, David. Ben became ill and passed away in 1945 and Bernice was remarried to Leland Grant. They later moved to California.

Bonter, Norman and Nancy: Norman and Nancy, who were both born in England, came from Vancouver to Bridge Lake in 1953 with their children, Bill, Mickey, and Karen. They purchased the Lucky Strike Ranch at the end of Wilson Lake from the MacLeans and developed it into a large resort. They sold out in 1980 and retired to Victoria. Mickey Bonter still lives in Bridge Lake.

Boultbee, Gardner and Mabel: Gardner Boultbee picked up where *The Rainbow Chasers* family, the MacDonalds, left off. In 1940, he purchased their ranch at Lac des Roches, married Mabel Larson of Roe Lake, and raised a family of five girls: Betty, Helen, Thea, Trudy, and Kathy. Gardner continued cattle ranching and instituted many agricultural improvements. The Boultbees were a vital part of Bridge Lake community life; most notably, Gardner founded the Cattlemen's Association there. They sold out and moved to Kamloops in 1955.

Boulter, Gertrude: Although Gertrude Boulter lived in Bridge Lake for only two years in 1924 and 1925, she was a notable character. Hailing from London, England, she was a single woman from a wealthy, privileged family who wanted to homestead in the wilderness. She survived only one winter before returning to London.

Boyer, Major Guy: Major Guy Boyer lived in Bridge Lake from about 1942 to 1945 on Lot 4290 on the west side of Bridge Lake. A retired military man, Guy Boyer came from a wealthy Montreal family. He left in 1945 after a scandal broke involving his son, Raymond. He moved back to Montreal and died there in 1955.

Boyle, Hugh (Paddy): Paddy Boyle was born in Donegal, Ireland, and immigrated to Canada not long before his arrival in Bridge Lake in 1910. He pre-empted land at Twin Lakes, but also spent time in Savona, where he married Mary Keefe (or O'Keefe). Paddy enlisted to serve in World War I in 1916 and returned alone to Bridge Lake in 1919. He lived at Twin Lakes until about 1935, at which time *Wrigley's British Columbia Directory* listed him as a trapper. He drifted away and died in the Savona area in 1958.

Bradford, William and Anna: Bill and Anna Bradford emigrated from Ireland to Canada in 1923. In 1926, they moved to Bridge Lake, first living in the Crooked (Webb) Lake area. In 1931, they purchased property on the east side of Bridge Lake and set up a fishing camp. Their eight children—Robert, Albert, Jessie, Harold, Lilly, Jim, Victor, and Stanley—all attended the North Bridge Lake School. Between 1947 and 1949, the whole family moved to the North Thompson area. Anna's brother, Bob McDowell, joined them in Bridge Lake in 1926 and worked for Lee Hansen. They eventually became partners and Bob stayed in Bridge Lake until about 1949.

Brookes, Arthur and Ella: Art Brookes served in World War II and came to Bridge Lake with his wife, Ella, and daughter, Barbara, about 1952, purchasing the land occupied by the North Bridge Lake School. Art farmed and was involved in community affairs. He and Ella parted ways, but Art continued to live in the area until sometime in the 1970s, when he moved to Vancouver.

Brown, Eugene: Eugene Brown, also shown in records as Charles E. Brown, came from the US and applied for pre-emptions in the Bridge Lake area in 1908. He eventually settled on Lot 1441 on a lake he called Brown's Lake, which is now known as Eugene Lake. He left sometime after 1912.

Bundrock, John and Mary: John Bundrock was born in Germany and immigrated to the US. In 1913, John and his wife, Mary, came to the Cariboo from Idaho with their three children: Roy, Ervin, and Clara. They were said to have lived for a while in the North Bonaparte at the old Price place. In 1914, John pre-empted Lot 4270 at Roe Lake and the family lived there until about 1917. The family may have moved to North Dakota since all the children were married and died there.

Burns Family: The Burns, who arrived in Bridge Lake in 1909, were from Montana. Along with their four grown children—Henry, Peter, Samuel, and Grace—they pre-empted land around Burns Lake and at Young Lake. (Strangely enough, Burns Lake is now officially named "Burn Lake," although it was named after the Burns family.) In 1918, Alex and Agnes Burns moved to Savona, leaving the Bridge Lake ranch for their sons Henry and Peter. After Peter's death in 1920, the remaining family members sold their Savona and Bridge Lake properties and moved to Clinton. Eventually, they moved to California.

Case, James Henry (Jim) and Lavena: Jim Case was born in Minnesota and after he came out west, he married Lavena MacDonald, the daughter of Archie MacDonald of *Rainbow Chasers* fame. They lived in various places, Jim working as a cook, until they joined the MacDonalds at Bridge Lake in 1919. By that time, they had two sons, Eddie and Richard (Buster). Jim pre-empted Lot 1489 on Crooked (Webb) Lake and the family raised hogs and cattle, trapped, and boarded schoolteachers. Around 1938, they moved to Little Fort.

Chapman, Elizur and Amelia: The Chapmans were a Mormon family who lived in Bridge Lake for about four years. Elizur, who was one of thirty-one children, eventually left Utah with his family and lived in several Mormon settlements in both the US and Canada. In 1922, along with his wife and two youngest children, Leo and Alfred, he came to the Cariboo. First filing for a pre-emption at the north end of Eagan Lake (an area still known as Chapman's Meadow), his son Leo filed for Lot 1483 in Bridge Lake and the family lived there for a few years. Their enterprise was listed in *Wrigley's British Columbia Directory* as "E. Chapman & Sons, Cattle." They left in 1926 and went to Cassia County, Idaho, where they spent the rest of their lives.

Chapman, Reginald and Edith: Originally from England, Reg Chapman immigrated to Washington, where he married Edith Whitmore. They had three children: Dorothy, Norman, and Joy. After suffering disabling injuries while serving with the US Army in World War I, Reg and his family immigrated to Canada. About 1933, they moved to Bridge Lake. The family lived on different properties in the North Bridge Lake area and sold out about 1942.

Chisholm, John and Adelia: see entry under North Bonaparte.

Conkey, John and Iva: In the mid-1950s, John and Iva Conkey of Vancouver purchased the Double T Ranch and along with their son, Todd, lived in Bridge Lake for about six years. They sold out about 1960 to the Peters family and moved to Kamloops.

Cornish, Arnold and Gwladys: Arnold Cornish and his wife, Gwladys, were from Vancouver and purchased property on Machete Lake Road in 1946, naming their farm Silver Birches. Later becoming a Department of Highways road foreman, Arnold moved to a location on Crooked (Webb) Lake, where their only child, Edward, was born in 1954. Ten years later, Arnold was transferred to Cherryville and they eventually retired to Vancouver.

Craddock, Bruce: Bruce Craddock was born in the US and immigrated to Canada in 1903, running a tobacco shop in Greenwood before he came to the Cariboo. He pre-empted Lot 1493 on the Machete Lake Road in 1909 and lived in Bridge Lake up to 1932. He was 79 at the time and died sometime after that date.

Craig, Norval and Alberta: The Craig family came from Washington in the early 1940s and purchased the former Paddy Boyle property at Twin Lakes, establishing a small tourist camp there. The family had five children: Joe, Tom, Joan, and twins Patrick and Michael, who were born while they lived in Bridge Lake. Because of the difficulty of attending school, the family sold out to the Petries and Blacks. They left sometime in the late 1940s and moved to Vanderhoof.

Currie, William (Bill): Bill Currie, who was from Ontario, came to Bridge Lake around 1943. For at least part of the time, he lived in a cabin built by Fred Larner on the south side of Otter Lake. About 1950, he moved to Vancouver.

Daniels, Walter and Florence (Nonie): Walter and Nonie Daniels came from Vancouver to Deka Lake and established the Deka Lake Resort. After selling out in the 1940s, they built a house on the shores of Bridge Lake, where they lived until the mid-1960s. They spent many of their winters in Vancouver and eventually moved there permanently.

Davis, William and Helene: William Davis, born in the US, along with his wife, Helene, filed for a pre-emption on Lot 1442 on Eugene Lake in 1920 and lived there for about three years.

Dean, Claude and Hannah: Claude Dean was born in England and immigrated to Canada. His wife, Hannah, was born in Scotland and later her family moved to what is now Belize. The two married in Vancouver and had a family of four girls: Pat, Dorothy, Elizabeth, and Claudia. Claude, a bookkeeper in Vancouver, wanted to try country life and in 1938, the family moved to Forest Grove in the middle of winter. They farmed there until 1945, when they purchased Major Boyer's property on Bridge Lake. They ran a successful tourist operation there for several years until they sold out in 1960 and moved to Quesnel.

Deane-Freeman Family: The Deane-Freemans arrived in Bridge Lake in 1945. Brudenell Deane-Freeman, along with his wife, Myra, and children, Deane and Elizabeth (Liz), settled at Knight Lake after Brudenell had a heart attack and decided "high country life" was the best thing for him. Pat, the son of his cousin Edward, joined them soon after. About four years later, Edward, his second wife, Isobel, and their daughter Molly joined the family group and settled on property on Eugene Lake. Brudenell died in 1950 and his wife, Myra, along with Pat, carried on with the Knight Lake property for many years. Members of the family still own some of the property and return every year.

DePutron, Bertram and Beatrice: The DePutrons arrived in Bridge Lake after World War II. Bertram was born in England and immigrated to Vancouver, where he married his second wife, Beatrice. By 1952, the couple had moved to Duncan, BC.

Doran, Daniel: Doran has the distinction of being the first settler at Sheridan Lake. He pre-empted Lot 1922 in 1910, but only stayed for a few years. He moved to Big Lake, near Williams Lake, and worked as a freighter on the Cariboo Road.

Dougall Family: Members of the large Dougall family were residents of Bridge Lake beginning in the mid-1930s. Ninian Dougall Jr. and his brother Alex came up as young men to work in the area, then returned after the war to settle. They were joined by their parents, Ninian Sr. and Marion, as well as sisters and brothers. Members of the family lived on the Rayfield River, at Half-Moon Lake and in South Bridge Lake. Clemmie Scott, a sister of Marion Dougall, also settled in the area along with her husband, Bill. Ninian Sr. and Marion's daughter, Rita Dougall, married Jack Larson, and their descendants still live in Bridge Lake today.

Ellingson, Ole Henry: Ole Ellingson, who lived at Roe Lake on Lot 1910 from 1909 to 1957, was one of the most well-known characters in the area. Originally from Iowa, he lived at Roe Lake for close to fifty years and then suddenly moved to Terrace. He died there in 1959 but his friends at Roe Lake had his body shipped back home and buried in the cemetery on land Ole once donated.

Faessler Family: The Faesslers of North Bridge Lake originally came from Switzerland and the two brothers Charlie and Ernie immigrated to Canada in the early 1920s. Charlie married Margarit Schurmann and Ernie married Josephine Sidler. After living in the Fraser Valley for some years, Charlie and his family, along with Arthur Barnes and his family, came up to the Cariboo. Charlie pre-empted Lot 1452 in North Bridge Lake in 1925. Ernie and his family followed three years later, pre-empting Lot 1458. Both families farmed, made cheese, trapped, guided, and did whatever it took to make a living. Both Faessler families were musical and participated in local bands, as well as being involved in community affairs. Charlie and Margarit's children were Marguerite, Charlie Jr., Bette, Paul, and Helen. Ernie and Josie's children were Ernie Jr., Elsie, Martha, Court, Lucille, Agnes, and Rudy. Of that generation, only Charlie Jr. and his family remained in Bridge Lake, where his descendants live today.

Fitch, Art and Monica: The Fitches arrived in Bridge Lake in 1943 and lived at the old Malm place at Montana Lake. They raised sheep, but had the misfortune to have their house burn down a year or two after they arrived. They rebuilt but left in 1946, Monica to Idaho and Art to Seattle. Art eventually returned to Canada and lived in Clinton.

Graf, Mike and Pauline: Mike and Pauline Graf were both born in Germany and came to Canada in 1928. They had three children: Mike, Joe, and Betty. In 1947, they purchased the Bridge Lake Guest Ranch. For nearly twenty years, they operated the tourist ranch. During this time, their daughter, Betty, married Deane Deane-Freeman. Mike and Pauline sold out in the mid-1960s to Gordon and Janine Brown and moved to Vancouver.

Granberg Family: Albert (Frank), Axel, and Ellis Granberg, brothers from Sweden, pre-empted property between Green Lake and Taylor Lake. Axel moved away after a short time; Frank remained in the area for the rest of his life. Ellis married Bertha Holland of Roe Lake in 1922 and they had a family of five children, Helen, Norman, Olga, Harold (Curly), and Janis. About 1926, Ellis purchased his father-in-law James Holland's ranch at Roe Lake. In their later years, their son Curly took over the home farm, and Ellis and Bertha spent their remaining years in Lone Butte.

Grauman, Paul and Mable: The Graumans came to Bridge Lake from Alberta in 1938 and lived in south Bridge Lake until about 1965, when they moved to Gibsons.

Greenall Family: Bill and Nora Greenall, along with their sons, Larry, Ken, John, and Matt, arrived in Bridge Lake from Burnaby in 1953. They purchased property at Crystal Lake from Ruth Wagner and Bill also operated a construction business. While in Bridge Lake, they were involved in community affairs. Bill and Nora left in 1966, moving to Heffley Creek. Larry and Ken remained in the Cariboo, Larry marrying Connie Leavitt of Roe Lake.

Grosset, Adam (Slim) and Edna: Slim Grosset moved to Bridge Lake from Chilliwack in 1931 and pre-empted land on the shores of Otter Lake, where he raised sheep. A few years later, his brother Tom joined him and filed a pre-emption on what is now Grosset Road. Tom left in 1943, and that year, Slim married Edna Barnes Higgins. They sold their Otter Lake property and moved to property on Grizzly Lake, near Wilson Lake. About 1970, they sold the place and retired to White Rock.

Hall, Marvin and Alice: Marvin and Alice Hall, who had owned a funeral home on the coast, moved up to Bridge Lake in the mid-1940s and purchased land on Montana Lake Road, along with a partner, Richard Redinhouser, calling their property the H & R Ranch. Eventually, the Halls bought out Redinhouser. In the mid-1950s, the Halls sold their place and returned to the coast.

Hansen Family: Frank and Dovie Hansen emigrated from Asotin County, Washington, to Roe Lake in 1910. With them were their children, John, Minnie, Robert Lee, and Wesley. Their last child, Evelyn, was born a year later at Roe Lake. In 1918, they pre-empted new land in the Crooked (Webb) Lake and Burns Lake area and settled there. Frank and Dovie's five children went on to be pioneers in their own right: Johnny took over the old Price homestead and established the Horsehead Ranch, later marrying Mabel Mercer; Minnie married Carr Cleveland of Eagan Lake; Lee married Jennie Jowsey of Bridge Lake and established a ranch that would become the Double T Ranch; Wesley married a local teacher, Mary Lockyer; and Evelyn married Duncan Scott and they created a hunting and fishing resort in the North Bonaparte.

Hart, Fred and Mable: Fred and Mabel Hart, along with their sons, Bob and Bill, moved to Bridge Lake from Vancouver in 1950. They purchased the former Morgan property in North Bridge Lake and developed a small tourist operation. During this time, another son, Stephen, was born, and they also took on the care of a foster son, Jim Broadfoot. They sold out in 1959 and moved back to the coast, eventually spending the last years of their lives in Fort St. John.

Higgins Family: Edward and Irene Higgins came from Lane County, Oregon, in 1913 and pre-empted Lot 4272 at Roe Lake. They became hugely instrumental in the development of the area, building roads, instituting mail service, and establishing a school. Both Ed and Irene and many of their descendants spent their entire lives in the district. Ed and Irene had eight children: Velma, Marion, Kenneth, Ronald, Noveta, Cecil, Beulah, and Forest, who died as a baby. Five of the children married local people and raised their families in the area: Velma married Ed Malm; Marion married Edna Barnes, then Lois Donnelly; Kenneth married Mary McMillan; Noveta married Frank Leavitt; and Beulah married Alex McMillan.

Hodges, Ernest and Florence: Ernie Hodges, who spent much of his life involved with the military, came to Bridge Lake with his wife, Florence, and daughter, Joyce, in 1933. They first pre-empted Lot 5198 in the Montana Lake area and lived there until 1936, when they purchased property on the shores of Bridge Lake. They called this the Lakeview Resort and ran a small operation until Ernie's sudden death in 1959. Florence eventually moved to Quesnel and Joyce married Peter Ross of Bridge Lake.

Holland, Bill and Martha: The Holland family of Bill and Martha and their children, Lawrence, Crate, Ivy, Nellie, Hugh, and Bertha, came to Roe Lake from Oregon in 1912. By 1927, all the family members had departed except for Bertha, who married Ellis Granberg; they purchased the original Holland homestead.

Horn Family: Brothers Hartwig and August Horn were born in Germany and first immigrated to the US as young men. In 1911, they came to Canada and, by 1913, were in the Cariboo. Hartwig pre-empted Lot 4269 and August Lot 3825 in the Horse Lake area. They were followed by their neighbour in Germany, Carl Nath, whose sister Anna was engaged to Hartwig. Anna came out from Germany that year and joined Hartwig on his homestead. They had a family of four sons: Stanley, Arthur, Walter (Shorty), and Chris. Two of the boys married local girls and pioneered in their own right: Shorty married Alice Eden of Watch Lake, and Chris married Helen Granberg of Roe Lake. Several of their descendants still live in the area.

Johnson, Jack and Doris: Jack and Doris Johnson had a small farm on the Shertenlib cut-off at Roe Lake during the 1940s and early 1950s. They were said to have come from Chicago and later moved to Sorrento, BC.

Johnston Family: The Johnstons of Bridge Lake were a family who originated in England and had immigrated to Montana. Three brothers, Percy, Fred, and Ernie, first came to North Bridge Lake in 1919 and were joined by their father, Charles, and another brother, Albert, two years later. They pre-empted Lots 1473, 1477, and 1465 around Wilson Lake and Percy purchased Lot 4290 on Bridge Lake. Albert left in 1930 and Ernie in 1940. Charles, Percy, and Fred spent the rest of their lives at Bridge Lake.

Jowsey, Fred and Fanny: Fred and Fanny Jowsey, along with their four children—Jack, Maggie, Betty, and Jenny—came to Bridge Lake in 1920. Fred and Fanny retired to Kamloops in 1935 and turned their ranch over to their children and their spouses.

Kallock, Amos and Anna May: The Kallocks and their children, Larry and April, came to North Bridge Lake from the Lower Mainland in 1947. They purchased Lot 1457 from Sid Reynolds, across from the old North Bridge Lake School, which was operating at that time. Amos worked the land, as well as working in local mills. The family sold out and moved to Williams Lake in 1960.

King Family: Archie and Eva King lived in Vancouver with their three children, Ernie, Agnes, and Harry. Agnes married Bill Williamson and they moved to Roe Lake for his health in 1942; her parents joined them not long after. In 1945, Ernie, his wife, Olive, and their children, along with Olive's parents, Harry and Ellen Cast, came up to Bridge Lake after purchasing the Bridge Lake Store from Jack Spratt. They ran the store, post office, and gas pumps until about 1981, when they sold out and retired. They had seven children: Joan, twins Patty and Polly, twins Michael and Gillian, Susan, and Robert. Polly married a local man, Jack Black; Michael married Linda Reed; and Susan married Steve Brown. Many of the King descendants still live in the area.

King, Gordon and Alice: Gordon King and Alice Shertenlib were married in 1918, and the next year they pre-empted Lot 1455 in North Bridge Lake. The couple established a ranch and had two children, Jack and Rita. Gordon died in 1959; Alice died in 1998 at 100 Mile House. Descendants of both Jack and Rita still own the home place on the shores of Bridge Lake.

Knight, Daniel and Josie: Daniel Knight and his family emigrated from Washington to the Cariboo in 1920. He filed for a pre-emption on Lot 1491 near a lake which now bears his name. With their blended family of three daughters, the Knights managed to subsist for almost three years. They left about 1923 and ended up in California.

Larner, Fred and Annie: The Larners lived off and on in the area for almost twenty-seven years, living at Roe Lake, Otter Lake, the North Bonaparte, Sheridan Lake, and Sharpe Lake. Fred first came up as a young man in 1928 and later brought his family—his wife, Annie, and their children, Pat, Donald, Freda, and Winnie. Because Fred was a log builder, they moved to wherever he could find work and, consequently, the Larner children attended many of the local schools. After Fred and Annie's marriage ended, Annie married Gilbert Price and lived in the Cariboo for the rest of her life. Fred eventually immigrated to Australia.

Larson Family: Ole and Hilda, born in Norway, settled on Lot 4296 at Roe Lake in 1913. They also acquired land at Sheridan Lake, where they lived for a few years. Ole died in 1950, and sometime after his death, Hilda turned the ranch over to their son Karel and moved to the coast. The children all lived and worked in the area for many years and descendants still live in Bridge Lake.

Law Family: The Law family of Allan and Patty and their two sons, Wilf and David, arrived in North Bridge Lake in 1941 and settled by Wilson Lake on Lot 1448, the first parcel of land ever settled in North Bridge Lake. Patty taught school for many years, while Al ran the farm. Eventually, they retired to a small house and turned the farm over to their son Dave. The property has expanded from the original quarter section on Wilson Lake to two and a quarter sections, and the family logs and raises cattle. Three generations of Laws now live and work together on the property.

Leavitt Family: Frank and Helen Leavitt, with their sons, Harry, Frank Jr., Ted, Raymond, and Chester, came from Saskatchewan to Roe Lake in 1932. They settled on Lot 4284 and their sons pre-empted several lots in the area as well. Frank and Helen retired to Kamloops in 1950, although Frank Jr., who married Noveta Higgins, remained in the area for the rest of his life. Another son, Ted, also married a local girl, Nina Bell.

Leith, Phillip: Phillip Leith was a rather shadowy figure who lived in Bridge Lake during the late 1940s. Originating from a well-off family in Toronto, he had been a banker and a self-styled "agriculturist." Leith lived in a cabin on Lot 1471 on Otter Lake for a few years and moved to West Vancouver sometime around 1950.

Lindros, Oscar: Oscar was born in Russia and pre-empted Lot 1883 south of Crooked (Webb) Lake in 1915. He built a homestead, then enlisted in World

War I. After his return, he was awarded title to his land but only lived there for a short while before moving to Lillooet.

MacDonald Family: The first settlers in the Bridge Lake area, the lives of Archie MacDonald and his children, Lavena, Angus, Donald (Dan), Ervin, and Ruth, are colourfully documented in *The Rainbow Chasers*. The MacDonalds arrived in 1907 at Lac des Roches and established a cattle ranch, the last member of the family leaving in 1929.

Mackay, Jock and Mary: The Mackays came from Vancouver in the early 1950s and purchased Lot 1493 on Machete Lake Road, where they lived for several years. Although they moved to Kamloops, their son Ken Mackay purchased the Bridge Lake Store from Ernie King and spent the rest of his life there.

MacLean, Donald and Jean: Don and Jean MacLean moved to Bridge Lake from Victoria in 1943 with their two daughters, Kerstie and Jean. They purchased Lots 1465 and 1464 on Wilson Lake and primarily raised sheep. Jean taught school in both Roe Lake and Bridge Lake. The MacLeans left in 1953 and eventually joined their daughter Jean in Clearwater. Kerstie moved to Denmark and Jean married Don Nelson of Blue River.

Malm, Edward (Ed) and Velma: Ed Malm, born in Finland, first immigrated to the US, then came to Canada. In 1919, he and a partner, John Naff, pre-empted land around Montana Lake. In 1930, he married Velma Higgins and the couple had six children: Howard, Marie, Irma, Nancy, Verna, and Grace. In 1939, they moved to Roe Lake. Ed, who ranched and trapped, died in 1962 and Velma in 1994. Several of their descendants still live in the area.

McCracken, James: James McCracken, a Canadian, pre-empted Lot 4288 on the south side of Lesser Fish Lake in 1915. He established a homestead but left by 1921. He died in Kamloops in 1937.

McLeod, James R. and Mary: James and Mary McLeod were an older couple who came to Bridge Lake about 1926 and possibly lived in the Montana Lake area. Mary died in 1938 and James moved to Campbell River two years later.

Mickle, Robert and Margaret: The Mickles, a middle-aged couple, arrived in Bridge Lake about 1930. Pre-empting Lot 1897 in the Crystal Lake area, they farmed as well as being beekeepers. They left about 1936 and moved to White Rock.

Morgan, Albert and Emily: The Morgans came from the coast to North Bridge Lake in 1934 with their sons, Richard and Arthur, and pre-empted Lot 4977. The family began building a lodge for guests and the sons pre-empted lots on Wilson Lake. However, after the sons returned from serving in World War II, they were no longer interested in living in the country, so the family sold out in 1950 to Fred and Mabel Hart and returned to the coast.

Mulvihill, Jim and Lora: Unrelated to the similarly named Mulvahills in the Chilcotin, Jim Mulvihill was born in Ontario. With his wife, Lora Smith, and their two daughters, Frances and Pat, he moved to the US for several years. In 1938, he pre-empted Lot 1465 in North Bridge Lake, land by Wilson Lake that had been lived on by Albert Johnston and then Tom Winters. Frances married local Floyd (Joe) Miller, who was tragically killed in the only traffic fatality ever to happen in the area, and soon after the accident the family moved away. They sold to Don and Jean MacLean in 1943 and moved to Clinton.

Naff, John and Irene: John Naff, originally from Washington, first came to Bridge Lake in 1918 or 1919, pre-empting Lot 1847 along with his partner Ed Malm. He then brought up his wife, Irene, their son, Vaughn, and Irene's daughter from a previous marriage, Viola. The family lived for several years in the Montana Lake area and left in 1927, first moving to Trail, then back to the US. After they divorced, John returned in 1950 to Mahood Falls.

Neal, Roy and Blanche: Roy and Blanche Neal, originally from Washington, came to Bridge Lake from Alberta in 1927. Pre-empting Lot 1483 between Stack Lake and Muddy Lake, they ran a small ranch for several years with their children, Billy, John, Mary, and Edith. They left about 1938 and moved to Deadman's Creek.

Potts, Charles: Although Charlie Potts was one of the early settlers in Bridge Lake, pre-empting Lot 1486 in 1911, he may have come to the North Bonaparte first, because he was a friend of the Andrus family and had connections with other people in that area. He seems to have lived part-time in the Vancouver area and, by 1918, was back there permanently, where he worked as a Canadian Pacific Railway employee for many years.

Potts, James: Jim Potts arrived in Bridge Lake about 1926, pre-empting Lot 1475 on Grizzly Lake. Not related to Charlie Potts, he had a small homestead and worked in lumber mills until his death in 1939.

Printzhouse Family: Hiram and Lilly Printzhouse came from Washington to Roe Lake about 1910 with their sons, Bill and Ernie, living on Lot 4299. About 1926, the family left the area and moved to Oregon.

Reed, Charles and Margaret: Charlie Reed, born in Sweden, immigrated to Canada in 1910. After serving in World War I, he ended up working for the Pacific Great Eastern Railway and lived in Lone Butte. He married Maggie Jowsey of Bridge Lake, and they had three children: Jim, Fred, and Audrey. In 1940, the family moved to the former Jowsey property in Bridge Lake and ran a cattle ranch. Charlie died suddenly in 1944 and his widow, Maggie, and her children carried on for another ten years. In 1954, they sold out and purchased another ranch at Eagan Lake. Maggie died at 100 Mile House in 1991.

Reichmuth, Meinrad (Roddy) and Wilhelmina: Originally from Switzerland, the Reichmuths arrived in North Bridge Lake in 1928. Roddy pre-empted two different lots on the Wilson Lake road and constructed sturdy buildings on both. They had some livestock and Roddy also witched wells and had experience with dynamite. After Wilhelmina's death in 1968, Roddy remarried and moved to Vernon.

Renshaw, Martin and Caroline: Martin Renshaw emigrated from Norway and moved to Kelowna, where he married Caroline Brent, the daughter of a German mill-owner, Frederick Brent, and his Indigenous wife Marianne. They lived in Kelowna for some years, along with three of Caroline's children, then came to Roe Lake in 1915. They lived on a couple of different properties, where Martin farmed and Caroline worked as the postmistress and later as a cook for Ma Porter at 70 Mile House. About 1930, Martin moved to Williams Lake and Caroline later moved there also.

Reynolds Family: The Reynolds family—Bob, Dorothy, and their sons, Cyril and Sidney—arrived in North Bridge Lake about 1933. Bob pre-empted Lot 1468, across from the North Bridge Lake School, and they established a small ranching operation there. The sons also pre-empted land in the area. About 1946, the family sold their properties and moved to south Bridge Lake, where they operated a garage and also a school bus. The family moved to Williams Lake around 1953 or 1954.

Rioux, Ernest (Ed): Ed Rioux, who was born in Quebec, first came to Green Lake in 1914. He pre-empted Lot 1915 but his interest soon turned from farming to trapping. His trapline extended for over 160 kilometres (100 miles), with his headquarters sometimes at Roe Lake, sometimes at Rioux

Lake near Clearwater. About 1934, he sold his lucrative trapline to Herb and Ben McNeil and moved to the East Kootenays. He died in 1953 in White Rock.

Roberts, Lee and Dorothy: Lee Roberts was born in Missouri, and he and his wife, Dorothy, came from the US to Canada about 1931. At that time, he pre-empted Lot 1491 on Knight Lake, where their son, Donald, was born. About 1945, they sold this property to Brudenell Deane-Freeman and lived on various properties in Bridge Lake. After Lee's death in 1962, Dorothy and Donald moved to 100 Mile House.

Roe, Claude and Addie: The Roes, with their young son, Raymond, came from Washington in 1910. They pre-empted land between Lesser Fish Lake and Roe Lake and built a house, but decided against staying. A year later, they moved to the Big Bar area.

Rose, Arthur: Arthur Rose came from Colville, Washington, in 1909, leaving a family behind. He pre-empted Lot 1444 at the end of Crooked (Webb) Lake. He left after acquiring title to his land in 1913.

Ross Family: John and Rosa Ross and their son, Peter, arrived in Bridge Lake in 1939, where John pre-empted Lot 1487. John became the village chronicler, writing a column about local people called "Round the Grass Roots." He died in 1969; his wife, Rosa, had died in 1952. Peter married Joyce Hodges of Bridge Lake and served in World War II, returning to Bridge Lake in 1946, where he trapped and ran a tourist enterprise. They had a family of five children: John, Peter, Judy, Sharon, and Steven. Peter and Joyce moved to Horse Lake in 1988 and finally retired in Kelowna.

Ross, Russell and Peggy: Although Russell's parents, Vi Shertenlib of Roe Lake and Norman Ross, moved frequently, Bridge Lake was always Russell's true home. In 1943, he moved back permanently and in 1951, purchased property in North Bridge Lake and developed a cattle ranch. He married Peggy Bell in 1953 and they had a family of four: Virginia, Kelly, Gordon, and Patti. Peggy passed away in 2010; Russell and his son Gordon still reside in Bridge Lake.

Rossi, Theophile François (Frank): Frank Rossi was born in Courroux, Switzerland, a town on the French border, and came to Bridge Lake from the US in 1908. He pre-empted Lot 1446 near the south end of Bridge Lake and raised horses there until 1920. After finally receiving title to his land, he travelled to Buenos Aires, Argentina, and possibly moved there permanently.

Rouse, Charles: Coming from Wyoming in 1908, Charlie Rouse pre-empted Lot 1443 on Crooked (Webb) Lake. He lived there for twelve years, then in 1920, he pre-empted Lot 1440 by Eagan Lake and spent the rest of his life there. One of the few Americans coming to the region who actually stayed, Charlie died in 1934.

Sargent, Harry and Alma: The Sargents arrived in Bridge Lake in 1910 with five small children. Two more children were born during the three years they lived in the area. They first lived on Lot 1883 near Burns Lake, then moved to the Port Price place in the North Bonaparte. In 1913, they left and moved to Australia. (Stories about the Sargents in the Australian outback can be found on the internet.)

Scott-Johns Family: In the early 1950s, Irene Scott, along with her brothers Albert (Red) Scott, Bill Scott, and Charlie Johns came to Bridge Lake from Atlin, BC. Irene married Dave Law and after they separated, moved to Alaska. Charlie and Red lived most of their lives in Bridge Lake, guiding and working on local ranches. Bill joined the air force; after he left the armed services, he returned to BC. Irene, Charlie, and Red all passed away at 100 Mile House.

Shertenlib, Frederick and Susanna: Fred Shertenlib was born in Switzerland and immigrated to the US in 1882. He married Susanna Green in Idaho, and they had a family of eight: Gladys, Nettie, Alice, Arvilla, Ernest, Viola, Edna, and Goldi. The family moved to Washington, where Gordon King met their daughter Alice and married her. Gordon and Alice moved to Bridge Lake, and in 1919, the Shertenlibs and some of their children followed them, pre-empting Lot 4301 at Roe Lake. Fred died in 1920 and Gladys took over the homestead; Susanna lived with her daughters until her death in 1943. Gladys sold out about 1946, and today there is nothing left of the old homestead on the Shertenlib cut-off.

Sick, Leo and Mary: Leo Sick was the youngest son of the family who owned Sick Breweries, which later became Molson's. He married Mary Wheeler, and in 1940, they moved to the Boyle property on Twin Lakes, along with Mary's father, Peter Wheeler. Peter died while they lived there and is buried on the property. Leo and Mary left about 1945, and Leo died in 1954 at Halcyon Hot Springs while on a holiday, his death caused by methyl salicylate poisoning.

Smith, Calvin and Jessie: Calvin and Jessie Smith came from Oregon to Bridge Lake in 1914 and pre-empted Lot 4290 at the west end of Bridge

Lake. They had a family of ten: Keith, Emma (Peggy), Maud, Leonard, Mable, Laketta, Rose, Calvin Jr., Jessie, and George (Tuffy). Four years later, they moved to land at Pressy Lake. Emma Margaret married Emmit Eakin of Little Fort and Maud married Dan MacDonald of Bridge Lake. In 1922, the family returned to Oregon and a few years later, they all migrated to the Peace River country of Alberta.

Smith, Edward and Martha: Ed and Martha Smith from Montana arrived in Bridge Lake in 1909. They pre-empted Lot 1485 and later Lot 1484 between Bridge Lake and Crooked (Webb) Lake. During their time in Bridge Lake, they had four children: Thelma, Clifton, Violet, and Goldi. Violet was probably the first white child born in Bridge Lake. They built up a dairy, then moved to Alberta in 1919.

Smith, Frank and Sarah: Frank may have been a relative of Ed Smith, since he came a year later and settled in somewhat the same area. However, the group of four adults and one child who came didn't last long and had left by 1913.

Sorenson, Henry: Sorenson came to Roe Lake in 1926 and pre-empted Lot 4291. He farmed there until his departure about 1935.

Spanks, George and Agnes: The Spanks came from Vancouver in 1946 and purchased Lot 1480 on Otter Lake from Slim Grosset. George worked for the Department of Highways and the family went back to the coast in 1958 so their children, Barbara and George, could go to senior high school.

Spickernell, Alan: Alan was born in Wales and immigrated to Saskatchewan as a young man. In 1931, Alan and his friend Duncan Scott went on a five-month horseback journey across Canada to British Columbia. Their original idea was to prospect but by the time winter had arrived, they were in Bridge Lake. Both of the men liked the area and decided to stay. In 1934, Alan married Marge Haines of the North Bonaparte and the next year purchased part of Lot 1896 by Crystal Lake. After the couple separated about 1944, Alan sold out to Ruth Wagner and moved to Quesnel.

Spratt, Edward (Jack) and Martha: Jack, his wife, Martha, and their two daughters, Evaline and Jean, came from Saskatchewan to Bridge Lake in 1937 or 1938. Jack built the Bridge Lake Store and ran a successful business for many years. Evaline returned to Saskatchewan, while Jean married Arthur Horn of Lone Butte. They sold out in 1945 to Ernie King and retired to Matsqui, BC.

Sprowl, Tom and Olive Walker: The blended family of Tom Sprowl and his children, Carol, Brian, Jon, and Judy, and Olive Walker with her sons, Clyde, Jim, and Rex, moved to Bridge Lake from Burnaby in 1951. Tom purchased land on the Wilson Lake Road at the east end of Otter Lake and had a small farm. Olive returned to the coast about 1956 and Tom remained until 1960, when he moved to Enderby.

Stokstad, Svend and Emily: The Stokstads arrived in Bridge Lake in 1937, along with their children Elsa and Ruth. Emily was a sister of Mabel Grauman's; Svend built log homes and cabins. In 1940, they moved to Kamloops.

Taylor, Grant: Said to be from New York, Grant Taylor and his wife purchased Lot 4287 on Bridge Lake in 1943 and worked at developing a small resort. They sold out a few years later to Mike and Pauline Graf.

Taylor, Richard and Edith: Dick and Edith Taylor, along with their daughter, Carol, and their partners, Mac and Maggie Thomasen, purchased Lee Hansen's ranch and tourist resort at Burns Lake in 1944. They renamed it the Double T Ranch, which it remains to this day. About 1950, they moved back down to the coast. After Dick's death in 1956, Edith came back up to Bridge Lake to teach for a few years. She then moved to Kelowna.

Thomas, David: Dave Thomas came to the Cariboo in 1924, first settling at Sheridan Lake, then pre-empting property by Jack Frost Lake. Sometime after 1935, he purchased property by Wilson Lake. Dave's wife had serious health problems and he managed to take care of her and look after the farm at the same time. After her death, Dave left and sold the place to the Alan and Patti Law family in 1941. It's not known where he went.

Thomason, David (Mac) and Margaret: The Thomasons arrived in Bridge Lake in 1944 with Dick and Edith Taylor and ran the Double T Ranch until its sale in the mid-1950s. Strong community supporters, Mac had many skills; Maggie was a nurse. They remained in Bridge Lake at their home on the south shore and about 1963 moved to Texada Island.

Thompson, Roy and Pearl: Roy Thompson came from Oregon as a young man and pre-empted Lot 4298 at Roe Lake in 1914. His parents, Everett and Mary, later joined him for a year or two. In 1916, Roy married Pearl Whitley of the North Bonaparte and they had a son, Ingles, born in 1918. The family left in 1923 and moved to Washington, where Roy worked in the dairy industry.

Trout Family: The Trouts, who came from Saskatchewan, were an enterprising family who pre-empted three parcels of land around Crystal Lake in 1920. Bill and Agnes Trout and their sons, Neil and Allan, and their families established a cattle operation that they ran until 1926. They then moved to Lone Butte where they operated a general store for a few years, and ranched. The last Trout, Allan, left the region in 1932.

Wagner, Ruth: Ruth Wagner arrived in Bridge Lake in 1945 with her twin teenaged sons, Calvin and Matthew. Purchasing the Spickernell place at Crystal Lake, the family remained until about 1950, when they moved back to the United States.

Webb, Harold: Born in England, Harold came to Canada from the US in 1907. In 1920, he built the Bridge Lake Trading Company close to the southeast end of Bridge Lake and operated it as a store and fur-trading post for about eighteen years. Before his death in 1938, he willed his operation to Beulah Higgins.

Wheeler, Tom and Nellie: Tom Wheeler came from Ontario and married Nellie Clark in England during World War I. They first settled at Sheridan Lake in 1922, then pre-empted Lot 4299 at Roe Lake in 1929. Both were an important part of community life, with Nellie working as the postmistress for many years. They retired to Winfield in the early 1950s.

Williams, Stanley and Dorothy (Dot): The Williams family, along with their daughters, Sharon and Sandi, came from Richmond to Bridge Lake in 1953. They settled on Tom Grosset's old place on what is now Grosset Road and established a small farm. During that time, a son, Stanley Jr., was born and with his congenital health problems, the family eventually had to leave. They sold out to John Sullivan and moved to Kamloops about 1970.

Wilson Family: The Wilson family, from Addy, Washington, headed by their mother, Sarah, arrived in the Bridge Lake area about 1908. There were four grown sons looking for land: Charlie pre-empted Lot 1439 at Eagan Lake; George, Lot 1445 in southeast Bridge Lake; and Albert, Lot 1448 in North Bridge Lake. Will chose to settle in Little Fort. The two daughters, Della and Lizzie, as well as Will, married people from the Little Fort-Blackpool area. Albert's property was by a lake that now bears his name, Wilson Lake; he returned to the US, which George did as well. Charlie moved to Little Fort and, by 1918, there was no trace left of the large Wilson family in Bridge Lake.

Wilson, Percy W. W.: W. W., as he was known, was born in England to a family with fourteen children. He made his way to Canada and arrived in the Cariboo around 1940. He lived on land in Sheridan Lake, Bridge Lake, and Roe Lake, and eventually left about 1949.

Wilson, William (Bill): Bill Wilson came to the area in the 1940s and had a small piece of property some kilometres south of Bridge Lake, where he barely managed to eke out a living. Working as a ranch hand in other areas to make ends meet, his good nature endeared him to many. He quietly left the area for parts unknown in the 1960s.

Winters, Tom: In 1932, Tom Winters filed for a pre-emption on Lot 1465 at Wilson Lake in North Bridge Lake and stayed for a few years. Little is known about him, other than a mention by Ernie Ades that "Tom Winters once played his harmonica at a dance all night long" and a photograph that Noveta Leavitt had of a young woman identified as "Dorothy Winters."

Woodrow, Horace and Anne: The Woodrows and their children (two of whom were Elizabeth and Teddy) moved to Bridge Lake about 1949. They lived in the old Grauman house not too far from the Bridge Lake Store. In the early 1950s, they also took in two foster children, Arthur and Shirley Martinson, who remained with them for a few years. By 1957, the family was living in 100 Mile House.

BIBLIOGRAPHY

Barriere & District Heritage Society. *Exploring Our Roots: North Thompson Valley McLure to Little Fort, 1763–1959.* Barriere, BC: Author, 2004.

Belshaw, John Douglas. *Becoming British Columbia: A Population History.* Vancouver: UBC Press, 2009.

Brundage, Mike. *Tales of the Cariboo.* Quesnel, BC: Self-published memoir, 2007.

Charyk, John C. *The Little White Schoolhouse.* Saskatoon, SK: Western Producer Prairie Books, 1968.

———. *Pulse of the Community.* Saskatoon, SK: Western Producer Prairie Books, 1970.

Cummings, J. M. "Saline and Hydromagnesite Deposits of British Columbia." BC Department of Mines Bulletin #4: Victoria, BC: Charles L. Banfield, 1940.

Downton, Geoffrey. Unpublished surveyor's diary, 1920–1923.

Faessler, Charlie. *Bridge Lake Pioneer.* Victoria, BC: First Choice Books, 2010.

Fry, Alan. *Ranch on the Cariboo.* New York: Doubleday, 1962.

Gagan, David. *Hopeful Travellers: Families, Land, and Social Change in Mid-Victorian Peel County, Canada West.* Toronto: University of Toronto Press, 1981.

Higgs, Reverend Stanley. Unpublished memoir, 1933, 1934.

Larson, Leonard. Unpublished memoir, no date.

Loggins, Olive Spencer. *Tenderfoot Trail: Greenhorns in the Cariboo.* Victoria, BC: Sono Nis Press, 1996.

MacDonald, Irvin. *The Rainbow Chasers.* Vancouver: Douglas & McIntyre, 1982.

MacInnes, Ian. *Cariboo Memories.* Unpublished memoir.

MacMillan, James R. *They Came to Lone Butte.* Victoria, BC: Trafford, 2008.

Marriott, Harry. *Cariboo Cowboy*. Sidney, BC: Gray's Publishing, 1966.

Mathers, Ken. *Frontier Cowboys and the Great Divide: Early Ranching in BC and Alberta*. Surrey, BC: Heritage House, 2013.

Patenaude, Branwen Christine. *Trails to Gold*. Vol. 2. *Roadhouses of the Cariboo*. Surrey, BC: Heritage House, 1996.

Patenaude, Branwen. *Golden Nuggets: Roadhouse Portraits along the Cariboo's Gold-Rush Trail*. Surrey, BC: Heritage House, 1998.

Paterson, T. W. *Outlaws of Western Canada*, 2nd ed. Langley, BC: Mr. Paperback, 1982.

Ross, Joyce. Unpublished memoir.

Ryder, Angus Gordon. "Recollections of Four Years at the Fifty Nine Mile House, Cariboo Road, 1910 to 1914." Unpublished memoir, January 1976.

Stangoe, Irene. *Cariboo-Chilcotin: Pioneer People and Places*. Surrey, BC: Heritage House, 1994.

Stokstad, Emily. Unpublished memoir, no date.

Tompkins, Floyd. *Honest Memories of One Mans' Life*. Chase, BC: Self-published memoir, 2007.

Van Osch, Marianne. *The Homesteader's Daughter*. Victoria, BC: First Choice Books, 2006.

———. *Along the Clearwater Trail*. Victoria, BC: First Choice Books, 2013.

Wade, Mark S. *The Cariboo Road*. Victoria, BC: The Haunted Bookshop, 1979.

Weir, Thomas R. *Ranching in the Southern Interior Plateau of British Columbia*. Ottawa: Department of Mines and Technical Surveys, 1955.

Wilson, Ian R., Kevin Twohig, and Bruce Dahlstrom. Archaeological Overview Assessment, Northern Secwepemc Traditional Territory: Final Report. August 1998. Available online at https://www.for.gov.bc.ca/ftp/archaeology/external/!publish/web/raad/WLAKE/SECWEP.pdf.

Witte Sisters. *Chilcotin: Preserving Pioneer Memories*. Surrey, BC: Heritage House, 1995.

Wrigley, Eva. *To Follow a Cowboy*. 3rd printing. Salmon Arm, BC: Self-published, 2003.

SOURCES

NEWSPAPERS
100 Mile House Free Press: obituaries and articles
100 Mile Free Press: "Cariboo Calling" articles
Clinton Pioneer
Ashcroft Journal: obituaries and articles
Quesnel Observer: obituaries and articles
Williams Lake Tribune: obituaries and articles
Vancouver Sun: articles

ARCHIVES AND FAMILY PAPERS
Ashcroft Museum and Archives
Bays, Kathie. Family papers. Bridge Lake, BC
Cleveland, Diane. Family papers. Bridge Lake, BC
Kelowna Public Archives
Papov, Gwen. Veda Papov school records. Nakusp, BC
Roy Eden fonds. Kelowna Public Archives, Kelowna, BC
Ryder, Faye. Andrus letter collection. Maple Ridge, BC
Scheepbouwer, Rose. Family papers. Vernon, BC
Village of Clinton Archives
Woodman, Audrey. Family papers. Merritt, BC

INTERVIEWS
Apostoluik, Claudia (Smith), Nelson, BC
Balziel, Lynn, Kelowna, BC
Bays, Kathie, Bridge Lake, BC
Belshaw, John, Vancouver, BC
Berkey, Sharon (Williams), Kamloops, BC
Black, Jack and Polly (King), Bridge Lake, BC
Boulanger, Caroline and Ray, 70 Mile House, BC
Boule, Rod, Chilliwack, BC
Boyd, Bob, Penticton, BC
Boyd, Diana, Vancouver, BC
Bradford, Georgina, Kamloops, BC
Burr, Olga (Prydatok), Kamloops, BC

Cahill, Bette (Faessler), New Westminster, BC
Cahill, Earl, Clinton, BC
Carras, Marion, Richmond, BC
Cleveland, Deann and Glen, Armstrong, BC
Cleveland, Diane, Bridge Lake, BC
Coldwell, Rodina (Reinertson), Quesnel, BC
Connolly, Karen (Reinertson), Tumbler Ridge, BC
Cornish, Edward, Vancouver, BC
Creed, Jeannie, Chilliwack, BC
Crutch, Deane, Chilliwack, BC
Cunningham, Bill, 74 Mile House, BC
Deane-Freeman, Betty (Graf), Abbotsford, BC
Dorger, Mitch, Los Angeles, California
Dougall, Isabelle, Richmond, BC
Ethier, Lily (Bradford), Clearwater, BC
Faessler, Merridee (McAnich), Bridge Lake, BC
Frame, Sharon (Ross), 100 Mile House, BC
Freisen, Kathie, Taber, Alberta
Fremlin, Robert and Gayle, 70 Mile House, BC
French, Leona, 100 Mile House, BC
Gammie, George, Kamloops, BC
Goldstone, June, North Vancouver, BC
Gowans, Judy (Ross), Kelowna, BC
Graf, Joe, Christina Lake, BC
Granberg, Anna (Nath), Lone Butte, BC
Granberg, Carla, Kamloops, BC
Greenall, Connie (Leavitt), Kamloops, BC
Greenall, Ken, 100 Mile House, BC
Grosset, Slim and Edna (Barnes), White Rock, BC
Hanson, Judy (Haines), Louis Creek, BC
Hanson, Sharon, Vancouver, BC
Hart, Fred and Mable, Fort St. John, BC
Haywood-Farmer, Frank, Kamloops, BC
Horn, Dimps, 70 Mile House, BC
Horn, Helen (Granberg), Lone Butte, BC
Hosler, Valborg (Tuovila), Kelowna, BC
Humphries, Sandy, Merritt, BC
Hutchison, Jean, Salmon Arm, BC
Janes, Alf, Langley, BC
Jeddeloh, Anne (Park), Plymouth, Minnesota
Johnson, Ivy, Barriere, BC
Johnson, Myrtle (Bryant), Kelowna, BC
Johnson, Wayne, Sturgeon, Alberta

Kaiser, Susan, Alberta
Kruger, Sheila (Francis), Kamloops, BC
Lamb, Freda (Larner), Winnipeg, Manitoba
Lance, Art and Chris, Bridge Lake, BC
Larner, Patrick, Sparwood, BC
Larson, Gail and Jack, Bridge Lake, BC
Larson, Mary, Kelowna, BC
Laviolette, Lani, Kamloops, BC
Law, Dave, Bridge Lake, BC
Lucas, Barbara (King), Williams Lake, BC
Lye, Betty (Boultbee), Port Coquitlam, BC
MacInnes, Ian, Duncan, BC
MacLean, Kerstie, Denmark
Maddocks, Raymond and Toni, Summerland, BC
Malm, Howard, Lone Butte, BC
Martin, Marilyn, North Vancouver, BC
Matson, Helen, Prince George, BC
Mawdsley, Jack and Joanne, London, Ontario
May, Andy, Clinton Museum, Clinton, BC
McBride, Helen (Boultbee), Kamloops, BC
McConnell, Mae (Bryant), 70 Mile House, BC
McConnell, Stallard, Ashcroft, BC
McGillivray, Keith, Kelowna, BC
McKechnie, Shirley (McGillivray), Armstrong, BC
McMillan, Mark, 70 Mile House, BC
McNeil, Glen, Clearwater, BC
McNeill, Sherri, Vancouver, BC
Miller, Johann (Faessler), Bridge Lake, BC
Mobbs, Harold, Lone Butte, BC
Mobbs, Walter, Falkland, BC
Monette, Marie (Malm), 100 Mile House, BC
Moonen, Irene (Johnson), Kelowna, BC
Moore, Sandi (Williams), Kamloops, BC
Morris, Ron, Smithers, BC
Nelson, Jean (MacLean), Clearwater, BC
Neufeld, Sharon, Clearwater, BC
Ouellette, Sharon, Weststock, Alberta
Park, David, Clinton, BC
Park, Gene, Langley, BC
Paulos, Kathie, Ashcroft Museum, Ashcroft, BC
Pease, Sharon, Kamloops, BC
Pete, Elizabeth, 100 Mile House, BC
Peters, Elsie, Bridge Lake, BC

Price, Tom, Monterey, California
Princehouse, Myrtle, Barriere, BC
Profili, Susan (Johnson), Castlegar, BC
Pyper, Bonnie (Boyd), Kamloops, BC
Quinn, Lynne (Wrigley), Salmon Arm, BC
Reinertson, Isabel, Salmon Arm, BC
Richards, Steve, Abbotsford, BC
Robertson, Mary (Adams), Smithers, BC
Ross, Russell, Bridge Lake, BC
Rousell, Thea (Boultbee), Kamloops, BC
Ryder, Faye, Maple Ridge, BC
Scheepbouwer, Bill, Castlegar, BC
Scheepbouwer, Jackie, Surrey, BC
Scheepbouwer, Rose (Park),Vernon, BC
Smith, Dorothy (Dean), McLure, BC
Spanks, George, Kelowna, BC
Sprowl, Jon, Edmonton, Alberta
Stephens, Marilyn (Coukell), Kamloops, BC
Sturges, Mona (McConnell), San Diego, California
Tasker, Patricia, Surrey, BC
Thomson, Ed, Surrey, BC
Vance, Carol (Sprowl), Chilliwack, BC
Walker, Clyde, Enderby, BC
Walker, Rex, Port Coquitlam, BC
Walsh, Marilyn, 83 Mile House, BC
Watrich, Lynn (Gammie), Kamloops, BC
Wilkinson, Chuck, Ashcroft, BC
Winterburn, Karen (Bonter), Lac La Hache, BC
Woodman, Audrey (Reed), Merritt, BC
Woodruff, Donna, Newport Beach, California
Ziercke, Liz (Wrigley), Salmon Arm, BC

WEBSITES
http://canimlakeband.com/about/our-people
https://www.for.gov.bc.ca/ftp/archaeology/external/!publish/web/raad/WLAKE/SECWEP

DIRECTORIES AND GUIDES
British Columbia Directory, 1882-1883
First Victoria Directory, Fifth Issue, and British Columbia Guide
Henderson's British Columbia Gazetteer and Directory
Wrigley's British Columbia Directory

INDEX

Main entries for these and other families can be found in the 70 Mile to Bridge Lake Settler's List